P9-CQW-524

3 1611 00210 2116

Current Issues and Trends in Education

Jerry Aldridge
University of Alabama at Birmingham

Renitta Goldman
University of Alabama at Birmingham

GOVERNORS STATE UNIVERSITY
UNIVERSITY PARK
IL 60466

Allyn and Bacon

Boston • London • Toronto • Sydney • Tokyo • Singapore

Executive Editor: *Stephen D. Dragin*
Editorial Assistant: *Barbara Strickland*
Editorial-Production Administrator: *Joe Sweeney*
Editorial-Production Service: *Colophon*
Composition Buyer: *Linda Cox*
Electronic Art and Composition: *Publishers' Design and Production Services, Inc.*
Manufacturing Buyer: *Chris Marson*
Cover Administrator: *Kristina Mose-Libon*

Copyright © 2002 by Allyn & Bacon
A Pearson Education Company
75 Arlington Street
Boston, MA 02116

Internet: www.ablongman.com

LA 217.2 .A42 2002

Aldridge, Jerry.

Current issues and trends in
   education

All rights reserved. No part of the material protected by this copyright notice may be
reproduced or utilized in any form or by any means, electronic or mechanical, including
photocopying, recording, or by any information storage and retrieval system, without
written permission from the copyright owner.

Between the time Website information is gathered and then published, it is not unusual
for some sites to have closed. Also, the transcription of URLs can result in unintended
typographical errors. The publisher would appreciate notification where these occur so
that they may be corrected in subsequent editions. Thank you.

Library of Congress Cataloging-in-Publication Data

Aldridge, Jerry.
   Current issues and trends in education / Jerry Aldridge, Renitta Goldman.
      p. cm
   Includes bibliographical references and index.
   ISBN 0-321-07978-7 (alk. paper)
      1. Education—United States.   2. Education—Aims and objectives—United
States.   I. Goldman, Renitta L.   II. Title.

LA217.2 .A42 2002
370′.973—dc21   2001045849

Printed in the United States of America

10 9 8 7 6 5 4 3 2 1   RRD-VA   06   05   04   03   02   01

CONTENTS

SECTION FOUR   Issues in Accommodating Differences

9 Teaching in Inclusive Settings   133

PREFACE

Both of us began teaching children over 25 years ago. Currently we work with teachers in classrooms on a weekly basis. One of the comments we hear again and again is that children today are different than they used to be. Teaching is very different today as well. We also present at conferences and attend book exhibits, where we often hear the question asked, "Do you have a source on current issues in education?" The book representative hurries around showing books that skirt current issues but finds none devoted solely to considering current trends facing educators. This book was written to address these issues, to examine how children and teaching are different today, and to explore the path of education in the 21st century.

Organization of the Text

This textbook provides an introduction to current issues in education. It is divided into four sections: Political, Economic, and Historical Issues and Trends; Evolving Notions of Human Development and Learning; Changing Views of Instruction; and Issues in Accommodating Differences.

Political, Economic, and Historical Issues and Trends

Chapter 1, Politics and Education, looks at the conservative backlash in public education and considers policy issues related to education. Chapter 2, Changing Demographics amid Diversity, maps the changing face of the American population and the growth of minorities, considers the demographics of families and teachers, and poses possible ways of working with quickly changing populations. Chapter 3, The Rights of Children, looks at advocacy for children with regard to children at risk—those in poverty, children who are homeless, those who are perpetrators or victims of violence, and children who are suffering from abuse or neglect. The chapter closes with a section written by Susan M. Hill, doctoral student at the University of Alabama at Birmingham, on the United Nations Convention on the Rights of the Child. The United States is the only member nation of the United Nations that has not ratified the convention.

Evolving Notions of Human Development and Learning

During the past three decades radical changes in the way we view human learning have occurred. Chapter 4, Theoretical Shifts in Our Understanding of Children, reports many of these changes. It begins by considering changing worldviews and moves to more specific theories. A shift in education has taken place from the ideas of dead, white, Western men to more critical, feminist, and postmodern perspectives. All of these changes have influenced curriculum models, which are also presented in chapter 4. Chapter 5, The Controversy over Brain Research, was written by Nina King, Instructor of Elementary and Early Childhood Education at Jacksonville State University in Jacksonville, Alabama. She begins by giving an overview of what we have learned about the brain during the past decade and then provides a fascinating account of both promoters and inhibitors of brain development.

Changing Views of Instruction

Chapter 6, Developmentally Appropriate Practice, is concerned with the National Association of Education for Young Children's (NAEYC) and the Association for Childhood Education International's (ACEI) published guidelines for early childhood and the middle grades. Noticeably missing from developmentally appropriate practice literature is an emphasis on secondary education. This chapter considers the research base for developmentally appropriate practice as well as current criticisms. Chapter 7, Progressive Education in the 21st Century, was written by Shelly Hurt-Chumley, a fifth-grade teacher with the Jefferson County, Alabama, Public Schools and a doctoral student in early childhood education at the University of Alabama at Birmingham. Shelly provides three current examples of progressive education and then describes, from a personal perspective, how it is particularly difficult to be a progressive teacher in the 21st century. Chapter 8, Social Promotion, Retention, and Alternative Possibilities, is the work of Janice N. Cotton of the Civitan International Research Center of the University of Alabama at Birmingham. Janice effectively describes the prevalence of both social promotion and retention. More importantly, she details the effects of both, provides alternatives to both retention and social promotion and offers suggestions for implementing these options.

Issues in Accommodating Differences

Chapter 9, Teaching in Inclusive Settings, begins by defining inclusion and considers whether or not we should be moving toward full inclusion. The reader is cautioned in this chapter to consider the complexities of special education and avoid seeking simplistic solutions to this salient issue. Chapter 10, Multicultural Education and the Cultural Curriculum, is concerned with *religious*, *cultural*, and *linguistic* differences in classrooms and begins by posing real-world scenarios for students to use in problem solving. Fifteen misconceptions concerning multicultural education are described and specific suggestions for working with limited-English-proficient learners are provided. Chapter 11, Gender Equity and Education, was written by L. Kay Emfinger, project coordinator of the Ready to Learn in School Program at the University of Alabama at Birmingham (funded by a grant from the Mayer Electric Foundation). She focuses on the differences between boys and girls in mathematics and science and considers the impact self-concept and internal variables have in exacerbating the differences between males and females. Chapter 12, Private Schools, examines private schools and looks at other variations of or alternatives to public schools, including charter schools and vouchers.

Acknowledgments

No book would be completed without the work of an outstanding and unbelievably supportive publication team. Grateful thanks are due to Steve Dragin, executive editor, and to Barbara Strickland for their undying encouragement and belief that we would eventually finish this book. Both are hardworking, incurable optimists. We would also like to thank the reviewers of the text for their kind and helpful suggestions. These include Rita Egan, Morehead State University; Alvin Futrell, Henderson State University; Dennis Herschbach, University of Maryland; Lynn Kirkland, The University of Alabama at Birmingham; Anthony Roselli, Merrimack College; and Susan Talburt, Georgia State University.

Many thanks go to our families. Jerry wishes to dedicate this book in memory of his father, J. Titus Aldridge, and in honor of his mother, Winnie Aldridge, who is still active and traveling throughout the world at 91 years of age. He would also like to thank the following friends and family for their support and encouragement: Susan Durant, Linda Steele, MaryAnn Pearson, Jessica Capp, Gay Trawick, Gwen McCorquodale, Trish Crawford, Anne Watson Bauer, Randall Scott, Pat Snyder, Patricia Kuby, Ricky Aman, Made Wertha, and Hitoshi Someya. Renitta wishes to dedicate this book to Jay.

1 Politics and Education

If I were a rich man, I wouldn't give any money to learning. I would amend the Constitution and Congress will do it if you suggest it to 'em. Have 'em pass a Constitutional Amendment, prohibiting anybody from learning anything. And if it works as good as the Prohibition one did, why, in five years we would have the smartest race of people on earth.

—Will Rogers

Power and knowledge are inseparable (Giroux, 1993). Politics has always played a major role in the relationship between power and knowledge. Since power is always deployed strategically to advance or restrict knowledge, we can look at education as a political endeavor fashioned by those in power (McLaren, 1998). For example, throughout the twentieth century most presidential elections in the United States emphasized education as a major issue, and this was still the case in the 2000 elections. We will explore the many ways in which politics drives education. We will describe the conservative backlash, the democratic-progressive discourse, and recent and future political challenges to postmodern education.

The Conservative Backlash

A conservative reasoning has dominated many political efforts at school reform over the past several decades (Carlson, 1998). This is especially true of urban school reform. This discourse has centered on such issues as the back-to-basics movement, instructional objectives, and minimum competency testing. Overtly, the basics-skills push, centered on standardized testing, has been in response to the changing character of work in postindustrial America.

Before the 1960s, urban school districts had students from predominantly white and working-class backgrounds. General and vocational education prepared these students for available clerical and trade union jobs. There was also a small college preparatory program for those who aspired to more. The jobs in industry available to high school graduates were often routine and unrewarding but the pay was relatively high and some jobs offered security. Manual skills took a priority over literacy requirements. The high school curriculum socialized the working class by teaching students how to be cooperative workers, with more offerings for technical skills than for college preparation.

By the 1960s, however, business and state leaders began to discuss the mismatch between the literacy skills of high school graduates and the literacy requirements of new jobs in urban areas. While enrollment in vocational education was relatively high, fewer jobs were waiting for these students (Gray, 1991). Developing countries became recipients of manufacturing jobs, and the good trade union jobs became less available. Data processing, janitorial, clerical, and service industry jobs replaced these. New entry-level jobs increasingly required more literacy because workers frequently had to refer to sets of standards in operating equipment and in recording data on forms. Students needed certain minimal reading and writing skills and competencies (generally defined at about ninth grade level of ability) that could be used and adapted to a number of diverse work settings (Livingstone, 1985).

To respond to the new jobs for Americans, conservatives believed the curriculum needed revision to include minimal language decoding, comprehension, and processing skills. These were needed for students to become effective workers in the new service industry, data processing, maintenance, and paraprofessional fields. The curriculum took the form of workbooks, drill sheets, and skills fragmentation. Students would encounter these year after year. Because the curriculum didn't work, many students had to enroll in remedial basic skills classes in order to pass minimum competency tests. Many were also placed in low ability groups or courses that emphasized basic skills over subject-area knowledge.

After several decades of this basic skills reform, schools still have failed to achieve even the most limited objective of certifying that students will be functionally literate by the time they graduate. In fact, many students from lower socioeconomic areas have not stayed in school long enough to graduate. Like the Vietnam War and the War on Poverty, the War on Illiteracy and the War on High School Dropouts in urban schools have become so problematic that little hope is held for solving these battles any time in the near future (Carlson, 1998).

Disparities between Curriculum and Student Needs

Why have schools not been more successful in ensuring that students from lower socioeconomic backgrounds learn the literacy skills necessary for gainful employment? One reason that stands out is how the curriculum is packaged. The curriculum is so highly rationalized and regimented that it lacks interest for students. How can students in the twenty-first century, who are used to being entertained, find anything interesting in routine workbooks, drill sheets, computer programs with similar formats, individual seatwork, and rounds and rounds of pre- and post-testing? The curriculum itself fails to hold much relevance for urban students once they leave school. The new working-class jobs pay low wages and leave little room for advancement. They offer little job security and few health benefits. Workers often have to hold several jobs just to maintain their families' level of poverty. While jobs may be out there, fewer "good" jobs exist, given the growing disparities between power and wealth in the United States. A "basics skills" curriculum has become increasingly more difficult to sell to the students who suffer through it (Carlson, 1998).

Who Controls the Schools?

Proponents of the conservative backlash give considerable credence to local control but local control does not seem to be how the school agenda works. Several conditions keep the control of schools basically out of local hands. State-mandated minimum competency testing, the growing financial dependency of urban schools on the state resulting from chronic fiscal crises in urban schools, and the growing threat of direct state takeover of failing urban schools keep local school districts under control. To challenge these curricular and educational power relationships, African American and Hispanic groups will need to fight for involvement in substantive rather than merely technical educational decisions (Carlson, 1998). Many African Americans and Hispanics were drawn to major urban areas in the 1970s and beyond because they were seeking a space to assume control of their own institutions that was away from the control of a repressive white power structure. Local control of school reform, however, still eludes both urban and rural areas (Carlson, 1998).

The conservative basic skills school reform movement has also affected gender power relations in the schools. The reforms have taken for granted the bureaucratic and hierarchical chain of command in urban schools that rigidly subordinates women teachers, particularly elementary teachers, to male administrators. In education, teacher-proofing the curriculum, advanced through basic skills reform, has also been based on masculine presumptions that (female) teachers are not intelligent enough to be seriously involved in important curricular decisions (Freedman, 1988).

The Democratic-Progressive Discourse

Although liberal groups have exerted some influence on policy *thinking*, they have had little influence on policy *making*. Liberal discourse has advanced concerns over equity and excellence and urged a curriculum organized around higher-order literacy skills, a college preparatory curriculum for all students, the need to professionalize teachers rather than "de-skill" them, personalize instruction rather than regiment it, and promote "site-based management" (McLaren, 1998; Sizer, 1984). Liberalism, however, has failed to deliver fully on its promises, even when liberal politicians have gained control of the state. This failure has to do with a failure to take on certain difficult questions about whose interests are being served by the current system of structured inequalities and what it will take to change the way power is arranged and distributed in schools (Giroux, 1993).

Other Choices?

We must have alternative ways of looking at education besides the traditional conservative-versus-liberal agendas. Carlson (1998) cites four ways a democratic-progressive discourse in education might better address the current crises in education. First, while a democratic-progressive discourse would move beyond an economically functional analysis of the curriculum, it would not completely reject economic or workplace considerations in curriculum decision making. On the contrary, the relationship between school work and work in other important institutional sites in society should be encouarged.

Second, while the conservative state discourse has promoted functional literacy and the liberal discourse has empasized higher-order literacy, a democratic-progressive discourse would reconceptualize the curriculum around *critical literacy*. In urban-, rural-, and low-income-area schools, students need to learn how to critique the practices that keep them subordinated and to reflect on their own role in the social construction of inequalities. For teachers, critical literacy education implies a reconceptualization of the role pedagogy plays. Teachers need to undertake social criticism and to engage themselves in the struggles of their students (Giroux, 1998).

Third, educators must insist on restructuring teachers' work and in organizing the school so that it is consistent with democracy in the workplace. A shift in substantive decision-making power from bureaucratic state officials to local communities, schools, and classrooms must take place.

Finally, a democratic-progressive discourse focuses attention on linking educational theory and practice with social and cultural movements. Social movements involve a collective articulation and appropriation of cultural values in advancing particular agendas for changing the distribution of power in society. Dominant groups in education have become quite adept at crisis management. However, should the various groups who have been disempowered by basic skills reforms—in ways related to their class, gender, and race—articulate their concerns as part of a common movement to challenge bureaucratic state discourse and practice in education, it might yet become possible to build a new democratic-progressive voice for change that looks beyond crisis management toward crisis resolution (Carlson, 1998; McLaren, 1998).

Recent and Future Political Challenges

Education and politics are inextricably intertwined. One of the real dangers facing education is the refusal of the general public to recognize how embedded power and privilege are at all levels of everyday life, preferring instead to act as if there were no such political linkages and thereby allowing the public sphere to exist relatively uncontested (McLaren, 1998). Current issues in education and politics include attitudes, policy, and misguided educational reform, trends that are likely to extend well into the twenty-first century.

Attitudes about Schooling

Who is most supportive of the public school system and its current reform efforts? Those groups most advantaged by wealth and power. Individuals disempowered on the basis of race, socioeconomic status, or gender are understandably less enchanted with the public school system and its current reform efforts. Groups lobbying for minority positions on issues dealing with social, racial, and welfare concerns are being labeled ethnocentric or separatist by conservative agenda spokespersons such as William Bennett (1988) and Rush Limbaugh (1994). The ideological position of these groups sounds an alarm to white culture, which would shroud domination in a sheet of white purity by prohibiting questions of racism, sexism, homophobia, and class oppression (McLaren, 1998).

Another attitude that stirs debate concerns values based on characteristics of nationhood and Christianity. The issue avoided in this debate has to do with how religion and nationalism work together in negative ways to construct racist formations within the wider citizenry. For instance, fundamentalists who make an issue of censorship have not been confronted by an educational system committed to curricular practices that examine the relationship between religion, nationalism, and racism in our schools (Seljack, 1991).

While conservatives push their agenda and attitudes, critical theorists also have notions related to education and politics. Those who support a critical pedagogy perspective present an attitude of discontent and outrage that contests the hegemony of prevailing definitions of the everyday as the "way things are." They believe teaching must be transformed into acts of dissonance, refusing to accept the existing relations of power. Students are encouraged to make critical judgments about what society might mean and what is possible or desirable outside existing configurations of power and privilege (Minh-ha, 1988).

Policy Issues Related to Education

Shapiro and Purpel (1998) have described the Clinton administration's response to the issue of education as policies without meaning. They acknowledge some accomplishments, though shallow in scope and effect. These include the welcomed and overdue shift in emphasis toward early childhood, the Clinton initiative to make college loans more available, and the administration's proposals to encourage more flexibility and innovation in teaching and educational programs at the lower levels.

However, the Clinton years brought an increased emphasis on the notion that public education exists to serve the needs of corporate America. Clinton defined education primarily in *vocationally related* terms. This discourse was not new, but it was disappointing that Clinton's administration tried to frame public discourse of education in economic terms. Public education is more than a place to teach workers how to use machines or master technology. Individuals need to learn about cooperative work, collective responsibility, the negotiation of priorities, and conflict resolution.

Little occurred during the Clinton years to change the decision-making process in schools. There was much rhetoric but little action. Schools have to adopt a different approach to decision-making in the twenty-first century. They will need to become what John Dewey called "laboratories of democracy" (Dewey, 1952). These are places where students of all ages begin to experience empowerment in their everyday lives. In this sense, vocational education becomes not simply job training but a genuine form of critical, cultural education where the broad human, economic, social, and environmental consequences of one's work can be and often are in question. Unfortunately, our public schools are rarely places where students learn what it means to live and work in a democratic environment (Shapiro & Purpel, 1998).

Goals 2000, the major education bill of the Clinton administration in 1994, was a push for national standards and methods of assessment throughout public education. This added an emphasis on so-called performance standards, thereby reinforcing the uncritical and uncreative character of public education. Trends toward conforming were exacerbated. With Goals 2000 came more testing and more emphasis on accountability. Schools were already consumed by and obsessed with testing. In fact, since the 1980s the number of standardized tests administered to students has increased by almost 400 percent. The laudable notion of public accountability in education has been reduced to obsessive and harmful charting of test numbers. Teachers have been forced to teach to the test in order to keep their jobs. The result for teachers is content that is without creative or imaginative character (Shapiro & Purpel, 1998). The greatest disappointment in the Clinton administration was not what has been proposed but *what was missing.* Clinton's approach was highly technocratic in its stress on making systems more effective and efficient and its view of education as an investment in human capital. Educationally, it was a perspective without heart or soul. In a time when the Right was so willing and able to invoke moral claims and purposes in its social and cultural agenda, the Left, in contrast, continued to defend church-state separation and academic freedom but offered a view of education that was largely bereft of spiritual affirmation or moral conviction.

Clinton and his advisors should have learned that education is more than raising test scores, advancing industrial productivity, and improving human capital. Real educational reform has to be linked to the struggle for a politics of meaning, asserting clearly that at the core of the educational enterprise are questions of human purpose and social vision. What does it mean to be human, and how should we live together? Education should be understood as a cultural act, a means by which adults and children learn what it means to live with others in a community (Dewey, 1952).

Today a deep sense of social irresponsibility exists. This irresponsibility is mirrored in the callous and ubiquitous use of guns, in fathers who refuse responsibility for their children, in the rapacious corporate behavior that produces a toxic environment, and in Wall Street speculators who make fortunes at the expense of the American workers. Communal values and concerns have declined (Shapiro & Purpel, 1998).

The George W. Bush Educational Initiatives

The current administration has identified three significant initiatives (George W. Bush Educational Initiatives, 2001). These are:

1. **Let no child be left behind.** Current statistics indicate nearly 70 percent of U.S. children entering the fourth grade are academically behind. This initiative is to be realized by:
   a. increasing accountability for student performance;
   b. focusing on what works;
   c. reducing bureaucracy and increasing flexibility;
   d. empowering parents; and
   e. limiting federal dollars to interventions that work.
2. **Rally the armies of compassion** through faith-based community initiatives by:
   a. welcoming charities as *partners*;
   b. creating a White House panel; and
   c. establishing five Cabinet Departments committed to this initiative.
3. **New Freedom initiative.** This is to be accomplished by:
   a. removing barriers for Americans with disabilities;
   b. continuing the spirit and process of the Americans with Disabilities Act (ADA) legislation signed by his father, George H. Bush;
   c. increasing federal funding for only those programs that have proven effective; and
   d. offering low-interest loans for educational use of technology.

Misguided Educational Reform?

Although to some extent all times are unsettling because cultural development never stands still, in education the very existence of public education hangs precariously in the balance. Educational reform has taken many forms, but recent reforms have centered on either neoliberal thinking or neoconservative causes. Still, a crisis exists in the massive failure of urban school systems to reach inner-city youth and meet their needs. This failure is compounded by the collapse of job opportunities and fiscal crisis of the postwelfare state. So where is authentic educational reform?

Giroux (1998) believes the United States is going through one of its most potentially dangerous historical junctures. Fear and racial hatred appear to be inspiring a major backlash against the gains of the civil rights movement as affirmative action is openly attacked. Anti-immigration sentiments and legislation are sweeping the nation. At the state level, financial cutbacks and the restructuring of the labor force have weakened unions. Social services for the most vulnerable, including the poor, women with small children, and older citizens, are severely inadequate. Across the nation we are experiencing increasing discrimination and violence. Conservatives have well-organized campaigns to limit the rights and gains women have made. Acts of violence are increasing against women, gays, lesbians, religious, and racial minorities. A significant subtext of this conservative backlash is the growing effort to decimate the public school system as part of a larger assault on the democratic foundations of political, social, and cultural life (Giroux, 1998).

As we have noted, schools are inextricably linked to the communities they serve through social, political, economic, and cultural interests (Dewey, 1952). Society has not realized the possibility for reforming public education or the need to fight for social justice in education, particularly for minority children. In the 1980s and 1990s, many school reform reports argued in favor of a wide range of additive reforms such as increased testing, more homework, a longer school year, and a longer school day. Others suggested a plethora of technical solutions ranging from the addition of specific course requirements to the public school curriculum to the addition or reduction of certain education requirements for teachers (Noll, 1997). For the most part, the reform efforts have been driven by what Giroux (1988) has called the ideology of the "quick fix."

Berliner and Biddle (1997) have tried to dispel some of the myths about educational reform created by federal politicians, maintaining that some proposals for educational reform reflect only the personal experiences and prejudices of legislators and that others are based on misunderstandings about problems of education (Waters, 1998). Many programs intended to improve our schools turn out to have little detectable effect and result in creating serious problems for students and teachers.

Educators from diverse ideological and cultural backgrounds have drawn on the works of early scholars such as Dewey and Baldwin to show the political and ideological nature of schooling and the ways in which schools often underserve nonmajority students. The arguments have largely been ignored or dismissed or have resulted in blaming the victims of educational inequalities.

Schools ultimately bear the brunt of the broader economic and social problems that structure their existence.

Recent school reform movements have systematically removed the problems of U.S. education from public debate (Kretovics & Nussel, 1994). Giroux (1983) and Freire (1985) believe that the schooling process is always structured on the values that embody specific cultural, social, political, and economic interests. Evaluators of educational reform must have a vision for change and the willingness to act on that vision. Evaluators must develop a framework that takes seriously issues of power and inequality as well as education practice in the difficult process of reforming U.S. public education (Shapiro & Purpel, 1998). Schools of education should adopt policies and practices that link their educational contributions closely with improved schooling for America's young, or they should surrender their franchise (Maruyama & Deno, 1992).

Educational reform has not received much help from educational research and evaluation, which have remained both morally and politically innocent in theory, practice, and policy. Part of the innocence comes from their failure to deal with moral and political issues. Reasearchers and evaluators should not consider the conception of social justice a privilege for some but rather a birthright for all (Sirotnik, 1990).

Another problem with educational reform is that issues of democracy, equality, race, gender, class, and poverty are rarely discussed in a comfortable forum of politics or education. The real potential for improving public education and the present crisis in education are relegated to a silent space. Inquiry and discourse between public intellectuals remain fixed in a nonpolitical environment without values, beliefs, and passions. Most researchers in the modern university have internalized an ideology of neutrality. However, no research, particularly on educational reform, can be politically neutral.

Social service institutions such as education are partly able to shape the systems they comprise to serve their own personal and professional goals, but they do so at the expense of equitable delivery (Freire, 1985). Problems created by the repressed voices of the politically weak are exacerbated in educational evaluation. When direct provision of services in virtual public monopolies of the "best teachers," the allocation of "best practices" in education, and the provision of high-quality curriculum and professional development training are centralized in higher socioeconomic communities, citizens in lower socioeconomic communities have a limited capacity to improve public education.

Meanwhile, theoretical differences also abound. Neoconservatives are fighting efforts by progressives to make the curriculum more multicultural. Criticisms vary, but most substantive critical analyses have come from neo-Marxist and postmodern perspectives (Carlson & Apple, 1998). However, postmodernism brings with it some baggage that limits its critical potential. Postmodernism implies a dualism between the old and the new, which discourages us from seeing continuities and differences within modern and postmodern categories. In addition, some postmodern theorists have used language in a highly esoteric way that is quite hard to pin down to referents in the real world. Postmodern theory also risks abandoning the very idea of progress in a culturally and politically dangerous way. For instance, postmodernism professes a growing cynicism about progress in education. However, some limited progress *has* been made in public education that is worth holding on to. Consequently, the term *postmodernism* is a marker for a constellation of loosely related, contradictory discourses and practices (Carlson & Apple, 1998). Once again we ask, where is authentic educational reform?

Challenges for Educators

Educators have three major challenges in the early part of the twenty-first century. First, we must be concerned with the purposes of schools. Why have schools? Whether a teacher, a school, or a district elects to emphasize academic core subject matter, vocational training, or critical thinking, that choice is building toward the *common purposes of helping students engage in lifelong learning, participate in a democratic society*, and *engage in productive life work*. However, these choices limit or enhance certain opportunities for students. Careful consideration of *what we teach, why we teach*, and *how the curriculum supports or marginalizes students is certainly one of the top-ten issues facing us*.

A second challenge is *to rethink how schooling in the twenty-first century will work*. Many school districts are developing standards and working to redesign their schools. Still, much work remains as to what these standards might be, how they can be framed, and how the curriculum, instruction, and organizational conditions can be reshaped to support the standards (Marsh, 1999).

A third challenge is how schools and districts can embrace the new millennium as a source of celebration and reflection. United States society and schools recognize the importance of historical milestones. For example, the world's fair in Chicago gave a sense of identity and momentum that shaped Chicago's progress for the next 50 years. The U.S. Bicentennial celebration and the 500th anniversary of Christopher Columbus' voyage were important events that shaped the American identity and the curriculum in U.S. schools (Marsh, 1999).

Change needs to occur in virtually all American school districts, including those serving the wealthiest suburbs. However, the success of the reform movement ultimately will be measured by its impact on our largest, most troubled public school settings. It is in our largest cities—and our most rural districts—that the job of schools is most difficult, given the often overwhelming social and economic circumstances of students who live in desperately impoverished neighborhoods (Oakes & Sirotnik, 1986).

Subsequent chapters in this book will address such challenges for educators. Our mission is certainly not easy but eminently worthwhile.

The statement "All men are created equal" is found in the Declaration of Independence and in Lincoln's Gettysburg Address. For educators, it has meant that U.S. schools are charged with *offering every child equality* of educational opportunity. Throughout the nineteenth and twentieth centuries, the concept of educational opportunity through public education has been implicit in most educational practices. No American white suburb, however, would tolerate the deplorable conditions taken for granted in the urban or rural public schools attended primarily by African American, Hispanic, and poor children (Waters, 1998). Equality of educational opportunity has remained theory, not a reality.

Big-city minority students are leaving school by the tens of thousands each year—some as dropouts, some as graduates—utterly unprepared to participate in and contribute to a democratic society (Oakes & Sirotnik, 1986). They lack the skills necessary for gainful employment and they lack the preparation to continue their education.

What are we going to do about public education? In everything we do, politics plays a salient part, whether we choose to recognize it or not. As we look to the future, we must consider the following personal questions:

1. How have politics played a part in the education system of my community?
2. What inequities exist in public education in my area?
3. What role do I play in education reform?
4. Who decides what is taught and how it is taught in my state?
5. Is it possible for me to make a difference?

REFERENCES

Bennett, W. (1988). *American education: Making it work*. Washington, DC: U.S. Government Printing Office.

Berliner, D., & Biddle, B. (1997). *The manufactured crisis: Myths, fraud, and the attack on America's public schools*. New York: Longman.

Carlson, D. (1998). *The manufactured crisis: Myths, fraud, and the attack on America's public schools*. New York: Longman.

Carlson, D., & Apple, M. (1998). *Introduction to critical educational theory in unsettling times*. In D. Carlson & M. Apple (Eds.), *Power/Knowledge/Pedagogy*, (pp. 1–38). Boulder, CO: Westview Press.

Dewey, J. (1952). *The school and society*. New York: Macmillan.

Freedman, S. (1988). Teaching, gender, and curriculum. In L. Beyer & M. Apple (Eds.), *The curriculum: Problems, politics, and possibilities*, (pp. 204–218). Albany, NY: SUNY Press.

Freire, P. (1985). *The politics of education*. South Hadley, MA: Bergin and Garvey.

George W. Bush Educational Initiatives, (2001, January 29) Updated. [On-line]. Available: http://pfie.ed.gov/inits.htm

Giroux, H. (1983). *Theory and resistance in education: A pedagogy for the opposition*. South Hadley, MA: Bergin and Garvey.

Giroux, H. (1988). *Teachers as intellectuals: Toward a critical pedagogy of learning*. South Hadley, MA: Bergin and Garvey.

Giroux, H. (1993). *Border crossings*. London and New York: Routledge.

Giroux, H. (1998). Education in unsettling times: Public intellectuals and the promise of cultural studies. In D. Carlson & M. W. Apple (Eds.), *Power/Knowledge/Pedagogy*, (pp. 41–60). Boulder, CO: Westview Press.

Goals 2000: Educate America Act, Improving America's School Act of 1994, Washington, DC. [On-line]. Available: http://www.ed.gov/legislation/ESEA/toc.html

Gray, K. (1991). Vocational education in high school: A modern phoenix? *Phi Delta Kappan, 72*, 437–445.

Kretovics, J., & Nussel, E. (1994). *Transforming urban education.* Boston: Allyn and Bacon.

Limbaugh, R. (1994). *See, I told you so.* New York: Simon and Schuster.

Livingstone, D. (1985). Class, educational ideologies, and mass opinion in capitalist crisis. *Sociology of Education, 58*, 8.

Marsh, D. (1999). Getting to the heart of the matter: Education in the 21st century. In D. Marsh (Ed.), *ASCD Yearbook: Preparing our schools for the 21st century*, (pp. 1–12). Alexandria, VA: ASCD.

Maruyama, G., & Deno, S. (1992). Research in educational settings. Newbury Park, CA: Sage.

McLaren, P. (1998). *Life in schools: An introduction to critical pedagogy in the foundations of education* (3rd ed.). New York: Longman.

Minh-ha, T. (1988). Not you/like you: Post-colonial women and the interlocking questions of identity and difference, *Inscriptions, 314*, 71–77.

Noll, J. (1997). *Taking sides: Clashing views on controversial educational issues* (9th ed.). Guilford, CT: McGraw-Hill.

Oakes, J., & Sirotnik, K. (Eds.). (1986). *Critical perspectives on the organization and improvement of schooling.* Hingham, MA: Kluwer-Nijhoff.

Seljack, D. (1991). Alan Davies on racism. *The Ecumenist, 29*, 13–14.

Shapiro, H., & Purpel, D. (1998). *Critical social issues in American education* (2nd ed.). Mahwah, NJ: Lawrence Erlbaum.

Sirotnik, K. A. (1990). Evaluation and social justice: Issues in public education. In K. A. Sirotnik (Ed.), *New directions for program evaluation* (Vol. 45). San Francisco: Jossey-Bass.

Sizer, T. (1984). *Horace's compromise: The dilemma of the American high school.* Boston: Houghton-Mifflin.

Sterling, B., & Sterling, F. (1996). *Will Rogers speaks.* New York: M. Evans.

United States Department of Education. (1998). *Twentieth Annual Report to Congress on the Implementation of the Individuals with Disabilities Education Act.* Washington, DC: Author.

Waters, G. (1998, November 3). Critical Evaluation of Education Reform [On-line]. Available: http://olam.ed.asu.edu/epan/v6n20.html

2 Changing Demographics amid Diversity

People who understand demographics understand two-thirds of everything.

—David Foote, *Boom, Bust, or Echo* (1996)

Canadian author David Foote titillates the reader by suggesting that most of us are not sure that we understand two-thirds of anything. We are swishing around the demographic tea leaves in an attempt toward enlightenment. Unfortunately, the future they predict may make us wish we had stuck with coffee.

Is Diversity a Myth?

We hear conflicting reports about diversity. Large numbers of international immigrants to the United States in the early 1990s foster the perception that the United States is becoming truly diverse. Riding in cabs in downtown New York City may lead you to think that America is growing more racially and ethnically diverse by the day. According to William Frey (1998), however, the "melting pot" simply is *not real*. Frey, a demographer and Ph.D. research scientist, analyzed Census Bureau population estimates for 1996 and 1997. His research concluded that population shifts during the 1990s show a continued geographic concentration of minority groups into *specific regions* and a handful of metro areas. Frey proposes that this concentration is particularly true for new immigrant minorities, namely Hispanics and Asians. These minorities typically enter the United States through limited gateway cities and remain in those regions.

Granted, the term *Hispanic* was invented in the 1980 census in an attempt to describe the large numbers of people from South and Central America who were moving to the United States. In Florida, they are not identified as Hispanics; rather they are called Latinos and Latinas. In Texas and California, they are identified as Chicanos and Chicanas (Hodgkinson, 1998). For the purposes of this chapter, however, the term *Hispanic* is used in its comprehensive sense to include all of these groups.

While some of the Asian minorities are trickling out of the gateway metros, the pace is relatively slow. According to Frey, the largest blocks of these minorities are clustered in only a few geographic areas. Most places beyond these "melting pots" are largely white, or white and black.

The Rapid Hispanic Migration to the United States

Although Frey's comments may have reflected the Hispanic migration six or seven years ago, the current data shows a more rapid and comprehensive migration to other metropolitan centers as well as to rural areas throughout the United States. One of the pitfalls of using demographics for predictive purposes is that some have targeted geographic locations where the number of minorities is growing rapidly, while the actual number of minorities in those areas may be quite small. Los Angeles, in contrast, yields both large numbers of minorities and a rapidly growing population of Hispanics. Among the nation's 271 urban areas, Los Angeles is home to fully one-fifth of the Hispanic population. It also ranks first in total Hispanic population growth, netting 18 percent of all Hispanic population gains in the nation between 1990 and 1996. The city's Hispanic growth comes not only from Mexican and Latin American immigrants, but also from continued high birth rates among long-term Hispanic residents.

On June 11, 2001, *Time* magazine published a special issue titled "Welcome to Amexica." The article, titled "Courting a Sleeping Giant," reports:

> The biggest political news of the 2000 Census was that Hispanics—more than half of them tracing their roots to Mexico—have become the largest minority group in the U.S., surpassing African Americans at least six years sooner than expected. Where that's happening is turning out to be as surprising as how fast. Of the congressional districts that saw the biggest increases in their Latino populations over the past decade, not a single one is in a state along the Mexican border. Rural areas saw huge growth in Hispanic populations. By the end of 2001, four of the eight largest U.S. cities may have Hispanic mayors (Tumulty, 2001, p. 74).

The political ramifications continue to intrigue us. Where Hispanics are newly arrived, they only have just begun to "crack" the city school boards, councils, and county commissions. As one seemingly savvy politician remarked, "We're on the ground floor of political empowerment" (p. 74).

Why has Hispanic political influence lagged behind the census? Several reasons are postulated. Hispanics in the United States are more dispersed than other minorities such as African Americans. This means that legislators have to work harder to identify districts where potential voters live. In addition, the census figures cannot yet accurately give the polls the true picture of voting power. More than one-third of Hispanics are under voting age and those who are eligible to vote often do not. Although the Hispanic and African American populations in the United States are roughly the same size, six million more blacks are registered to vote. Turnout rates for Hispanics are even more disappointing for the more educated and affluent.

People on the Move

An incredible number of people move every year—about 43 million. It may be possible, if not probable, for an elementary school teacher to report that she started the year with 24 students in September and still had 24 the following May, but that 22 of them are different children (Hodgkinson, 1998).

Three states—California, Texas, and Florida—account for half of the country's population growth. When examining population movement in the eastern half of the country, a picture emerges of suburban growth around declining urban cores in major cities. This pattern is very important when considering poverty among children. While poverty is not increasing in cities as a whole, it is increasing in the *inner ring of suburbs*. If the criterion for poverty status is the increased number of children eligible for free and reduced-price lunches, then poverty exists in those inner rings of older suburbs.

Size-Begets-Growth Phenomenon

The importance of the immigrant gateways in both attracting and maintaining large Hispanic populations is evident in the rankings of the top metropolises for numerical gains in Hispanics during the 1990s. The ten metro centers with the largest Hispanic populations also had the largest population gain. Together they attracted more than half (52 percent) of new Hispanic immigrants between 1990 and 1996. The top ten collectively house 58 percent of the nation's Hispanic residents.

These metropolises include Miami, where Cubans have come; New York City, gaining Dominicans, Puerto Ricans, and other Caribbean-origin Hispanics; and Chicago, a continuing magnet for Mexicans. The other seven metro areas lie close to the Mexican border and continue to build on large, existing Latin American residents.

As with Hispanics, Asians have given the large gateway metros the greatest numerical growth. Together, Los Angeles, New York City, and San Francisco account for 39 percent of the nation's gains in Asian residents since 1990. Forty-three percent of all U.S. Asians live in these three urban areas. Chinese immigrants are heavily drawn to New York City, Filipinos to Los Angeles, and both show a large presence in San Francisco.

Blacks and the New South

Tracking the movement of America's black population may be even more challenging than tracking Hispanics and Asians. Many blacks are still concentrated regionally in Northern urban centers and in the South. The popularity among blacks for the revitalized "New South" represents the greatest gain in Southern metros for blacks in the 1990s. The Atlanta metro area is representative of these new attractive markets. With a booming economy and a large black middle class, working-class and middle-class blacks from all national origins made Atlanta the biggest gaining metro area for blacks between 1990 and 1996.

Two generations ago, freed slaves and sharecroppers moved from regions like this to the North, where they got jobs in manufacturing, especially the auto industry. Their children prospered, often were able to go to college, and their grandchildren are now the ones who are moving back to the South to take leadership positions in government and business. Other growing metros with similar metropolitan characteristics that dot the Southeast and have also attracted blacks include Raleigh-Durham and Charlotte, North Carolina, and Houston-Dallas-Fort Worth, Texas.

In northern metros such as New York City and Chicago, large population gains are deceptive. The numbers represent a natural increase among already-existing black populations who migrated in previous decades. If the domestic trend had continued, the number of new black residents in these northern metro areas would have been even greater. Instead, these areas are losing blacks to domestic migration to the South.

White Migration

As the largest ethnic population in the United States, whites are even more widely dispersed than blacks across the nation. The white migration tends to be toward different metropolitan areas than that of Hispanics and Asians. Whites appear to be more responsive to growing economic opportunities in western and southern states. White growth is occurring mostly in Texas, the Southeast, and the Rocky Mountain states near California. White employment in services and construction is driving white migration to Las Vegas and Orlando.

Weather is another attraction for white migrants. The allure of temperate climates is especially appealing to retirement-age whites. Unlike migrants of other ethnicities, whites seem to feel less tied to family and friends for economic and social support and more free to move (Hodgkinson, 1998).

Between 1990 and 1996, more than one-fourth of the nation's 271 metros lost populations. These included cities with struggling economies in the Northeast such as Providence, Rhode Island; Pittsburgh, Pennsylvania; and Springfield, Massachusetts. Yet the three greatest white population losses occurred in metros whose economies were viable, namely, New York City, Los Angeles, and San Francisco. They are also the greatest-gaining metro areas for Hispanics and Asians (Hodgkinson, 1998).

Melting Pots and Salad Bowls: How Elusive Can Demographics Be?

Most communities lack true racial and ethnic diversity, given the ongoing growth in the numbers of Hispanics and Asians in large gateway metros, the domestic migration of whites to the South and West, and the movement of blacks to the South (Frey, 1998). Instead, the United States has only a few "multiple melting pots," counties and metro areas with a significant presence of two or more minority groups. These places may evolve into unique markets as intermarriage and blending cultures lead to unique politics, tastes for consumer products, and community personalities.

Frey (1996) identified 21 melting-pot metros using a relatively stringent demographic definition. These are areas where the percentage of non-Hispanic whites is lower than its share of the national population (73 percent). These communities must also have at least two minority groups with a population percentage that is greater than their national representations—12 percent for non-Hispanic blacks, 11 percent for Hispanics, and 5 percent for Asians or Native Americans/Eskimos. The 21 multiethnic metro areas include the three largest gateways—New York City, Los Angeles, and San Francisco—as well as Washington, D.C., Chicago, San Diego, and Houston. The remaining metros are relatively small and are located in Texas and California. Only New York City has overrepresentations of three minorities: Hispanics, Asians, and blacks. The multiethnic California metro areas have a uniform overrepresentation of Hispanics and Asians, while Texas metro areas and Chicago are multiethnic by virtue of blacks and Hispanics. Although the list of multiple-minority metros is short, there are many more areas with a significant share of only *one* minority group.

A most striking characteristic of U.S. demographics is the broad swath of states in the Northeast, Midwest, Rocky Mountains, and Northwest that are mostly white, and where none of the minority groups comes close to approximating their national percentages of population. Of the over 3,000 counties identified as of 1996, only 745 show white populations below the national white percentage (73 percent). Well over half are at least 90 percent white.

The salad bowl analogy refers to various racial and ethnic groups who maintain their own identity, as opposed to the melting pot analogy, in which everyone comes out the same (Aldridge, 1993). As previously mentioned, most communities in the United States lack true racial and ethnic diversity given the ongoing growth in the numbers of Hispanics and Asians, the domestic migration of whites to the South and West, and the movement of blacks to the South (Frey, 1998). Instead, the United States has only a few salad bowl cities, counties, and metro areas with a significant percentage of two or more minority groups. These places may evolve into unique markets, as intermarriage and blending cultures leads to unique politics, tastes for consumer products, community personalities, and relationships with schools.

Minority Majorities, or, Where Have the White People Gone?

In 1996 only 226 counties in the United States had white minorities. Most of these were small counties in the rural South where blacks are the majority or in Texas and other parts of the Southwest where Hispanics are in the majority. The largest of these areas suggest the location of counties that will have minority majorities in the future. Many of the new minority-majority counties are inner counties of older, largely white-black metropolitan areas such as St. Louis and Philadelphia. The change in these areas is being fueled primarily by traditional white flight to the suburbs and beyond. But the shift also is due to infusions of new minority populations, namely, Hispanics and Asians in some California counties (i.e., Alameda, Fresno, and Monterey); blacks in the Georgia counties of DeKalb and Richmond; and all three in Fort Bend County, Texas. According to Frey (1998), outside of these distinct regions, racial and ethnic diversification is likely to occur at a more "glacial" pace.

Small Numbers, Fast Growth

For the foreseeable future, the greatest numbers of minorities will probably continue to live in large metro areas. But evidence exists that some minorities, particularly Hispanics, are migrating to parts of the country where foreign languages are alien to the residents. The major lure for these ethnic pioneers is economic, namely employment opportunities. Ethnic minorities with or without college degrees are taking advantage of booming job markets that previously have mostly attracted whites and blacks.

   One criterion for identifying these new minority frontiers is to look at counties where the growth rate is high. For Hispanics, these counties include both the cities and suburbs of white-black metropolitan areas like Atlanta and, in North Carolina, the communities of Raleigh–Durham–Chapel Hill and Greensboro–Winston Salem–High Point as well as other counties in the Southeast. Other Hispanic "hot spots" include urban and rural counties in the largely white parts of Rocky Mountain states (Idaho and Nevada) and America's midsection (Nebraska and Iowa).

Asian Americans are even more concentrated than Hispanics in gateway metropolitan areas. Fast-growing areas for them are typically where there is an existing Asian American presence. However, when they migrate nationally, the pattern appears as a "chain migration," with friends and family following the lead of the first pioneering movers. Still, the migration is relatively circumscribed.

Middle-class blacks are the vanguard of the new migrant movement to the South. For blacks, the 1990s represent a return to the South from the industrial cities of the Northeast and Midwest. Included in this migration are fast-growing metros like Atlanta, Dallas–Forth Worth, and Washington Baltimore. Parts of Florida that previously did not have a large African American presence are also feeling the growth. But black retirees who have spent most of their adult lives in northern and western cities are also attracted to many of the smaller, rural counties of the South.

Cities Still Have the Most Minorities

While both whites and people of color show migration preferences for non-metropolitan areas, it is important to remember that most minorities reside in urban areas. They are much more likely than whites to live in cities and metro counties. As of 1996, nearly 95 percent of Asians, more than 91 percent of Hispanics, and better than 85 percent of blacks resided in metropolitan areas (Frey, 1996). The plurality of all three groups is located in metropolises with populations that exceed 1 million. In contrast, the share of the U.S. white population residing in nonmetropolitan areas is approaching one-fourth, and less than half reside in the nation's biggest metropolitan areas.

How Rapid and Diverse Population Growth Challenges the Public Schools

Population growth continues to challenge an already strained educational system. In the school year 2000, 53 million children entered public and private schools, the highest enrollment in history (*Yearbook*, 2001). In 20 years the expected growth rate will increase by 7.2 percent to 55.2 million. This increase begins as a "small dip" in the next five years, then surges through 2020. Why does this happen? Demographers point to the "baby boom echo," which is the continuing growth of children entering the public schools from the children of baby boomers to the grandchildren of baby boomers.

A Small Number of Schools Carry the Heaviest Burden

Schools comprised largely of minorities are historically understaffed and under-financed and carry the largest burden of educating our children (*Yearbook*, 2001).

One hundred of the largest public school districts that represent 0.06 percent of all U.S. school districts are responsible for educating 22.9 percent of all public school students. Among those 100 schools, 52 percent of students—as compared with 38 percent of *all* reporting schools within the United States—were eligible for free lunch. Three states—California, Florida, and Texas—accounted for about 40 percent of the largest school districts. These same three states are experiencing the largest influx of immigrants and need to meet the demands that population changes make on public schools.

Student Enrollment at an All-Time High

American schools presently enroll the highest number of students in the history of the country, 49 million students in public school districts and 5 million students through the private sector. Fewer than 1 million students are taught through homeschooling or charter schools. This enrollment is causing shortages and funding crises in many communities (Frey, 1998).

Hispanics: The Greatest Growth of Immigration and Its Impact on Public Schools

"In the next 20 years, Hispanic school-age population is predicted to increase about 60 percent. In 25 years, it is predicted that one in four school-age students will be Hispanic" (*Yearbook*, 2001, p. 65). These projections will force school districts to accommodate distinctive needs such as linguistic challenges, immersion into the mainstream curriculum, and the need to recruit more minority teachers and/or teachers who have been educated to meet these challenges.

Teacher Shortages: Both Quantity and Quality?

For years we have heard about teacher shortages. School reformers demand that we not only meet teacher shortages in numbers we recruit but also that these teachers are willing and able to meet the challenges that await them. In the forthcoming decade, estimates place the teacher shortage at 2.2 million. "Unfortunately, in order to meet these new demands, many states have lowered standards and hired teachers with marginal qualifications. More than 30 percent of newly hired teachers lack full certification when they enter the profession, more than 11 percent enter the classroom without a license, and more than one-quarter of public school teachers are teaching subjects out of their field" (*Yearbook*, 2001, p. 66). The irony remains that students with the greatest need are less likely to have the most qualified teachers. Teachers who will be most challenged by their students' needs are less likely to pursue advanced degrees or work with poor and minority students.

Education and licensing are major problems, but high turnover is also a serious problem. More than 20 percent of new teachers leave the profession within three to four years. How do we retain teachers? Professional development through continued coursework, improved working conditions, peer mentoring, and higher salaries must complement new licensing requirements.

Leaving Poor and Minority Students Behind

A major factor that contributes to poor achievement levels is the dramatic disparity in resources provided to the poorest children. A U.S. Department of Education (USDOE) analysis of data from 1997 showed that the richest school districts spent 56 percent more per student than the poorest did. If we extrapolate this factor by poor schools serving large numbers of poor children and having teachers with less training and fewer supplies, the picture looks bleak. "Children of color concentrated in underfunded urban school districts, disproportionately suffer the consequences of these unequal resources. Nearly five decades after the *Brown versus Board of Education* decision, too many minority children still do not have equal opportunity to succeed in school and their future careers" (*Yearbook*, 2001, p. 63).

Demographics of Students

Student demographics continue to shift toward greater racial and ethnic diversity (Education Market Conditions, 1999). Forty percent of U.S. students are racially and ethnically diverse populations, with big-city districts and some border states having significantly higher percentages of enrollment. Midwestern and rural communities also face expanding diversity. The School District of Lawrence, Kansas, for example, documents more than 40 languages spoken in homes of its student population; however, this data may be particular to a college town, the location of the University of Kansas.

Special Needs Children and Youth

Culture and language are not the only diversities in the new demographics of the classroom. Other differences such as children with special needs integrated into the regular classroom pose challenges, too. According to the Nineteenth Annual Report to Congress (U.S. Department of Education, 1997), a total of 5,573,350 U.S. children and youth with disabilities, ages 3–21, were served under the Individuals with Disabilities Education Act (IDEA), Part B, during the 1995–1996 school year. This number comprises 12.4 percent of the total school-age population and reflects an increase of 3.5 percent from the previous year. As in past years, the total number of special students, those with specific learning disabilities, represent by far the largest disability category in special education (SPED), currently comprising 51.2 percent of those served under IDEA, Part B. Students with speech or language impairments, mental retardation (MR), and emotional disturbance (ED) represent 20.2 percent, 11.5 percent, and 8.6 percent, respectively, of the SPED population served under IDEA, Part B. Together these four disabilities categories represent over 91 percent of all children and youth with disabilities currently served in SPED.

The number of special needs youth served under federal law has steadily increased. The percentage of students with disabilities ages 6–21 served in *general education* classes gradually increased from 32.8 percent in 1990–1991 to 42.5 percent in 1994–1995. According to the U.S. Department of Education (1997), the largest relative increases from 1994–1995 to 1995–1996 were in the areas of traumatic brain injury (TBI), autism, and other health impairments (OHI). Most states attributed these increases to the addition of the two newest categories to IDEA (i.e., TBI and autism). The increase in the OHI category was generally attributed to increased services to children and youth with attention deficit hyperactivity disorder (ADHD) (USDOE, 1997).

One of the most significant changes that has occurred in SPED over the past 15 years has been the movement toward greater *inclusion* of students with disabilities into general education classrooms (McLeskey, Henry & Hodges, 1998). The "rightness" of inclusion continues to incite considerable controversy among parents and educators. Chapter 9 will address these issues in a comprehensive manner. Data provided by the USDOE (1997) suggests that over 44 percent of students with disabilities currently spend at least 80 percent of their school day in the general education classroom and more than 95 percent of all students with disabilities attend regular schools. While progress toward more inclusive placements has been made, only 9.5 percent of students with MR are served in general education classrooms and the degree to which students with disabilities are educated in general education classes has varied greatly across states and districts. In larger urban areas, fewer than 60 percent of all students with disabilities are educated primarily in general education classrooms (USDOE, 1997).

Long-term outcomes for students with disabilities have been discouraging (USDOE, 1997). A significant number drop out of school or graduate through certification only. Students who do not graduate from high school usually experience lower rates of employment, lower incomes, and higher rates of incarceration. Whereas 75.6 percent of students without disabilities graduate from high school, only 57.1 percent of students with disabilities do.

A major concern is the continued overrepresentation of minorities in SPED (USDOE, 1997). National data compiled by the Office for Civil Rights, suggest that whereas blacks account for approximately 16 percent of the total student population, they represent 32 percent, 29 percent, 24 percent, and 18 percent of students with mild mental retardation, moderate mental retardation, serious emotional disturbance, and specific learning disabilities, respectively. As noted by the USDOE (1997), the consequences of misclassification or inappropriate placement in SPED are serious and may result in a denial of access to the core curriculum, increased segregation, and ultimately, reduced access to postsecondary education and employment opportunities.

Kea (1997) has summarized numerous studies related to the overrepresentation of black students in SPED. Her review suggested that black students, particularly *males*, are:

- three times more likely than white males to be included in the categories of ED and MR;
- more likely to be separated in special classrooms or buildings;
- more likely to be expelled or suspended; and
- more often employed in low-paying and minimum-wage jobs once they leave public schools.

Black students are at greater risk for early behavior problems than their white counterparts and are more likely to disrupt the classroom environment and to be suspended and expelled *even* when socioeconomic status is controlled (National Center for Education Statistics, 1997). Although the reasons why black youth are at high risk for school-related behavior problems are unclear, several researchers have speculated that the increased incidence is related to cultural conflicts these students encounter in the school setting (Barr & Parrett, 1995). These findings are disconcerting when we consider the following:

- When suspension and expulsion rates are high, juvenile crime increases.
- Suspension or expulsion of students only makes the problem worse by pushing out those students who need to be in school the most.
- Suspension or expulsion of students results in "relocating" the problem.
- More positive, proactive supports for youth result in more positive outcomes (National Association of Child Advocates, 1998).

Voltz (1998) has argued that many factors may contribute to this overrepresentation. Some of these factors are due to larger social problems such as the disproportionately higher poverty rates among blacks. Voltz (1998) also reported that when differences in income are controlled, the disproportionate representation of black students decreases substantially. In contrast, when income is controlled, increases in the numbers of white students occur. Research has indicated that poverty is a significant risk factor because of its enduring association with unhealthy home and work environments, poor nutrition, insufficient prevention and treatment services, and infant mortality.

Demographics of Teachers

The retirement of college professors and school district superintendents is at an all-time high. About 90 percent of these retiring leaders are white men. Their vacated positions will be filled with significant numbers of minorities and women. Many states are already experiencing shortages in teaching positions.

The average teacher in America is between 45 and 50 years old and has taught more than 20 years. Unfortunately, as older teachers jump through the window of opportunity into early retirement they take much of the institutional memory of the profession with them. While teachers eligible for retirement rarely need intensive support for classroom management, new teachers often do.

Demographics of Families: An Increasing Number of Nonparents as Taxpayers

The demographics of families, taxpayers, and communities are changing. Typically, the fate of the schools rests with the priorities and political clout of parents (Foot, 1996). Fewer families today have children of school age than in any other period in the history of our nation and fewer than 35 percent of taxpayers have direct family ties to school systems (Education Market Conditions, 1999). In future decades *nonparents* will outnumber and probably outmaneuver parents in setting priorities for public spending. As populations decrease in fertility, they age rapidly. In 1900, the average American was 21 years old whereas today the average American is 37. If not for immigration, we would be similar to Italy, which has as many people over 80 as it has children under 4. The youngest children in the United States are also the most diverse. While 26 percent of all Americans are nonwhite, among school-age children the figures move up to 37 percent. Among preschool children younger than 5, that figure is 38 percent. It seems that children entering our schools will be the most diverse population ever experienced (Hodgkinson, 1998). Another significant demographic principle to consider is how many people were born during the 17-year baby boom that began in 1946. A 37 percent increase in births occurred that year, and that means that in 2011 the percentage of people who apply for Social Security will go up 37 percent followed by 16 more years of rapid increases. Because of our aging population, only one home in four now has a child enrolled in school.

Public Schools No Longer Have a Monopoly on Education

Most urban school districts do not have, nor will they have in the near future, the vision, leadership, capacity, resources, political leverage, or community support to continue as centralized systems (Frey, 1998). Depending on local conditions, most will abdicate centralized authority more and more to the local school site, be taken over by the state, or be reorganized in ways yet to be identified. Thirty-six states now have charter school legislation, and well over 1,000 charters are operating nationally. We have come to recognize that learning can take place anywhere, at any time, and at any age. Schools, therefore, do not monopolize education. Education and human development are a $350 billion market. The nonprofit and for-profit sector are focusing on learning systems for the lifelong educational market. During their careers, 90 percent of all American workers will be involved in some formal postsecondary education. The educational "experience" is merging into service industries, retailing, and cultural markets as a significant sector of the economy (Frey, 1998).

Immigrant Education Issues Related to Demographics

Since the 1980s the wave of Hispanic and Asian immigration has rapidly changed school demographics across the country by expanding racial, cultural, and linguistic diversity within classrooms (Frey, 1998). The number of language minority students has increased dramatically, particularly in urban school districts such as New York City and Los Angeles, which carry much of the responsibility to meet the needs and interests of their immigrant students. The number of limited English proficient (LEP) students who live in non-English-language homes is estimated to be approaching 40 percent of all school children (Frey, 1998). At the beginning of the twenty-first century, 77 percent of the total limited English proficient population in the United States were Spanish-speaking. Educators are currently dealing with these new issues of increased cultural and linguistic diversity in schools. The need to reframe the national agenda to create progressive and inclusive classrooms for all students is critical (Frey, 1998).

Life Expectancy and Population Growth

A pattern emerges as we look at life expectancy in countries around the world. With the exception of China, the nations with the longest life expectancies for its citizenry are all in the Northern Hemisphere, namely, in North America and Europe. Populations in the Northern Hemisphere are basically old, white, rich, well educated, and *barely maintaining themselves in terms of numbers*. By contrast, populations in the Southern Hemisphere are mostly young, nonwhite, poor, less educated; they account for 98 percent of the world's population growth.

Seventy percent of the world's resources reside in the Northern Hemisphere where only 30 percent of the world's population exists. Immigration has come mainly from relatively poor, uneducated minorities in the Southern Hemisphere moving north. This northern migration is seen also in Europe. People in Africa are moving to Europe at about the same rate as people from Central and South America are moving to the United States (Hodgkinson, 1998).

This data is important if we consider the future student body. With fertility rates on the decline everywhere in the world, the world's population of 5.7

billion will level off at about 11.5 billion (Hodgkinson, 1998). In Southeast Asia, the fertility rate is declining from 8 to 7.8 children per female. That drop is small given the average white fertility rate of 1.7 children per female. By 2010, whites will account for only about 9 percent of the world's population. This projection is compared to the 17 percent white representation in 1997. Whites, then, will be the world's smallest ethnic minority.

Only 12 percent of immigration to the United States is from Europe. Almost all the rest is from Central and South America and Asia. Children from these areas represent the new America. Some of these immigrant children are remarkably adept in school. Many classrooms today have children who can speak several different languages. In the 1900s the immigrant children spoke Polish, French, German, or Italian. Today, they speak Hindi, Urdu, Arabic, and several other languages. The issue today, as it was in 1900, is to create a socially responsive environment. Demographics may be able to help. With demographics, it is possible to predict how many children are at risk for academic failure before they even begin kindergarten. The Casey Foundation annually produces a map that ranks states in terms of teen pregnancies, high school dropouts, single mothers, low-income families, violent teenage deaths, and infant and child mortality. Combining all of these factors can help make predictions about which children will be in the most trouble and which will graduate from high school and go to college (Hodgkinson, 1998). However, these predictions have to be critically questioned and not used to stereotype individuals or have low expectations for children.

Currently, the population of youth under the age of 18 is increasing only slightly—2 million over a 10-year period. This represents a big increase in student population in the outer suburbs, particularly offset by a decline in the inner suburbs and core cities. Young workers ages 18–44, who were born after the baby boom, represent numbers that are down by over 1 million people over the 10-year period. In comparison, the 45–64 year old boomer group is up 17 million. Those over age 65 are up 4 million (Hodgkinson, 1998).

Are U.S. Residents Represented Fairly in the Schools?

Currently there are 24.6 million people living in the United States who were born in another country, according to the 1996 Current Population Survey (Miller, 1997). This figure represents 9.3 percent of the population, the highest percentage since 1940. Every one of the 215 nations in the world has someone living in the United States. The leading birth nations of the foreign-born are Mexico, the Philippines, China, Cuba, and India. Mexican Americans constitute 6.7 million (27 percent) of all foreign-born. Almost half have not completed high school, in contrast to 16 percent of natives. Thirty-five percent of the Mexican-born are in poverty. This figure is significantly higher than the 22 percent of all foreign-born and 13 percent of all Americans.

Another 27 percent of the foreign-born are from Asia, including 1.2 million Filipinos, who are more likely than natives to have a bachelor's degree or higher and to have incomes over $35,000. Only 5 percent of Filipinos live below the poverty level of subsistence. Included among the Asian-born immigrants are 801,000 Chinese. These individuals are generally older than the national average and are more likely than natives to have incomes over $50,000. Although 85 percent of the China-born population live above the poverty level, the China-born are more likely than natives to have no income (Miller, 1997).

Cuban-born Americans number 772,000 and tend to be older than natives, 57 percent over the age of 45. They are more likely than natives to have less than a high school degree. Just behind them are Asian Indians with 757,000 residents. They tend to be very well educated, with 52 percent holding a 4-year college degree and 29 percent holding professional or graduate degrees. Asian Indians are also likely to be middle-aged, which may explain why their $50,000 plus incomes are higher than natives (Miller, 1997).

People in the United States are marrying others of different ethnic origins. A quarter of the marriages today among Hispanics are to non-Hispanics. A quarter of the marriages among Asian Americans are to non-Asians.

Three million children in U.S. schools are of mixed ethnic ancestry. For example, golf champion Tiger Woods calls himself a "Cablinasian." This designation is because he is Caucasian, black, and Indian Asian.

Between the years 2000 and 2010 the future national increases among ethnic groups suggest the population of whites rising by 5 million. Hispanics should rise by 9 million and blacks by 3.8 million. Asians will be up 3.8 million and native Americans up over 250,000. These statistics imply considerable diversity within the public schools (Hodgkinson, 1998).

For the first time in history more Hispanic youths than black youths will be coming to school. This trend will likely not turn around since there is no black immigration to compare with the large pool of potential Hispanic immigrants, the largest group coming from Mexico. In the past when we talked about diversity in America we thought in terms of black and white. We need to start thinking about black, white, Hispanic, Asian, and Native American.

Changes are to be predicted in the religions of America as well. In the past we thought primarily of Catholic, Protestant, and Jewish. The most rapidly growing religion in this nation is Islam.

Given the changes in the racial/ethnic composition of students for the future, a greater degree of heterogeneity of language and culture in our nation's schools should be anticipated. Certainly a variety in the backgrounds and interests of students can enhance the learning environment; however, the variety can also create new or increased challenges for our schools (Aldridge, Calhoun, & Aman, 2000).

The Awesome Challenge

"What we have called the 'triple dilemma,' or 'trilemma' is the mutually damaging collision of individual human rights, cultural diversity, and global human opportunities. Today the damage from that collision is suddenly all around us. Finding ways to become unified despite diversity may be the world's most urgent problem in the years ahead" (Cleveland, 1995, p. 26).

Darling-Hammond (1997) projects demographics that impose challenges: "Meeting America's twenty-first-century challenge is not just a matter of improved teaching of academic content in schools that are now failing . . . Repairing the torn social fabric that increasingly arrays one group against another will require creating an inclusive social dialogue to which individuals can come to understand diverse experiences and points of view" (p. 30).

Williams (1999) poses the following challenges to society and educational institutions as a result of diversity:

1. We need to comprehend and accept the paradigm shift in conceptualizations of diversity supported by new understandings of human development.
2. We need to centrally position these new understandings of human development in reform proposals introduced to increase the learning success of a diverse student population.
3. We need to integrate available models and strategies into efforts to develop the abilities and attitudes necessary for current populations of diverse students to successfully participate in the global market economy of the twenty-first century.

What we know about diversity and human development has been shaped and limited by inadequate theoretical assumptions and historical, political, and economic conditions (Banks & Banks, 1995; Cleveland, 1995; Orfield, Bachmeier, James & Eitle, 1997). In addition, rapid changes in the society have superseded an understanding and acceptance of the complexities of human development (Williams, 1999).

Inadequate Assumptions about Human Development

Hundreds of theories of human development and intelligence have been offered since the recorded philosophical assumptions of Plato (428–347 B.C.) (Ceci, 1996). Modern psychological theories have been motivated by either genetic (Jensen, 1973) or contextual (Coles, 2000) assumptions. The nature/nurture controversy debated elsewhere (Ceci, 1996; Kamin, 1974) has revolved around assumptions and interpretations of IQ tests. Kamin (1974) argues that the IQ tests used in the United States have been fostered by men committed to a particular social view. The view, basically, is that those at the bottom of the scale are genetically inferior; consequently the tests serve as instruments of oppression against the poor, the foreign-born, and racial minorities.

Research and theories of scholars from diverse disciplines (Ceci, 1996; Coles, 2000; Dewey, 1938; Wozniak & Fischer, 1993) currently have converged to support a framework of human development that builds on developmental, cognitive, and social psychology, as well as anthropology, sociology, and genetics. Ceci (1996) suggests, "One's cultural context is an integral part of cognition because the culture arranges the occurrence or nonoccurrence of events that are known to affect cognitive developments, e.g., literacy" (pp. 95–96). Coles (2000) shares an illuminating quote from the anthropologist Theodor Adorno: "Culture might be precisely that condition that excludes a mentality capable of measuring it" (p. 7).

What is culture? How and by whom is it defined? Culture is closely intertwined with concepts of ethnicity, social class, and race. Williams (1999) offers the following definition, "Culture is the lens, crafted by history, tradition and environmental conditions: through which groups view themselves, their environment, and their future, and shape their decision making, problem solving, and behavioral responses" (p. 93).

Rapid Social Changes

Within a span of 200 years we have made the transition from Agricultural Age through the Industrial Age and into the Information Age. Toffler (1990) and Resnick (1995) suggest that success in the twenty-first century will be defined by an access to information and the ability to process it. Ensuring that success will be the central challenge for educational institutions.

Possible Solutions?

The 21st Century Learning Initiative, a program of 40 researchers, educational innovators, and policy makers from 10 countries, was established in 1996 to synthesize the best of research and development into the nature of human development/learning and to examine its implications for education, work, and the development of communities worldwide. An interim report that summarizes the work in progress presents four findings:

1. a shift in perception—Current conceptualizations of knowledge and learning reflect a shift from a science of analysis of discrete parts, i.e., behaviorism, toward a science of organizing principles and dynamics, and interactive relationships.

2. new understandings of what it means to be human—Recent research is defining the co-evolution of the human and the environment, and the development of multiple forms of intelligence that help make sense of the environment in different ways.
3. new understandings about the brain—Traditionally, the study of learning was largely limited to psychologists and philosophers and, more recently, cognitive scientists. Neurologists, as a result of functional MRI and CAT scans, are now able to indicate how individual learning actually occurs.
4. evolving ideas about learning—The process of learning has passed from simple, self-organization to social problem-solving activity, collaborative and interpersonal dependence on conversation, meaningful involvement, and practical real-world experience and application. Learning is viewed as a consequence of experience, thinking, and an integral part of living.

In summary, these findings represent a shift in perspective with the focus on the learner, from information transmission views of traditional learning environments to a constructivist/cultural environmental view (Greeno, Collins & Resnick, 1994). There is little evidence that the deeper meanings are understood and internalized in the conversations and decision-making processes in schools, communities, and government agencies.

Greeno, Collins, and Resnick (1994) have identified elements found in most teaching and learning environments that, when combined, are most effective. The recognition that learning and work are not separated has resulted in efforts to focus on the role of *motivation and effort* in learning and to incorporate some of the characteristics of work environments into school learning and environments. Current research indicates that motivation is sensitive to contexts. For example, a student may be highly motivated in algebra but not in geography. Students may be very unmotivated in some school environments but very motivated in others. Teachers vary in setting motivation as a priority. Motivation also reflects cognitive factors such as the way in which individuals differ in how they interpret their success and failure. Many schools have not focused on improving student motivation as an important outcome. Rather they have focused mainly on improving test scores or achievement (Greeno, Collins & Resnick, 1994).

Resilience literature offers another opportunity to more adequately address the educational supports of learning necessary for populations of economically diverse students. Researchers (Rutter, 1987; Werner & Smith, 1992) have identified the following attributes as those that enable youth to cope with risks in their environment: (1) social competence, (2) problem-solving skills, (3) autonomy, and (4) a sense of purpose/future. To facilitate the development of resiliency in students, schools, as well as families and communities, should provide: (1) caring and support, (2) high expectations, and (3) opportunities for children to participate.

Current major reform proposals that deal with issues of *decentralization, site-based management, curriculum and assessment standards,* and *schoolwide projects* have not centrally positioned the new understandings of human development outlined by the 21st Century Learning Initiative. A review of reform proposals reveals that many important issues of human development have been left to chance (Stringfield, Rossie & Smith, 1996).

Other attempts at reforming school will be addressed in great detail in a later chapter regarding private schools, charter schools, and other alternative school settings. Although these reform initiatives have attempted to improve the educational outcomes for diverse students as well as others, and achievement gains are impressive in some cases, those gains are often uneven and not adequate to close the achievement gap that limits the opportunities for culturally and linguistically diverse students to be competitive in the twenty-first century (Walberg & Greenberg, 1998).

Teachers' Responses to Diversity

Research has identified a positive correlation between the higher achievement of culturally diverse poor students and teachers who demonstrate culturally responsible instructional strategies (Ladson-Billings, 1994). There is an assumption that teachers will do what is best to improve academic outcomes for students. Lipman (1998) reports research describing teacher *decision making* that negates this assumption. Issues at the core of many black students' experiences in school—misinterpretation of discourse (language, style, social interactions), academic tracking, negation of student strengths, the exclusion of diverse students' experiences and histories in the curriculum, and the problematic implications of an emphasis on individual competition—were not touched.

A large-scale, systematic study reporting the instructional practices of approximately 140 classrooms in 15 elementary schools serving diverse students reports a range of teacher responses to diversity (Knapp, Shields & Turnbull, 1995). Teachers approached the tasks of dealing with cultural and social diversity in a variety of ways. Responses to diversity ranged from approaches that actively excluded children from learning opportunities because of their backgrounds to attempts to use students' backgrounds as a positive basis for learning in the classroom.

Corbett, Wilson, and Williams (1997) researched another dimension of teachers' responses to diversity. They found that teachers overwhelmingly agreed (79 percent of 50 teachers interviewed) that "all students could succeed in school and that the teachers themselves could make a difference" (p. 102). One segment of the teachers maintained that it is the *teachers' responsibility* to ensure that diverse students do so. Another segment claimed that all children can succeed if the students put forth the necessary effort.

Teachers vary in their perceptions of recognizing and valuing the diverse experiences of students. Many believe that the responsibility for learning in school resides in the student, a perception that may affect a teacher's approach to classroom instruction. The assumption or perception that all students should come to school ready to learn and that it is the teacher's job to teach them and to treat them equally raises issues and questions about the understanding of equity.

Equity Issues for Diverse Students

If current reform proposals such as site-based decision making are to improve academic outcomes for all children, issues of equity must be scheduled for discussion, defined, and clarified. Boisvert (1998) cites a useful definition of equality offered by John Dewey:

> . . . equality is a manner of regarding others which refuses any absolute scale by which to judge them. People are equal in the sense that life offers multiple contexts within which to evaluate others. Democratic equality is postulated on the denial of any single, atemporal universal context for judgment. (p. 68)

The question, then, is what is the "universal context" for judgment in public schools serving students of diversity? Williams (1999) cites the conclusions of the 1992 Commission:

> Most Americans assume that the low achievement of poor and minority children is bound up in the children themselves or their families. "The children don't try." "They have no place to study . . . Their parents don't care." "Their culture does not value education." These and other excuses are regularly offered up to explain the achievement gap that separates poor and culturally diverse students from other young Americans. (p. 3)

The assumptions of *Brown v. Board of Education* (1954) were a most significant attempt to define and address *equity* in education. Society and schools accepted the determination that equity was simply defined as all children having equal access to the same schools, classrooms, teachers, and instruction. Unfortunately, in poor urban and suburban schools, tracking, disproportionate placement in remedial programs, and underrepresentation in advanced placement and gifted programs are the strategies that are replacing school segregation (Oakes, Wells & Associates, 1996).

> Darling-Hammond (1997) suggests that successful democratic learning communities for diverse groups of students are possible by allocating resources of staff and time to the central task of classroom teaching and teachers' learning. These schools organize teachers and students to work together in ways that get beyond bureaucracy to produce:
> 1. active in-depth learning
> 2. emphasis on authentic performance

3. attention to development
4. appreciation for diversity
5. opportunities for collaborative learning
6. a collective perspective across the school
7. structures for caring
8. support for democratic learning
9. connections to family and community. (pp. 331–332)

Preservice and inservice support for teachers requires broad, clear perceptions, restructuring, and shared responsibility (Darling-Hammond, 1997). Three
examples of the kind of changes that need to occur follow.

1. To develop knowledge and skills for teachers in the 21st century teacher
   preparation institutions must revise the courses required for certification
   by integrating new conceptualizations of cultural diversity and human
   development into the pedagogy.
2. Educational leaders and policy makers must identify opportunities to
   schedule and facilitate deeper conversations about the role of cultural
   diversity in human development, and must implement strategies to impact
   learning.
3. Parents and communities must be informed of and included in conversations about the role of cultural environments in human development and
   the implications of this role for community, home, and school.

Innovations that Seem to Be Working

Williams (1999) gives samples of innovative resources that can help inform the
educational community about the current conceptualizations of human development and diversity and can suggest ways to prepare diverse populations of students for the global market economy of the twenty-first century.

*Educating Culturally and Linguistically Diverse Students (ASCD Professional
Inquiry Kit).*   This kit provides an active approach to learning for school study
groups and improvement teams. The material includes theories, research, and
practice activities for educating diverse student populations. Readings and activities to explore personal cultural perspectives and how they can affect classroom
practices; brain-based research; multiple intelligences; language development;
and change strategies are included.

*The Urban Learner Framework (ULF) (Research for Better Schools/Northeast
and Islands Regional Educational Laboratory at Brown University).*   The
major features of the ULF are (1) four research-based themes (cultural diversity,
unrecognized abilities, motivation and effort, and resilience) and (2) ramifications

of these research-based themes for decision making in curriculums, instruction, and assessment; in professional development; in management/leadership; and in community, home, and school environments.

Samples of programs and strategies that engage diverse student populations include:

The Responsive Classroom (Northeast Foundation for Children).   The Responsive Classroom is a teaching approach used in classrooms from prekindergarten through eighth grade. The program has the following aims:

- to create community (each day begins with a whole-group circle)
- to foster response interactions by sharing, listening, inclusion, and participation
- to teach through daily patterns and rituals the skills needed to be a responsive member of a classroom and school.

MicroSociety: A Real World in Miniature.   MicroSociety is a program structured explicitly to connect formal instruction to the daily experiences of students and the authentic world of work. In this program:

- Children learn by working, playing, and doing. They become both contributors and producers in the miniature community and in the world outside the school.
- Children confront moral issues and dilemmas both in theory and in practice.
- A partnership exists among children, teachers, administrators, and parents to improve the quality of life in school. Adults and children build new relationships based on the work experiences that unfold.

Additional innovations to promote true understanding of diversity abound. A principal in the Midwest undertook a bus trip for his entire school staff to the neighborhood surrounding the school so that the teachers, who do not live there, could become familiar with the community and the daily experiences of their students. The staff got off the bus to talk to people who lived in the community and who owned the local businesses to identify available opportunities. In another school district, a school newsletter, written to strengthen parental involvement, featured interviews with parents and community individuals. Other innovations include student-scheduled and -led conferences in schools that resulted in increased parental involvement. Teachers involved in looping (remaining with the same students for two to three years) report improved parental involvement, student attendance, and knowledge of their students.

Conclusions

No single way to ensure success for all student learners appears best. An increased awareness among staff of the need to *know the learner* and to strengthen their relationships with culturally diverse students seems to be a key element. Williams (1999) states that the challenge is to *systematize* such an awareness by providing caring environments and strategies that connect learners to instruction. She further acknowledges that much remains to be resolved. Brain research continues; new information will influence perceptions of diversity and learning. Technology continues to explode and changes rapidly occur. Populations continue to move and grow. Will adjusting learning experiences to ensure success for diverse populations continue to be ignored and resisted?

Educators must continue to learn about human development and learning. We must continue to *learn about ourselves*—the strengths and concerns (i.e., skill deficiencies and/or biases) we may bring to the learning relationship. We must continually evaluate the implications of technology for skill development. New professional development studies (e.g., study groups, action research) face a constant challenge to reach all students. We need to define "success" in terms of the twenty-first century. We need to stress cooperation, not competition. We have a wonderful opportunity . . . let's go for it!

REFERENCES

Aldridge, J. (1993). *Self-esteem: Loving yourself at every age*. Birmingham, AL: Doxa Books.

Aldridge, J., Calhoun, C., & Aman, R. (2000). 15 misconceptions about multicultural education. *ACEI Focus on Elementary, 12*, 1–6.

Banks, J. A., & Banks, C. A. (1995). *Handbook for research on multicultural education*. New York: Macmillian.

Barr, R., & Parrett, W. (1995). *Hope at last for at-risk youth*. Boston. Allyn & Bacon.

Boisvert, R. D. (1998). *John Dewey: Rethinking our time*. Albany, NY: State University of New York Press.

Brown v. Board of Education of Topeka, 347 U.S. 483, 493 (D. Kan. 1954).

Ceci, S. (1996). *On intelligence: A bioecological treatise on intellectual development*. Cambridge, MA: Harvard University Press.

Cleveland, H. (1995). The limits to cultural diversity. *The Futurist, 29*, 23–26.

Coles, R. (2000). *Lives of moral leadership*. New York: Random House.

Corbett, D., Wilson, B., & Williams, B. (1997). *Assumptions, actions, and performance: First-year report to OERI and the participating school districts*. Philadelphia: Unpublished report.

Darling-Hammond, L. (1997). *The right to learn: A blueprint for creating schools that work*. San Francisco: Jossey-Bass.

Dewey, J. (1938). *Experience and education*. New York: Macmillan.

Education Market Conditions, (April 21, 1999). [On-line]. Available http://www.lx.org/edmarket.html

Foot, D. (1996). *Boom, bust, and echo: How to profit from the coming demographic shift*. Toronto: Macfarlane, Walter & Ross.

Frey, W. (1998). The Diversity Myth. [On-line]. Available: http://www.demographics.com/ publications/ad98_ad/9806_ad/ad/980626.htm

Greeno, J. G., Collins, A. M., & Resnick, L. B. (1994). *Cognition and learning*. In D. Berliner, & R. Calfee (Eds.), *Handbook of educational psychology* (pp. 137–154). New York: Teachers College Press.

Hodgkinson, H. (1998). Demographics of diversity. *Education Digest, 64*(2), 1–4.

Jensen, A. R. (1973). *Educability and group differences*. New York: Harper & Row.

Kamin, L. J. (1974). *The science and politics of IQ*. Hillsdale, NJ: Lawrence Earlbaum Associates.

Kea, C. (1997). Focus on ethnic and multicultural concerns. *CCBD Newsletter, 11*(2), 6.

Knapp, M. S., Shields, P. M., & Turnbull, B. J. (1995). *Academic challenge for the children of poverty: Summary report*. Office of Policy and Planning, Washington, DC: U. S. Department of Education.

Ladson-Billings, G. (1994). *The dreamkeepers: Successful teachers of African American children*. San Francisco: Jossey-Bass.

McLeskey, J., Henry, D., & Hodges, D. (1998). Inclusion: Where is it happening? *Teaching Exceptional Children, 31*, 4–10.

Miller, B. (1997). Foreign-born diversity. [On-line]. Available: http://www.demographics.com/ publications/ad/97_9707_ad/970727.htm

National Association of Child Advocates. (1998). Why school suspension and expulsion are not the answer. *Reclaiming Children and Youth, 7*, 87–90.

National Center for Education Statistics. (1997). *The condition of education, 1997*. Washington, DC: Department of Education, Office of Educational Research and Improvement.

Oakes, J., Wells, A., & Associates. (1996). *Beyond the technicalities of school reform: Policy lessons from detracking schools*. Los Angeles, CA: UCLA Graduate School of Education & Information Studies.

Orfield, G., Bachmeier, M., James, D., & Eitle, T. (1997). *Deepening segregation in American public schools*. Harvard University: Taubman Center for State and Local Government.

Phillips, C. B. (1994). The movement of African American children through sociological contexts: A case of conflict resolution. In B. Mallory, & R. New (Eds.), *Diversity and developmentally appropriate practice* (pp. 137–154). New York: Teachers College Press.

Resnick, L. (1995). From aptitude to effort: A new foundation for our schools. *Daedalus, 124*, 55–62.

Rutter, M. (1987). Psychosocial resilience and protective mechanisms. *American Journal of Orthopsychiatry, 57*, 316–331.

Stringfield, A., Rossi, S., & Smith, L. (1996). *Bold plans for school restructuring: The new American schools designs*. Mahwah, NJ: Lawrence Erlbaum.

Toffler, A. (1990). *Powershift*. New York: Bantam Books.

Tumulty, K. (2001, June 11). *Courting a sleeping giant. Time*, Special Edition: Amexica.

United States Department of Education. (1997). *Nineteenth annual report to Congress on the implementation of the Individuals with Disabilities Education Act*. Washington, DC: Author.

U.S. Department of Education, National Center on Education Statistics. (2000). Characteristics of the 100 largest public elementary and secondary districts in the United States: 1998–1999. [On-line]. Available: http://nces.ed.gov/pubs/2000/100largest.highlights

Voltz, D. L. (1998). Cultural diversity and special education: Critical issues confronting the field. *Teacher Education and Special Education, 21*(1), 63–70.

Walberg, H., & Greenberg, R. (1998). The diogenes factor: Why it's hard to get an unbiased view of programs like "Success for All." *Education Week, 17*, 52.

Warger, C., & Repect, S. (1998). Partnership in place: Positive behavioral supports. *Reclaiming Children and Youth, 7*(2), 99–103.

Werner, E., & Smith, R. (1992). *Overcoming the odds: High risk children from birth to adulthood*. Ithaca, NY: Cornell University Press.

Williams, B. (1999). Diversity and education for the 21st century. In D. Marsh (Ed.), *Preparing our schools for the 21st century* (pp. 89–114). Alexandria, VA: ASCD.

Wozniak, R., & Fischer, K. (Eds.). (1993). *Development in context: Acting and thinking in specific environments.* Hillsdale, NJ: Lawrence Erlbaum.

Yearbook 2001: The state of America's children. (2001). Washington, DC: Children's Defense Fund.

CHAPTER

3

The Rights of Children

A child is a person who is going to carry on what you have started. He is going to sit where you are sitting, and when you are gone, attend to those things which you think are important. You may adopt all the policies you please, but how they are carried out depends on him. He will assume control of your cities, states, and nations. He is going to move in and take over your churches, schools, universities, and corporations. All your books are going to be judged, praised, or condemned by him. The fate of humanity is in his hands.

—Abraham Lincoln (1862)

America is jeopardizing its future and its soul.

- Every 44 seconds, an American baby is born into poverty.
- Every minute, a baby is born without health insurance.
- Every 2 minutes, a baby is born at low birth weight.
- Every 11 minutes, a child is reported abused or neglected.
- Every 2 hours and 20 minutes, a child or youth under 20 is killed by a gun—10 every day!

(Children's Defense Fund, 2001, p. xiv)

In a great nation such as the United States where resources abound and democracy is the rule, individuals should be able to live in safety, security, and at a manageable comfort level. Unfortunately, this quality of life is not the case for many of our youngest residents. Although adults are vulnerable to injustices, children, by the nature of their dependency, are particularly vulnerable to victimization. This chapter will address the rights of children and what that means as an issue in education. Topics presented include children and youth at-risk for failure, for poverty, homelessness, violence, abuse, and neglect. The chapter concludes with the United Nations Convention on the Rights of the Child.

Children and Youth At-Risk: An Overview

Maria comes from a large family, originally from Mexico. She is a first grader who does not speak English and has been identified by readiness tests and by her teacher as a child at-risk. But the issue is "at-risk" for what? from whom? Is Maria at-risk for failure because others believe she is not ready to learn in school? If so, what does this mean? Children from Mexico come to school with a wealth of knowledge (Moll, Amanti, Neff & Gonzales, 1992). It is a mistake to believe that children who do not speak Standard English "must first be filled in by the school before they can learn" (Erickson, 2000, p. 19). A massive school readiness problem exists, but who owns that problem? The children are ready for school. Are the teachers ready for the children?

Beth Swadener and Sally Lubeck (1995) prefer to look at children and families "at promise." They believe that the whole notion of "children at-risk" places a negative perspective on how we define children, youth, families, and communities who are different—who are poor, of color, or speak a primary language other than English. Indeed, the term *at-risk* is an entire issue unto itself.

At-risk is a generic term used to describe a range of problems of school-aged children and youth. Low achievement, absenteeism, grade retention, and behavior problems indicate that a student may be at-risk of school failure (Henley, Ramsey & Algozzine, 1999). Risk factors most often relate to home, school, and community (Barr & Parrett, 1995). Risk factors interact synergistically. As the number of risk factors increases, chances rise for teenage pregnancy, incarceration, unemployment, welfare, suicide, and other negative long-term outcomes (Barr & Parrett, 1995).

During recent years, research has successfully identified and documented factors that place children at risk (Barr & Parrett, 1995). Using only a relatively few identified factors, schools can now predict with better than 80 percent accuracy students *in the third grade* who will later drop out of school. These factors are so powerful that researchers agree if a poor child (a) attends a school composed largely of other poor children, (b) is reading a year behind by third grade, and (c) has been retained a grade, the chances of this child ever graduating from high school are near zero (McPartland & Slavin, 1990). Two of the three characteristics are school related. Learning (or not learning) to read and grade retention are related to school issues. Why are these children at-risk? Is it because of their own personal and familial characteristics or are they at-risk because the schools are failing to meet their needs?

Approximately 15 percent of all high school students leave school before their graduation date. After infants, the most vulnerable at-risk population is adolescents, according to Henley, Ramsey and Algozzine (1999).

Overwhelmingly, the appearance, culture, language, values, communities, and family structures of at-risk students did not match those of the dominant white culture the schools were designed to serve and support (Hixson & Tinzmann, 1990). School efforts to help at-risk children and youth have focused almost exclusively on students from low socioeconomic backgrounds. The term *compensatory education* is used to describe federal programs targeted for disadvantaged children who are at-risk for academic failure (Henley, Ramsey & Algozzine, 1999; Peterson, 1987).

Too often these at-risk students are identified and placed in special education classes. This overrepresentation occurs also among culturally diverse students. When students are identified as at-risk for low achievement or school failure, schools often respond by *labeling* them as disabled and placing them in restrictive educational programs. These practices appear to be especially problematic in urban settings (Gottlieb, Atler, Gottlieb & Wishner, 1994). Since the passage of the Individuals with Disabilities Education Act (IDEA), the number of students with learning disabilities has increased beyond all reasonable expectations. Slavin (1989) points out that ". . . special education has assumed a substantial burden in trying to meet the needs of students at-risk of school failure. Yet research comparing students with mild handicaps in special education to similar students left in regular classrooms finds few if any benefits for this expensive service" (p. 15).

The annual dropout rate for students with disabilities is 5.1 percent. Students with behavior disorders have a higher rate than any other type of disability, and older secondary students are more likely to drop out than younger ones.

The tendency to blame school failure on characteristics *within* the students, their families, and communities has supposedly diminished somewhat or at least has become less overt. The terminology used is less pejorative, although some educators still use the term *educationally disadvantaged* (Natriello, McDill & Pallas, 1990).

Defining *at-risk* continues to remain controversial because it reflects ideological and philosophical divisions among educators, policy makers, and the general public about the role and responsibility of schools, families, and students themselves. Hixson and Tinzmann (1990) offer three general approaches used by educators and policy makers to define at-risk youth. Unfortunately, each of these approaches is flawed.

The Predictive Approach.   Students who live under some conditions are considered at-risk. These conditions include a single parent, membership in a minority group, or limited English proficiency. Statistically, students in these categories are more likely to be among the lowest achieving groups or drop out of school altogether. This predictive approach, frequently used, has the advantage of being relatively straightforward. The information is already available from schools and other agencies. Moreover, this approach is based on an early intervention philosophy for preventing rather than remediating academic school problems.

A major problem with this approach is its basis as a *deficit model* of students, their families, and communities. It rarely examines fundamental aspects of schools (Natriello et al., 1990). Though well-meaning, it emphasizes ways to change the children in order to fit into existing school structures and programs (Goodlad &

Keating, 1990). Even more problematic is that it categorizes students so that teachers' expectations of school potential may be lowered. By using categorical indicators, students often get blamed for characteristics over which they have little or no control.

The Descriptive Approach.   This approach waits until *after* school-related problems occur and then identifies the student as at-risk. Unfortunately, categorizing students happens long after a pattern of difficulty and negative expectations from both teachers and students have occurred. Once identified, the problems may be too severe to make successful intervention/remediation likely.

The Unilateral Approach.   With the complexity of modern life faced by today's youth, all students are at risk in some way. This approach is attractive because it addresses egalitarian ideals and values. It also allays fears of many parents, educators, and policy makers that disproportionate attention is paid to poorly performing students at the expense of average and gifted students. Although the logic of this approach is appealing, it ignores the urgent need to focus attention on those students for whom structural and organizational impediments in the current model of schooling have led to school failure. To treat people fairly does not mean to treat them the same.

A Promising Approach for Addressing At-Risk Students

An ecological approach (Bronfenbrenner, 1989; Hixson & Tinzman, 1990) can be used to recognize education as a process that takes place both inside and outside school and is affected—not determined—by (a) the social and academic organization of the school, (b) the personal and background characteristics and circumstances of students and their families, (c) the community contexts within which students, families, and schools exist, and (d) the relationship of these factors to one another (Natriello et al., 1990).

Maria would be better served by this approach because the teachers would consider how the school was organized to meet her needs with regard to her personal characteristics, family background, language, and neighborhood, which is predominantly Mexican. All of these factors and the relationship among them will influence whether Maria succeeds in first grade.

When Maria gets to high school, promising practices will help her complete her schooling. These practices address the ecological or contextual systems in which Maria lives and attends school. According to Werner and Smith (1992), some factors that may help are: (a) individual attention such as tutoring, (b) smaller class sizes, (c) help from an instructional aide or peer tutor, (d) job-specific vocational education, and (e) socialization with other students outside of school and involvement in extracurricular activities.

Poverty

> America, at its best, is compassionate. In the quiet of America's conscience, we know that deep, persistent poverty is unworthy of our nation's promise. And whatever our views of its cause, we can agree that children at risk are not at fault.
> —President George W. Bush, Inaugural Address, January 20, 2001.

Raymond is five years old and has just begun attending a public kindergarten. Raymond and his family live below the poverty line. He comes to school hungry most mornings. He has just survived a summer of oppressive heat because there is no air conditioning in his building. In the winter he will suffer from limited heating in his home. How will all of this affect Raymond's experiences in school?

A twenty-year review of poverty rates for children under the age of 6 analyzed data from all states in the United States and 12 large cities. Their findings paint a portrait of poor young children in America, where they live, and how they are changing (National Center for Children in Poverty, 1997). Let us consider the following data:

"Poor children come in all colors and live in every family type and region" (Children's Defense Fund, 2001).

- 78 percent of poor children live in families where somebody worked all or part of the time in 1999.
- 62 percent of poor children are white, up from 60 percent in 1969.
- 31 percent of poor children are black, down from 39 percent in 1969.
- 57 percent of poor children live in suburban and rural areas, down from 67 percent in 1969.
- Young children in the United States have about a 50-50 chance of escaping the risks of poverty. In 1994, nearly half of all children under the age of 6 lived in poor or nearly poor families.
- More than any other age group, young children are more likely to be extremely poor, poor, or nearly poor—and that disparity continues to grow. The poverty rate for young children was well over double the rates for adults or the elderly. The poverty rate for young children is also significantly higher than the poverty rates for children age 6 through 17 (Children's Defense Fund, 2001).

Scientific evidence indicates that life in *near* poverty is almost as detrimental to children's development and health as living *just below* the poverty line (Zill, Moore, Smith, Stief & Coiro, 1991). Moreover, extreme poverty early in life is especially deleterious to children's chances for a future life (Duncan, Brooks-Gunn & Klebanov, 1994). "A three-person family was poor in 1999 if it made less than $13,290. The average poor family with children had just $9,211 in total income: $768 a month, $177 a week, or $25 a day" (Children's Defense Fund, 2001).

Between 1979 and 1999, the number of children living in poverty increased 16.9 percent from 9,691,000 to 12,109,000 (Children's Defense Fund, 2001). In 1995 the U.S. Bureau of the Census reported a modest—but statistically insignif-icant—0.8 percent drop in the poverty rate for children under age 6. The long-term growth in poverty among young children over the past two decades presents a disturbing picture. The rate of young children in extreme poverty has doubled (Population Reference Bureau, 1997). While Social Security and Medicare helped transform the financial situation for older Americans, public policies did less to reduce poverty among the young.

The Changing Face of Poverty among the Young

The problems of poverty among young children extend beyond the stereotypi-cal image of the poor minority child in an urban setting. Young child poverty is a *mainstream* problem, affecting children from all racial and ethnic backgrounds, from all types of residential areas, and from all regions of the United States. Poverty among young children has grown much faster in the suburbs than in rural or urban areas. The poverty rate for young children has grown twice as fast among whites as among blacks. Among young Hispanic children the rate of poverty is high and increasing more rapidly than among other racial and ethnic groups (National Center for Children in Poverty, 1997). Less than one-third of the families of poor young children depend exclusively on public assistance.

The age of the household head appears to be a telling factor. Among fam-ilies with children in which the household head is under age 25, the poverty rate rose from one-fourth in 1974 to nearly half in 1994 (National Center for Chil-dren in Poverty, 1997).

Families headed by a single parent run an exceptionally high risk of being poor. In 1994 the poverty rate for female-headed families with children was 44 percent as compared with 8.3 percent for married-couple families with children. The poverty rate for single mothers has hovered around 45 percent for the last 20 years. Several reasons are proposed: (a) single-parent families have fewer poten-tial breadwinners than two-income families; (b) most single-parent families are headed by women, who traditionally earn less than men; (c) single mothers with dependent children, on average, have lower levels of educational attainment than married mothers, thus limiting their employment opportunities further. Educa-tional attainment has been one of the most powerful personal protections against poverty. The economic penalty for failing to attain at least a high school diploma has risen steadily since the 1970s. In 1994, the poverty rate was 31 percent for high school dropouts ages 22 to 64 (Poverty in America, 1997).

The Costs of Poverty among Young Children

Poverty takes a serious toll on young children. Young children in poverty are more likely to:

- be born at a low birthweight;
- be hospitalized during childhood;
- die in infancy or early childhood;
- receive lower quality medical care;
- experience hunger and malnutrition;
- experience high levels of interpersonal conflict in their homes;
- be exposed to violence and environmental toxins in their neighborhoods;
- experience delays in their physical, cognitive, language, and emotional development, which will affect their readiness for school (Klearman, 1991).

Children in poverty are more likely to experience difficulty in adolescence and adulthood. They are more likely to drop out of school, have children out of wedlock, and be unemployed (Klearman, 1991).

In addition to the costs to the children themselves, large economic costs to the nation result from the poverty of children. Several economists working with Nobel laureate economist Robert Solow placed the cost of child poverty to the United States at between $36 billion to $177 billion annually (Sherman, 1994). If one in four children continues to grow up in poverty, enormous constraints will be placed on our nation's labor force in terms of productivity and competitiveness.

Concentration of Poverty

The rate of poverty among children is significantly higher in the United States than in other Western industrialized nation. This rate is at least a third higher and usually two to three times as high as the poverty rate of young children in any of the 12 other Western industrialized nations (National Center for Children in Poverty, 1997).

The poor most often live in neighborhoods in which their neighbors are also poor. This geographic concentration of poverty exacerbates the negative social and economic consequences of being poor, especially for children (Duncan et al., 1994). Few neighbors have the financial resources to help a poor family through a poverty spell or the social connections to pass along information about job possibilities. The trend toward a geographic concentration of the poor is most evident in the cities. An expanding share of the urban poor live in high-poverty neighborhoods in which the near majority of residents are below the poverty level. Rates for child poverty, however, vary greatly from city to city, state to state, and region to region. For example, among the nation's 12 largest cities, the child poverty rate ranged from 14 percent in San Jose, California, to 60 percent in Detroit, Michigan.

Homelessness

Katrina, a fourth grader, lives with her father under a bridge in a large urban area. They sometimes stay in a homeless shelter on cold nights, but most evenings they huddle with other homeless families just beneath the bridge. Katrina's attendance at school is sporadic, but in some ways she's lucky to even attend school. Just a few years ago she would have been denied schooling because she did not have a permanent address.

The experience of homelessness can devastate a family. It disrupts virtually every aspect of family life, harming the physical and emotional health of family members, interfering with children's education and development, and frequently leading to the separation of family members (National Coalition for the Homeless, 1997).

Families with children are the fastest-growing segment of the homeless population. Approximately 40 percent of people who become homeless include families with children (Shinn & Weitzman, 1996). A 1997 survey of 29 U.S. cities found that children accounted for 25 percent of the homeless population (Waxman & Hinderliter, 1997). In rural areas these proportions are likely to be higher. Research (Vissing, 1996) indicates that single mothers, families, and children constitute the largest group of people who are homeless in rural areas. Moreover, the 1997 survey revealed that about one-third of the requests for shelter by homeless families were denied access due to lack of resources. Over 90 percent of the cities surveyed expected an increase in the number of requests by families with children for emergency shelters in 1998.

Causes of Homelessness

The National Coalition for the Homeless (1997) found that the principal causes of homelessness are poverty and lack of affordable housing. Stagnating wages and changes in welfare programs (principally, the erosion of benefits and restrictive eligibility requirements) account for increasing poverty among families. Before its repeal in 1996, Aid to Families with Dependent Children (AFDC) was the largest cash assistance program for poor families with children. It was replaced with a block grant program called Temporary Assistance to Needy Families (TANF). Current TANF benefits are below the poverty level in every state. In most states they are below 75 percent of the poverty level (Kauffman, 1997). The welfare benefit levels have not kept up with increases in the cost of rent and therefore do not provide families with adequate allowances for housing.

Affordable housing is also shrinking. The gap between affordable housing units and the number of people needing houses is currently the largest on record

(Lazere, 1995). Households with "worst-case housing needs" (U.S. Department of Housing and Urban Development, 1998) pay over half their incomes for rent. They often live in severely substandard housing. With less income available for food and other necessities, these families are only an illness, accident, or paycheck away from becoming homeless.

Domestic violence also contributes to homelessness among families with children. When a woman leaves an abusive relationship, she often has nowhere to go, particularly women with limited resources. Lack of affordable housing and long waiting lists for assisted housing may mean that women are forced to choose between homelessness or abuse. A recent estimate put the range of homeless women and children fleeing abuse at 25 to 35 percent (National Coalition for the Homeless, 1997).

Consequences of Homelessness

Homelessness severely impacts the health and well-being of all members of a family. When compared with housed poor children, homeless children experience more severe consequences: worse health, more developmental delays, more anxiety, depression, and behavioral problems; and lower educational achievement (Shinn & Weitzman, 1996). Homeless children face barriers to enrolling and attending school including problems with transportation, inability to obtain previous school records, lack of a permanent address and/or immunization records, and lack of clothing and school supplies. A study (Bassuk, 1996) of mothers of homeless and poor housed families found that both groups experienced higher rates of depressive disorders than the overall female population. One-third of homeless mothers had made at least one suicide attempt as compared to one-fourth of housed mothers. In both groups, over a third of the sample had at least one chronic health condition.

Families often break up under the stress of homelessness. Shelter policies that deny access to older boys or fathers may separate families. Separations may also be caused by placement of children into foster care. Moreover, parents may leave their children with friends or relatives to permit them to continue attending their regular school or to save them from the ordeal of homelessness. Shinn and Weitzman (1996) have documented the phenomenon of the break-up of families because of homelessness. In New York City, 60 percent of the residents in shelters for single adults did not have children with them. In Chicago, although 54 percent of the homeless samples were parents, 91 percent did not have children with them.

Homelessness frequently deprives children of their right to a free, public education. It demeans their sense of worth. The following *profiles* (State and Local Profiles, 1997) reflect the experiences and feelings of homeless children:

> I've been in four schools this year. It's rough. Always having to move
> and change and get used to people and make new friends. It takes a

little while. And right when I get it, then right when I get friends and get used to stuff, then we have to move again.

Ryan (Public Justice Center, 1997)

Kendrick Williams, a homeless boy who was excluded from Washington, D.C., schools for one month while officials searched for his records, spoke the following words while giving his testimony before the Congressional Subcommittee on Employment and Productivity of the Senate Commission on Labor and Human Resources, May 22, 1990.

It's hard being homeless and going to school. People make fun of you and tease you . . . I love to read and learn, so that month was hard on me. I really missed school . . . They shouldn't try to ruin the one chance we've got.

Policy Issues on Homelessness

To end homelessness we must support jobs that pay livable wages. To work, families with children need access to quality, affordable child care. However, jobs and child care are not sufficient. Decent housing is necessary so that people can keep their jobs and remain healthy. Welfare reform must include serious efforts to link cash benefits and job assistance to affordable housing. Preventing homelessness and poverty also requires access to affordable health care. No known community or school has solved all the problems homelessness presents (Reach for the Child, 1999). Federal, state, and local housing, education, and health agencies must work collaboratively in order to enhance homeless children's access to needed services. Only concerted efforts to meet these needs will end the tragedy of homelessness for America's families and children (National Coalition for the Homeless, 1998).

Violence and Child Development

Let us consider the following statistics:

- More children died in 1998 from gunfire than from cancer, pneumonia, influence, asthma, and HIV/AIDS combined.
- Ten children and teens die each day from gunfire in America—one child every two and a half hours.
- Juvenile arrests for violent crime have declined 23 percent since 1995.
- The United States accounts for one-third of the world total of persons sentenced to death for crimes committed while under age 18.
- Between 50 to 75 percent of incarcerated youths have a diagnosable mental health disorder.

- The average American child watches 28 hours of television a week and by age 18 will have seen 16,000 simulated murders and 200,000 acts of violence.
- The unemployment rate for teens is more than four times the adult rate. (Children's Defense Fund, 2001, p. 100)

Violence continues to run rampant in the United States, claiming thousands of lives and costing annually hundreds of millions of dollars in medical care and lost wages (Wallace, 1994). Violence refers to child abuse or other domestic conflict, gang aggression, and community crime, including assault. The developmental consequences of violence for children who are victims of, or witnesses to, family and community violence can be enormous.

Violence in the Preschool Years

Children growing up surrounded by violence are at considerable risk for pathological development. According to Erik Erikson's (1968) theory on developmental milestones, an infant's primary task during the first year of life should be learning to trust. Trust provides the foundation for later development of self-confidence and self-esteem. The infant's ability to trust is dependent upon the family's ability to provide consistent care and to respond to the baby's need for love and nurturance. Caregiving is greatly compromised when the baby's family lives in a world racked by violence and when the family fears for its safety. In such a world, otherwise simple tasks like going to work or shopping take careful planning and extra effort.

During toddlerhood, children are learning to walk, jump, and climb—skills best learned in playgrounds and parks, not crowded apartments. Because of fear of the outside, parents restrict their children's activities to indoors. Toddlers do not understand these restrictions and often resent them, leading to disruptive relationships with the rest of the family (Wallace, 1994).

During the preschool years, children seek new relationships to learn about other people. Because of fear for safety, adults limit children's activities. Child care programs may be located in areas where violence occurs frequently.

Violence in the School Years

During the school years, children develop academic and social skills that are necessary to function as adults and citizens. Violence in the community or at home takes its toll:

- When children's energies are drained because they are defending themselves against outside dangers or internal fears, difficulty in school may ensue (Craig, 1992).

- When children have been victims or witnesses to violence, they may have difficulty getting along with others.
- Children learn social skills by identifying with adults in their lives. Children may have difficulty learning nonaggressive ways of interacting with others when their only models, including those of the media, use physical force to solve problems (Garbarino, Dubrow, Kostelny & Pardo, 1992).
- Children who live with violence may repress feelings in order to control their fears. This defensive maneuver may lead to pathological development. It can interfere with their ability to feel empathy for others. They are more likely to become insensitive to brutality in general (Gilligan, 1991).
- Children need to feel they have some control over their current existence and future.
- Children who live with violence learn that they have little say in what happens to them. Beginning with the restrictions on autonomy when they are toddlers, this sense of helplessness continues as they go through their school years.
- Research indicates that children who experience some form of violence in their homes are more likely to behave violently throughout their adolescence and into adulthood (Children's Defense Fund, 2001, p. 100).

Child Abuse and Neglect

Child abuse thrives in the shadows of privacy and secrecy. It lives by inattention.

David Bakan, *Slaughter of the Innocents*

Child abuse and neglect rob children of their right to safety and security. Usually the victims know their perpetrators. If a child is victimized, it is likely the perpetrator is an adult who should be ensuring the well-being of children. Instead, the adult has betrayed the child, and the child's innocence is lost.

The topic of child abuse is so abhorrent that it shocks the collective conscience of all people of goodwill. So alarming is its existence that most people are reluctant to bring it to a conscious level yet alone to *discuss, understand, remedy, or prevent it.*

Tragic stories of child maltreatment occur regularly. The following tragic story is one of three that appeared in a newspaper within a three-month period.

John Daniel "Little Man" Powell died: May 15, 1996
He was buried in a tiny red baseball cap and long-sleeved T-shirt to hide the bruises caused by adult hands and the scars of an autopsy. The 19-month-old Theodore (AL) boy did not choke to death on powdered milk in May as his mother Shelley Orso, 21, and her

boyfriend claimed. "Little Man" had the life beaten out of him, suffering multiple blows to the head and abdomen, police said. Ms. Orso has been charged in her son's death. (Littlest Victims, 1996)

What Do Abuse and Neglect Mean?

The definition of *abuse* and *neglect* is generally unclear since both are generic terms. A universally accepted understanding of the construct is difficult to achieve (Goldman & Wheeler, 1986). The definition of abuse and neglect, according to Meier and Sloan (1984), varies over time, across cultures, and between dissimilar cultural and social groups. Maher (1985) noted that "different societies accept and condone different levels of violence toward its members, including the children" (p. 54). Despite the problems of offering a definition that is acceptable to various professionals and that satisfies differing community standards, one must attempt to facilitate and establish a language of understanding. Therefore, for the purposes of this discussion, the following descriptions are used:

Physical abuse, according to the National Center on Child Abuse and Neglect (1986), includes violent assault with an instrument such as a knife or strap, burns, fractures, or other nonaccidental inflictions or actions that lead to possible injury or harm of a child. *Neglect* includes abandonment; inadequate physical supervision; refusal to seek, allow, or provide medical treatment; poor nutrition; disregard of health hazards in the home; inadequate or inappropriate clothing; and chronic school truancy.

Sexual abuse according to the federal definition of child maltreatment included in the Child Abuse Prevention and Treatment Act, is defined as: "(a) the employment, use, persuasion, inducement, enticement, or coercion of any child to engage in, or assist any other person to engage in, any sexually explicit conduct or simulation of such conduct for the purpose of producing a visual depiction of such conduct; or (b) the rape, molestation, prostitution, or other form of sexual exploitation of children, or incest with children" (National Clearinghouse on Child Abuse and Neglect Information, 1997).The federal statute applies to the maximum age of 18 for other types of maltreatment, but also indicates that the age limit as set forth in the state law shall apply. Since chronological age is a significant determining factor, what happens to children and youth who are developmentally delayed, i.e., those whose cognitive abilities are immature? Consider, for example, a 20-year-old woman living in an institutional setting, whose mental age has been measured as that of a child. She is unable to understand adult relationships and make adult choices and decisions regarding her well-being. A caretaker has lured her into sexual intercourse. Is she a consenting adult or does she fall under the category of a *child* victim of sexual abuse?

Emotional abuse, according to Brenner (1984), occurs when adults attempt to shape children's behavior through the use of severe disparagement, humiliation, rejection, guilt, and fear. This type of abuse seems to be inherent in all kinds of earlier identified types of abuse since in the vast majority of instances, emotional or psychological injury is a consequence of physical abuse, neglect, and sexual abuse.

The National Incidence Study (1996) employed two definitions of maltreatment. The more restrictive one, called the *Harm Standard*, parallels the definitions used above. Under this standard, children were considered to be maltreated only if they had *already* experienced harm from abuse or neglect. The second definition, termed the *Endangerment Standard*, was used to compensate for the stringency of the Harm Standard and to broaden the definition to include those children who experienced abuse or neglect that put them at risk of harm.

Statistics

In 1997, over 3 million (3,195,000) children were reported for child abuse and neglect to child protective service (CPS) agencies in the United States. The figure represents a 1.7 percent increase over the number of children reported in the previous one-year period (National Committee to Prevent Child Abuse, 1998). Child abuse reporting levels have increased 41 percent over the 9-year period between 1988 and 1997. Experts attribute much of the increase in reporting to greater public awareness of and willingness to report child maltreatment, as well as changes in how states now collect reports of maltreatment (Wang & Daro, 1998). Since 1986, significant increases (300–500 percent) have occurred in the rates at which professionals recognize maltreated children. This includes school staff, hospital staff, mental health agencies, police departments, and social service agencies. School staff members predominate as the main source of recognition of children who had been maltreated (National Incidence Study, 1996).

The number of cases being investigated by CPS agencies has remained stable since 1986. Given the absolute number of cases increasing across all types of abuse, however, the percentage of cases being investigated has significantly lowered. These findings suggested that the CPS system might have reached its capacity to respond to the growing population of children who are maltreated (National Incidence Study, 1996).

According to a 1997 survey (National Committee to Prevent Child Abuse, 1998), neglect represented 54 percent of confirmed cases, physical abuse 22 percent, sexual abuse 8 percent, emotional maltreatment 4 percent, and other forms of maltreatment 12 percent. Currently, about 47 out of every 1000 children are reported as victims of child abuse or neglect (Wang & Daro, 1998). Regarding child fatalities, more than three children die each day as a result of child abuse or neglect. This rate of child abuse fatalities has increased by 34 percent since 1985 (Wang & Daro, 1998).

Reports of child maltreatment involving day care centers and foster care homes attract considerable attention. Such publicity has created the perception that abuse is more commonplace in these out-of-home settings than in in-home settings (Finkelhor, 1979). Reports from 18 states on abuse in day care, foster care, or other institutional care settings represented only about 3 percent of all confirmed cases in 1997. This percentage has remained consistent over the past 11 years (National Committee to Prevent Child Abuse, 1998). Sadly, these statistics merely continue to underscore two tragic facts: (1) that most perpetrators are family members—adults who have failed in their primary responsibility to protect their children—and, (2) that although private homes should be considered safe havens, they are not, (i.e., most abuse occurs within the confines of the child's home).

The link between *substance abuse* and child abuse has increased over the years. In 1997, 88 percent of respondents named the influence of substance abuse as one of the top two problems presented by families reported for maltreatment. This percentage is higher than those reported in previous years, suggesting that after several years of some improvement, substance abuse again is surfacing as a primary contributor to child maltreatment.

Is Child Maltreatment on the Rise?

Significant increases across all categories of abuse and neglect have been noted (National Incidence Study, 1996). More than 1.5 million children were estimated to be maltreated in the United States in 1993 under the Harm Standard. Using the Endangerment Standard, it is estimated that nearly 3 million children were abused and neglected in the United States.

Characteristics of Victims

Age.   According to recent statistics (Child Maltreatment, 1997), about 27 percent of victims of maltreatment were 3 years old or younger. Elementary age children comprised about Children 4 to 6 years old represented about 52 percent of the victims. Teenagers (13–18 years old) constituted about 21 percent.

Gender.   Girls are sexually abused about three times more often than boys; a disturbing statistic that has been stable over time (Goldman, 1994). Boys, however, had higher incidence rates than girls in some arenas. Boys were at somewhat greater risk of serious injury (24 percent higher than girls' risk) and boys were significantly more likely to be emotionally neglected (18 percent higher than girls' risk). Trends in the incidence of fatal injuries from maltreatment, moreover, indicated that fatally injured girls declined slightly since the NIS-2, while incidence of fatally injured boys rose (Sedlak & Broadhurst, 1996).

Race/Ethnicity.   Whites represented almost 56 percent of all victims of maltreatment according to data provided by 47 States. African American victims constituted the second largest group at about 26 percent; Hispanic victims made up about 9 percent, Native American victims made up about 2 percent, and Asian/Pacific Islander victims accounted for less than 1 percent. The remaining 6 percent of all victims were of unknown or other racial/ethnic backgrounds

(Child Maltreatment, 1997). Service providers may find these results somewhat surprising in viewing of the disproportionate representation of children of color among the child welfare population and among clientele of other public agencies. The NIS-3 findings suggest that the *different races receive differential attention* somewhere during the process of referral, investigation, and service allocation (Goldman, 1994).

Characteristics of Perpetrators

People Known to the Child.   Nearly 80 percent of perpetrators of child maltreatment were parents according to NIS-3 data from 41 states. An additional 10 percent were other relatives of the victim. People who were in other caretaking relationships to the child victims represented only 2 percent of the perpetrators (e.g., foster parents, facility staff, and child care providers). The remaining 8 percent of all perpetrators were noncaretakers (Child Maltreatment, 1997).

Gender.   Female perpetrators were somewhat more likely than males to maltreat children: 65 percent of maltreated children had been maltreated by a female, whereas 54 percent had been maltreated by a male. Of the children who were maltreated by their birth parents, the majority (75 percent) were maltreated by their mothers and a sizable minority (46 percent) were maltreated by their fathers. Both parents maltreated some children. In contrast, children who were maltreated by parent substitutes or by other persons were more likely to have been maltreated by a male than by a female (80 to 85 percent were maltreated by males; 15 percent by females) (Sedlak & Broadhurst, 1996). Abused children presented a different pattern in connection with the sex of their perpetrators than did the neglected children. Children were more often neglected by female perpetrators, congruent with the fact that mothers and mother substitutes tend to assume the role of primary caretakers and persons held responsible for omission of care (Goldman, 1994).

Are Some Children at Greater Risk for Maltreatment than Others?

The relationship between disabling conditions and abuse has received increasing attention (Akuffo & Sylvester, 1983; Sobsey, 1992). Finklehor (1979), Straus and Kaufman-Kantor (1994), and Zirpoli (1986) have noted that research shows some common characteristics among victims that increase their vulnerability—particularly victims with *special needs* (i.e., persons with a wide variety of physical, mental, and sensory disabilities). These characteristics include a greater dependency on adults and more difficulty with communication, impulse control, social interaction, and people-pleasing behaviors (Zirpoli, 1986).

A disproportionate number of children and youth with intellectual disabilities appear as victims of sexual abuse (Goldman, 1994; Sobsey & Doe, 1991). Stimpson and Best (1991) found in their survey of 85 women with disabilities that 70 percent indicated that they had been sexually violated.

The detrimental effects that abuse and neglect play on cognitive development and language acquisition was chronicled by American psychologist H. Skeels (1966) in a longitudinal study which spanned 30 years. He showed the positive effects adult intervention played in the lives of institutionalized and adopted children. Conversely, children who are subjected to abuse show more intellectual and physical disabilities than previously suspected (Akuffo & Sylvester, 1983).

Low socioeconomic status also seems to place children at higher risk for abuse and neglect. Two National Incidence Studies (1996) conducted with similar research protocols over a seven-year period (1986–1993) support this finding. Children from families with annual incomes below $15,000 were 22 times more likely to experience maltreatment as compared with children from families with annual incomes above $30,000. Other strongly implicated family characteristics that contributed to abuse and neglect risk were single-parent status, substance-abusing parents, and large family size, especially when considering neglect (National Incidence Study, 1996).

Prevalence Data: An Issue of Uncertainty

Although the above-cited collection of prevalence data is a significant step forward, experts agree that the figures are underestimated (Goldman, 1994; Sobsey, 1992). Reasons for the underestimation of abuse and neglect are numerous.

- Inconsistencies among reporters still exist as to what constitutes child abuse.
- Cases of child abuse cover several types of abuse and may be recorded differently.
- Children who have truly been abused may recant their testimony.
- Children are reluctant to report abuse because they fear repercussions from perpetrators and have been "sworn to secrecy."
- Adults are reluctant to become involved and/or fear repercussions from perpetrators.

Although teachers and other professionals are mandated by law in the United States to report suspicions of abuse, many fail to do so (Goldman, 1994; Sobsey, 1992). Some reasons given for failure to report include: (a) insufficient information and/or signs of abuse, (b) fear of reprisal, (c) discouragement by supervisors, (d) concern for the destruction of the family unit, and (e) avoidance of the emotional and legal "hassle" likely to ensue once disclosure has occurred (School of Education majors, personal communication, June, 1998).

Child Abuse Is Not New

Child abuse and neglect are not recent phenomena. Unfortunately, the maltreatment of children has endured a long and tragic history (Goldman, 1994). Segal (1970), citing the child historian, De Mause, noted that "the history of childhood is a panorama of incredible cruelty and exploitation" (p. 171):

> A child, only seven, but appearing ancient, has become a grotesque satire of youth—the product of chronic abuse and mutilation by his elders. His feet are crushed, his shoulders bent out of shape, his head held at a tilt, the result of repeated insult to the brain. As he walks alone in the busy market, he excites the curious gaze and revulsion of passersby. (p. 171)

This description is chronicled in the archives of ancient Rome. One of the earliest recorded descriptions of child abuse occurred more than 5,000 years ago in ancient Sumer where a clay tablet tells of a young girl who was sexually abused (Goldman & Wheeler, 1986). Religious beliefs and practices frequently contributed to maltreatment. Boys were flogged by their parents before altars erected to the goddess Diana. Isaac, accompanied by his father, Abraham, went to the mountain top where he was to be slaughtered as a test of his father's obedience to his lord. In the days of the Roman Empire, the doctrine of *Patria Potestas* gave a father absolute authority over his children and allowed him, should he desire, to sell, kill or otherwise dispose of his offspring in any manner he desired. Throughout history, adults assumed that they had the right to treat children in any way they desired regardless of whether they were rich or poor, famous or unknown. Henry VI was regularly beaten by his tutor, as was Charles I, although Charles I was fortunate enough to have a whipping boy accept punishment meant for him. In the typical English and American schoolhouse, the hickory stick was a common instructional tool. Beethoven was known to have abused his pupils with a knitting needle and, on occasion, to have bitten them. The advent of the Industrial Revolution introduced a systematic means to use children as sources of cheap labor. Stories are rampant about the maiming and deaths of children in industrial settings (Goldman & Wheeler, 1986).

During the Victorian Era, human sexuality was not understood. Women were viewed as basically sexless. Men, however, were encouraged to be ambitious in the pursuit of wealth and sex (Goldman & Wheeler, 1986). These views were promoted to control women and keep men in power. Men of letters were preoccupied with the "cult of the little girl"; Edgar Allan Poe, Charles Dickens, John Ruskin, and Lewis Carroll all extolled the virtues of little girls. Child pornography, which has been in existence since at least 1780, became widespread when the industrial and technological advances of the nineteenth and twentieth centuries made possible its widescale production and distribution.

Prostitution in Europe was prevalent by the mid-nineteenth-century. In London alone it was estimated that 1 out of 16 women was a prostitute. Great numbers of homeless children lived by any means available. Often the boys became involved in thievery, whereas the girls became prostitutes. In the late 1900s, more than 20,000 street children lived and died of disease or starvation in London. In the United States, children were also victimized. Indentured girls often were sexually exploited. Prostitution in the United States flourished. Children brought premium rewards as much as $60 to $70 a night in a bordello.

Whereas the physical maltreatment of children has occurred throughout human history, its roots in Western Judeo-Christian culture are in perceptions of youngsters as easily spoiled, stubborn, or in some instances "born with original sin." John Calvin reportedly preached that it was the parent's duty to God to "break the will" of the child at the earliest possible age (Segal, 1978).

In some instances, children were flogged for displaying inappropriate behaviors. In 1646, Massachusetts adopted a law whereby unruly children encountered the death penalty. Connecticut soon followed the lead of its neighboring state. Fortunately, public whippings were frequently substituted for the death penalty for many young persons (Radbill, 1974).

Corporal punishment is historically and currently a major issue among critics of child abuse. The U.S. Supreme Court has upheld the right of schools to utilize corporal punishment. In a 1977 decision (*Ingram v. Wright*), the Court ruled, by a 5 to 4 margin, that corporal punishment administered by public school teachers and administrators was not a violation of the cruel and unusual punishment clause of the Eighth Amendment. Although some states have abolished corporal punishment in schools, many states have continued to maintain this practice if not endorsing it. Critics of corporal punishment would emphasize that this commonly used practice is harmful to children and can lead to physical injuries which, if inflicted by a parent, would be considered child abuse. American organizations opposed to corporal punishment in schools have included The American Academy of Pediatrics, the American Psychiatric Association, the American Psychological Association, the National Education Association, and the National Mental Health Association (Parents and Teachers, 1987).

Child Victims and the Law

The law has traditionally treated children differently than other adult victims. State criminal codes define many crimes against children separately from the same offenses committed against adult victims. Those crimes include

- abduction by stranger or by family;
- neglect or abandonment;
- physical, emotional, or sexual abuse;
- pornography or exploitation of children; and
- statutory rape (Child victims, 1996).

All states recognize their duty to protect children. Specified classes of professionals in every state must report child abuse. Those professionals usually include educators, child care workers, and medical professionals. States are also establishing child victim and offender registries to assist in the investigation and prevention of child maltreatment. The expanded awareness of the potential for child abuse in institutions such as school or day care facilities has prompted some states to require criminal history background checks for employees and to license applicants for child care facilities and other institutions.

In order to protect children, state laws allow police and other officials to take a child into protective custody in emergency cases. State laws also permit courts to issue protective orders and to require hearings at which the accused have an opportunity to contest reports and present evidence in their favor. The law of most states provides privacy protection for child victims by deleting identifying information or prohibiting the release of information regarding an offense committed against a child. States have also adopted laws relating to missing children. States often require a child's birth certificate or school records to be marked in some way when a child is reported missing (Child victims, 1996).

The Need for Prevention

For the past 14 years, the National Committee to Prevent Child Abuse (NCPCA) has commissioned national public opinion polls to determine the public's attitudes and actions regarding child abuse prevention. Since the first survey in December 1986, and each year subsequently, the survey has sought to identify shifts in public attitudes and behaviors in several areas: (a) the public's attitudes toward specific parenting behaviors; (b) the frequency of various discipline practices, and (c) the public's optimism toward and involvement in child abuse prevention. Each survey involved a representative telephone survey of 1,250 randomly selected adults across the country, of which approximately 36 to 38 percent were parents with children under 18 living at home. Key findings were:

- Physical punishment and repeated yelling and swearing continues to be viewed by the majority of respondents as potentially detrimental to a child's well-being. For the past 11 years, the public consistently expressed greater ambivalence over the potential harm of physical punishment (i.e., hitting or spanking).
- Parents in the samples continue to report less use of physical punishment today than was true in the initial 1988 survey. One-quarter fewer parents reported the use of corporal punishment and repeated swearing and yelling today than did so in 1988. Further, the use of alternatives to these behaviors, such as denying privileges or "time out" strategies, has been consistent or has increased.
- The decrease in potentially harmful discipline practices has been virtually universal across income levels, race, educational status, residential locations, and political and religious preferences.

- In contrast to the general decline, an increase has been seen in the reported use of spanking among the youngest survey respondents, those ages 18 to 24. During the 11-year reporting period, the percentage of young parents who reported the use of spanking and hitting rose from 45 percent in 1988 to 59 percent in 1998.
- Public commitment to and involvement in the prevention of child abuse virtually has been unchanged over the past 12 years. Each year, roughly one in four of the general public and one in three parents have taken personal action to prevent child abuse and neglect. (Prevent Child Abuse, 1998)

Implications

Are the observed increases in the incidence of child maltreatment real increases in the scope of the problem or do they instead reflect improved recognition on the part of the sentinels and other reporters to CPS? More children than ever are victims of maltreatment, regardless of increased sensitivity. Numbers of serious injuries have quadrupled since the previous NIS-2 study was undertaken in 1984 (Sedlak & Broadhurst, 1996).

Another important finding was that the percentages of maltreated children who receive CPS investigation have decreased since the NIS-2 of 1984. *Better targeting* is needed to ensure CPS investigation for the children who most need it. The number of children who are investigated by CPS has remained fairly stable; however CPS agencies have been unable to keep up with the dramatic rise in the incidence of maltreatment among these children. Forging working relationships between CPS agencies and schools is necessary since schools play a central and critical role in identifying children who are maltreated (Sedlak & Broadhurst, 1996).

The United Nations Convention on the Rights of the Child[1]

"Children are born with fundamental freedoms and the inherent rights of all human beings. This is the basic premise of the Convention on the Rights of the Child, and the International Human Rights Treaty that is transforming the lives of children and their families around the world." So reads the Information Publication from UNICEF at http://www.unicef.org/crc/ (UNICEF: The Convention, 1999).

Actually, the Convention is a treaty written in broad language with far-reaching implications for the member states who vote to ratify it. According to

[1]This section was written by Susan Hill, doctoral student in early childhood education from the University of Alabama at Birmingham.

this treaty, a society is held *legally accountable* for meeting the obligations that make those rights meaningful.

In 1959 the United Nations General Assembly unanimously adopted the *Declaration of the Rights of the Child*, ten principles asserting the message that mankind owes to the child the best it has to give. The text of the *Convention on the Rights of the Child* was written by Poland in 1979 after discussion and revision by the 42-nation Working Group of the UN Commission on Human Rights. After the UN General Assembly unanimously adopted the convention on November 20, 1989, it was opened for *signature* on January 26, 1990. The Convention entered into force after the 20th State had ratified it. To date, the United States is the only member nation that continues to withhold ratification of the Convention.

The *Convention on the Rights of the Child* is composed of 54 articles that attempt to spell out the basic human rights to which children everywhere should be entitled. They can be categorized into four broad groups:

1. The right to *Survival*
2. The right to the *Development* of their physical and mental potential
3. The right to *Protection* from harmful influences
4. The right to *Participation* in family, culture, and social life.

Most Americans agree on certain things concerning children. We want them to be raised in a positive, nurturing environment, to have optimum medical attention, to have the opportunity of education to its fullest, and to be protected from abuse, neglect, and exploitation. However, there are strong *proponents* and *opponents* of this treaty within the United States. It is important to realize that people of good conscience who are acting reasonably and responsibly can honestly differ in their views. Most U.S. citizens easily support some articles of the Convention of the Rights of the Child. However, others are questionable, particularly to conservatives. In light of the U.S. impact on global issues and due to the fact that the United States is the only member nation not to have ratified the Convention, sharing differences of opinion should be imperative in determining perceived obstacles from U.S. citizens. Ultimately, our decision is whether "on the whole" the treaty is worthy of ratification by the United States.

In looking closely at the Convention text, it becomes evident that this treaty is not so much about education for children, which is presumed by most middle-class Americans to be given, as it is about problems associated with poverty, homelessness, child labor, children in the middle of armed conflict, abuse, neglect, preventable diseases, unequal access to education, and gender inequality. Child labor is a major issue addressed by the Convention. For example, where do most child laborers work? In which countries is child labor a problem? The answers to questions concerning child labor can be found at http://www.unicef.org/ (UNICEF: Child labor, 1999).

Controversy over the Convention

In the United States, opponents of the ratification of this treaty include James Dobson, president of *Focus on the Family*, and Gary Bauer, president of the *Family Research Council*. The *Family Research Council's* publication, *Family*, produced an article titled "Unconventional Rights—Children and the United Nations." The author, James P. Lucier, makes the following statements:

> In a free country there can be no autonomy of the individual. All elements of society—the individual, the group, and the sovereign power of the state—participate in a dance of checks and balances, with each bowing to the necessary authority of the other, and all submissive to the Divine power which is over all. (Lucier, 1992, p. 15)

Beverly LaHaye, president of Concerned Women of America and wife of Tim LaHaye (author of the *Left Behind Series*), recommends

> ... that the U.S. not ratify it in its present form because it would not match its noble purpose of protecting children and could serve to abolish the rights of parents more than to advance the rights of children. (U.N. treaty, 1991, p. 3)

Phyllis Schlafly, president of the Eagle Forum calls the treaty "dangerous" (UN treaty, 1991, p. 3). Her stand is partially based on the fact that the U.S. Constitution states that "all treaties made . . . shall be the supreme law of the land" (U.S. Constitution, art. 6).

An examination of some of the more controversial articles of the *United Nations Convention on the Rights of the Child* yields a deeper perspective and better understanding of the controversy.

Article 3, section 2, states that through the legal system, "The State assumes ultimate responsibility to ensure the care and protection of children, realizing that parents and legal guardians have broad discretion in caring for their children" (UNICEF: The Convention, 1999). John Rosemond (1995), family minister and social critic from North Carolina, writes that the government is primarily responsible to take whatever steps are necessary to provide for the well-being of children. What Rosemond is saying, then, is that it is no longer the role of the parents but the state to take care of its children! In reality, most states do this anyway. For example, in the State of Alabama, the Department of Human Resources is charged with the responsibility of making sure children are not abused, neglected, or abandoned. There are three groups of children under the protection of the State: *Dependent Children*, including those who are in foster care under the goal of reuniting with their birth families, *Children in Need of Supervision* (CHINS), who are the truants, runaways, and ungovernables, and *delinquents*, or children who have committed a criminal act (Code of Alabama, 1975).

Article 13, section 1, gives children the right of unfettered access to information and ideas. It additionally provides for dissemination of such through any media of the child's choice (UNICEF: The Convention, 1999).

Gary Bauer, President of the Family Research Council, has problems with this article. He says,

> From the point of view of a child-slave in Bangkok, Article 13 makes sense. The media might be the only way he could find out that things can be different. But in this country, where limiting kids' TV time is necessary for preserving both their values and their incentive to read, making "access to the media" a "right" is absurd. (U.N. treaty, 1991, p. 2)

Article 15, section 1, gives children the right to peacefully gather and associate with persons of their choice (UNICEF: The Convention, 1999). John Rosemond retorts, Article 15 guarantees "freedom of association." This implies parents would not be allowed to restrict a child's choice of friends. If your 14-year-old daughter wants to date an 18-year-old dropout with a police record, who are you to say she can't? (Rosemond, 1995).

Article 19, section 1, requires that member nations take all steps necessary to protect children from violence, injury, sexual abuse, neglect, mistreatment and exploitation (UNICEF: The Convention, 1999). Focus on the Family advocates say that this article "could be used to outlaw corporal punishment, including spanking, as has happened in Sweden" (U.N. treaty, 1991, p. 3). John Rosemond adds, "Given what many 'helping' professionals consider inappropriate discipline, this might well include spanking, confining a child to his room and putting a child to bed early" (Rosemond, 1995).

Article 20, section 1, mandates that children who are removed from their family environment be given the protection and assistance of the State (UNICEF: The Convention, 1999). Again, Focus on the Family responds, "Article 20 grants children the right to be removed from families for their own best interests when necessary. Pro-family leaders recognize that there must be intervention in certain cases, but fear that some social service agencies will abuse their power" (U.N. treaty, 1991, p. 3).

Article 37(a) states that no child under 18 years of age shall be given the sentence of life without parole or capital punishment (UNICEF: The Convention, 1999). In the State of Alabama Code, a 16- or 17-year-old child *must* be tried as an adult if that child commits capital murder (murder plus another felony). If children are under 16, then they must be certified by a judge to stand trial as an adult. If children are under 14 years of age, they go to Juvenile Court where they will be sent to the Department of Youth Services (Code of Alabama, 1975). A few years ago in Saint Clair County, Alabama, three boys, one age 14, and two age 16, robbed and murdered a convenience store clerk as a requirement of a game they were playing. One of the 16-year-olds shot the clerk, then committed suicide the night before he was to be sentenced. The 16-year-old who watched the murder inside the store was sentenced to life without parole. The 14-year-old who drove the car did not enter the convenience store and was sentenced to life imprisonment. He has already come up for parole more than once, but he has been turned down each time. He remains in prison to date.

Article 43, sections 1 and 2, provide for a board of ten members whose function is to examine the progress made by member states in realizing their obligations to children in light of the Convention (UNICEF: The Convention, 1999). John Rosemond had this to say in his newspaper column:

> Article 43 sets up an international body of 10 child and family "experts" to make recommendations to signatories regarding compliance. In January, this committee admonished the United Kingdom for insufficient welfare spending, allowing spanking by parents, and for plans to incarcerate hard-core juvenile criminals. In short, the U.K. is being told to raise taxes to support more socialism and to coddle kids— the worse the kid, the more the coddling. This same committee has recommended that schools develop programs to educate children concerning their rights under the Convention. In other words, American parents would pay taxes to support schools that would teach children and how to challenge their parents' rules. (Rosemond, 1995)

Issues also must be considered and evaluated related to the *United Nations Convention on the Rights of the Child*. Representative Christopher Smith, Republican from New Jersey, said, "The Convention is not a perfect document, but it is a solid foundation on which the entire gamut of protections can be structured within the legal framework of each country" (U.N. treaty, 1991, p. 4).

Although Gary Bauer, who is opposed to the Convention, does say, "If the U.N. Treaty is ever sent over for ratification, the Senate could minimize the treaty's harm by attaching to it a declaration that states, 'In the event of conflict between this treaty and the U.S. Constitution, the latter shall prevail' " (U.N. treaty, 1991, p. 4).

Kofi Annan, Secretary-General of the United Nations has said, "Much of the next millennium can be seen in how we care for our children today. Tomorrow's world may be influenced by science and technology, but more than anything, it is already taking shape in the bodies and minds of our children (UNICEF: Why make a special case for children? 1999).

The American dream has been built on the hopes and lives of immigrant peoples. With children being the most precious resource of any country on earth, it is imperative for those who have power to exert whatever legal and political pressure is possible on the nations of the world in support of children everywhere. The question is, will the *United Nations Convention on the Rights of the Child* make a difference in the United States? We will never know unless the Convention is passed.

REFERENCES

Akuffo, E., & Sylvester, P. (1983). Head injury and mental handicap. *Journal of Royal Society of Medicine, 76,* 545–549.

Bakan, D. (1971). *Slaughter of the innocents.* San Francisco, CA: Jossey-Bass.

Bassuk, A. (1996, August 28). The characteristics and needs of sheltered homeless and low income housed mothers. *Journal of the American Medical Association, 276*(8), 640–646.

Barr, R., & Parrett, W. (1995). *Hope at last for at-risk youth.* Boston: Allyn & Bacon.

Brenner, A. (1984). *Helping children cope with stress.* Lexington, MA: Lexington Books.

Bronfenbrenner, U. (1989). Ecological systems theory. In R. Vasta (Ed.), *Annals of child development,* (Vol. 6) (pp. 187–251). Greenwich, CT: JAI Press.

Child Maltreatment. (1997). Child maltreatment 1995: Reports from the states to the national child abuse and neglect data system [On-line]. Available: http://www.acf.dhhs.gov/programs/cb/stats/ncands/index.html

Child Victims. from msp. 86d

Children's Defense Fund. (2001). Yearbook 2001: The state of America's children. Washington, DC: Author.

Code of Alabama, 12-15-1, Recompiled 1975.

Code of Alabama, 12-15-34, Recompiled 1975.

Craig, S. E. (1992). The educational needs of children living with violence. *Phi Delta Kappan, 74,* 67–71.

Duncan, G. J., Brooks-Gunn, J., & Klebanov, P. K. (1994). Economic deprivation and early childhood development. In A. C. Huston, C. Coll, & V. C. McLoyd (Eds.), Special Issue: Children in poverty. *Child Development, 65*(2), 296–318.

Erikson, E. (1968). *Childhood and society* (2nd ed.). New York: W. W. Norton.

Finkelhor, D. (1979). *Sexually victimized children.* New York: Free Press.

Garbarino, J., Dubrow, N., Kostelny, N., & Pardo, C. (1992). *Children in danger: Coping with the consequence of community violence.* San Francisco: Jossey-Bass.

Gilligan, J. (1991). Shame and humiliation: The emotions of individual and collective violence. Paper presented at the Erikson Lectures, Harvard University, Cambridge, MA, May 23, 1991.

Goldman, R. (1994). Individuals with intellectual disabilities. *International Journal of Disability, Development, and Education, 41*(2), University of Queensland Press.

Goldman, R., & Wheeler, V. (1986). *Silent shame: The sexual abuse of children.* Austin, TX: Pro-Ed.

Goodlad, J., & Keating, P. (Eds.). (1990). *Access to knowledge: An agenda for our nation's schools.* New York: The College Entrance Board.

Henley, M., Ramsey, R., & Algozzine, R. (1999). *Characteristics and strategies for teaching students with mild disabilities* (3rd ed.). Boston: Allyn and Bacon.

Hixson, J., & Tinzmann, M. B. (1990). Who are the at risk students of the 1990s? [On-line]. Available: http://www.ncre/.org/sdrs/areas/rpl_esys/equity.htm

Kauffman, T. L. (1997). Out of reach: Rental housing at what cost? Available from the National Low Income Housing Coalition, 1012 14th Street, NW, #610, Washington, DC, 20005-3410, (202) 662-1530.

Klearman, L. V. (1991). The association between adolescent parenting and childhood poverty. In A. C. Huston (Ed.), *Children in poverty: Child development and public policy.* New York: National Center for Children in Poverty, Columbia University School of Public Health.

Lazere, E. (1995). *In short supply: The growing affordable housing gap.* Washington, DC: Center on Budget and Policy Priorities.

Littlest victims: Why are these children dead? (1996, January 21) *The Birmingham News,* special reprint, pp. 1–16.

Lucier, J. P. (1992, August). Unconventional rights: Children and the United Nations. *Family, 5,* 1–16.

Maher, P. (1985). Child abuse: The secret epidemic. *Early Child Development and Care*, 22, 53–64.
McPartland, J. M., & Slavin, R. E. (1990). *Increasing achievement of at-risk students at each grade level.* Office of Education Research and Improvement, Policy Perspectives, Washington, DC: U.S. Government Printing Office.
Meier, J., & Sloan, M. (1984). The severely handicapped and child abuse. In J. Blacher (Ed.), *Severely handicapped young children and their families* (pp. 247–272). New York: Academic Press.
Menken, K., & Look, K. (2000). Making chances for linguistically and culturally diverse students. *Education Digest*, 65(8), 14–19.
Moll, L. C., Amanti, C., Neff, D., & Gonzales, N. (1992). Funds of knowledge for teaching: Using a qualitative approach to connect homes and classrooms. *Theory into Practice*, 31(2), 132–141.
National Center on Child Abuse and Neglect. (1986). *Child neglect: A guide for intervention.* Washington, DC: U.S. Department of Health and Human Services, Administration for Children and Families.
National Center for Children in Poverty. (1997). [On-line]. Available: http://www.cpmcnet .columbia.edu/dept/nccp/resports/longterm.html
National Coalition for the Homeless. (1997). *How many people experience homelessness?* [On-line]. Available: http://www.nationalhomeless.org/numbers.html
National Commission to Prevent Child Abuse. (1998, November). [On-line]. Available: http://www.childabuse.org/fs13.html
National Clearinghouse on Child Abuse and Neglect Information. (1997). What is child maltreatment? [On-line]. Available: http://www.calib.com/nccanch/pubs/whatis.htm
National Incidence Study: Implications for prevention (1996, November). [On-line.] Available: http://www.childabuse.org/fs13.html
Natriello, G., McDill, E. L., & Pallas, A. M. (1990). Schooling disadvantaged children: Racing against catastrophe. New York: Teachers College Press.
Parents and teachers against violence in education (PTAVE). (1987). Can be reached at 560 South Hartz Avenue #408, Danville, CA, 94526.
Peregoy, S. F., & Boyle, O. F. (1997). *Reading, writing, and learning in ESL.* New York: Longman.
Peterson, N. (1987). *Early intervention for handicapped and at-risk children.* Denver, CO: Love Publishing Company.
Population Reference Bureau. (1997). QuickFacts. [On-line]. Available: http://prb.org
Poverty in America. (1997). Appropriate economic development: Communities creating opportunities. [On-line]. Available: http://www2.ari.net/home/poverty/welcome.html
Prevent Child Abuse. (1999). Child abuse bucks U.S. crime trends and continues to rise. [On-line]. Available: http://www.preventchildabuse.org/media/03_30_99_3.html
Radbill, S. (1974). A history of child abuse and infanticide. In R. Helfer & C. Kempe (Eds.), *The battered child* (pp. 3–21). Chicago, IL: University of Chicago Press.
Reach for the Child. (1999). [On-line.] Available: http://www.wmpenn.edu/PennWeb/LTP/DOEMAT/ReachVid.html
Rosemond, J. (1995, May 14). U.N. treaty pushing child rights is outrage. *The Charlotte Observer.*
Sedlak, A. & Broadhurst, D. D. (1996). *Executive summary: Third national incidence study of child abuse and neglect.* Washington, DC: National Center on Child Abuse and Neglect.
Segal, J. (1978). *A child's journey.* New York: McGraw-Hill.
Shepard, L. A., & Smith, M. L. (Eds.). (1989). *Flunking grades: Research and policies on retention.* London: The Falmer Press.
Sherman, A. (1994). Wasting America's future: The Children's Defense Fund report on the costs of child poverty. Boston MA: Beacon Press and Washington, DC: Children's Defense Fund.
Shinn, M., & Weitzman, B. (1996). Homeless families are different. In *Homelessness in America.* Washington, DC: National Coalition for the Homeless.

Skeels, H. (1966). Adult status of children with contrasting early life experiences: A follow-up study. *Monograph of the Society for Research in Child Development*, I–65 (Serial No. 105).

Slavin, R. E. (1989). Students at risk of school failure: The problem and its dimensions. In R. E. Slavin, N. L. Karweit, & N. A. Madden (Eds.), *Effective programs for students at risk*, (p. 319). Boston: Allyn and Bacon.

Sobsey, D. (1992). Sexual offenses against people with developmental disabilities: An international comparison. Paper presented at the 9th World Congress of the International Association for Scientific Study of Mental Deficiency, Gold Coast, Australia.

Sobsey, D., & Doe, T. (1991). Patterns of sexual abuse and assault. *The Journal of Sexuality and Disability*, 9, 243–259.

State and local profiles. (1997). [On-line.] Available: http://nch.ari.net/edsurvey97/profiles.html

Stimpson, L., & Best, M. (1991). *Courage above all: Sexual assault against women with disabilities.* Toronto: Disabled Women's Network.

Straus, M. A., & Kaufman-Kantor. (1994). Corporal punishment of adolescents by parents: A risk factor in the epidemiology of depression, suicide, alcohol abuse, child abuse, and wife beating. *Adolescence*. 29, 543–561.

Swadener, B., & Lubeck, S. (Eds.). (1995). *Children and families "at promise."* Albany, NY: SUNY Press.

Undergraduate majors in School of Education. 1998. Personal communication with authors, June 7.

UNICEF. (1999, January). *Child labour: What do you know about child labour?* [On-line]. Available: http://www.unicef.org/

UNICEF. (1999, January). *The Convention on the rights of the child.* [On-line]. Available: http://www.unicef.org/crc/

UNICEF. (1999, January). *Why make a special case for children?* [On-line]. Available: http://www.unicef.org/crc.htm

U.N. treaty strips parents of rights. (1991, July 17). *Citizen*, 5, 1–4.

U.S. Department of Housing and Urban Development. (1998). The crisis continues: 1998 report to congress on worst case housing needs. Rockville, MD: HUD User.

Vissing, Y. (1996). *Out of sight: Out of mind.* Lexington, KY: The University Press of Kentucky.

Wallace, L. B. (1994). Violence and young children's development [On-line]. Available: http://ericeece.org/pubs/digests/1994/wallac94.html

Wang, C. T. & Daro, D. (1998). *Current trends in child abuse reporting and fatalities: The result of the 1997 annual fifty state survey.* Chicago, IL: The National Committee to Prevent Child Abuse.

Werner, E., & Smith, R. (1992). *Overcoming the odds: High risk children from birth to adulthood.* Ithaca, NY: Cornell University Press.

What Is Child Maltreatment. (1999). [On-line]. Available: http://www.calib.com/nccanch/pubs/whatis.htm

Yearbook 2001: The state of America's children. (2001). Washington, DC: Children's Defense Fund.

Zill, N., Moore, K., Smith, E., Stief, T., & Coiro, M. J. (1991). The life circumstances and development of children in welfare families: A profile based on national survey data. Washington, DC: Child Trends.

Zirpoli, T. (1986). Child abuse and children with handicaps. *Remedial and Special Education*, 7(2), 39–48.

CHAPTER

4

Theoretical Shifts in Our Understanding of Children

People living in the twenty-first century will experience more rapid changes than in any other period in human history. These changes have necessitated theoretical shifts in our understanding of children. This chapter will explore the rapidly changing perspectives held about children and education. We will explore changing worldviews; theories that inform our educational practices; problems with these theories; critical, modern and postmodern conceptions of children; changing curricular practices; and finally, what all of this means for education in the new millennium.

Changing Worldviews

We cannot fully address current issues in education without exploring major shifts in worldviews. Worldviews (sometimes called paradigms or metatheories) are the big picture. Paradigms are very general models of humankind. While they are neither true nor false, they are used as reference points for interpreting the world around us (Vander Zanden, 1989). Such worldviews were first discussed in detail by S. C. Pepper (1942), and T. S. Kuhn (1970) provided an early explanation of paradigms and how they are adopted.

Three worldviews have significantly influenced practices in education and child development: the organismic worldview, the mechanistic worldview, and the contextualist worldview (Miller, 1993). Table 4.1 provides an overview and comparison of these three worldviews and their influence on education.

As the table shows, there are some irreconcilable differences among the three worldviews—in defining the nature of children, the nature of development, and solutions related to teaching and learning. Over the past three decades, both organismic and mechanistic paradigms have been criticized (Bronfenbrenner, 1989; Ford & Lerner, 1992; Lerner, 1986; Thomas, 1999). Pelligrini and Hor-

An earlier version of this chapter was published in *No Easy Answers: Helping Children with Attention and Activity Level Differences*, by Jerry Aldridge, E. Anne Eddowes, and Patricia Kuby, Olney, MD: Association for Childhood Education International, 1998.

TABLE 4.1 A Comparison of Organicism, Mechanism, and Developmental Contextualism

	Organismic Worldview	Mechanistic Worldview	Developmental Contextualist Worldview
The nature of children	More active (passive environment)	More passive (active environment)	Interactive
Driving forces of development	Biological; predisposition; genetics; factors indigenous to the child	Environmental; adults; factors outside the child	A bidirectional interaction between the child and the environment
Nature of development	Qualitative changes; emphasizes stages or steplike development; big changes	Quantitative changes; emphasizes linear development; small changes	Both qualitative and quantitative changes; emphasizes both large and small changes
Humans are like . . . (Metaphors used)	Growing plants	Machines	Multifaceted individual and social beings
How children learn	From the inside out	From the outside in	In many ways based on numerous factors both within the child and between the child and context
Where the difficulty is when the child is not learning or developing as expected	Within the child	In the child's environment	Interactions between the child and the multiple contexts that influence the child
Examples of theorists	Gesell, Piaget, Freud	Watson, Skinner, Thorndike, Bijou	Vygotsky, Bronfenbrenner, Lerner

vat (1995) "argue against the simplistic dichotomizing of biology and experience" (p. 14) and favor a more developmental contextual view. Both organismic and mechanistic paradigms are unidirectional. By organismic paradigms, learning difficulties are described as problems *within* the child, while in mechanistic paradigms the environment is considered a major unidirectional contributor. "In contrast, a transactional model posits that children and their environments influence each other (e.g., special children elicit different reactions from different teachers; the reactions/expectations of these different teachers feed back to affect individual children's behavior)" (Pelligrini & Horvat, 1995, p. 15). Responsibility for any differences in learning would be a result of the transaction between the two systems.

Changing Theories

Theories of development are much more specific than paradigms or worldviews (Miller, 1993). A theory of development deals with change over time and is usually concerned with three things. First, it should describe changes over time within an area or several areas of development. Second, it should describe changes among areas of development. Finally, it should explain those changes.

No one theory has proven adequate to describe and explain learning or development. Numerous theories of development have influenced educational practices during the twentieth century (Aldridge, Kuby & Strevy, 1992), and currently a shift is affecting theories of child development and education. Some of the historical and current theories that have influenced education include Gesell's (1925) maturational theory, Skinner's (1974) behaviorist approach, Freud's (1935) psychoanalytic theory, Piaget's (1952) constructivist theory, Vygotsky's (1978) sociohistorical approach, Bronfenbrenner's (1989) ecological systems theory, and Gardner's (1983) multiple intelligences theory. More recently, critical theory (see Kessler & Swadener, 1992) has influenced education and child development practices, even though critical theory is not a theory of development. Finally, postmodern conceptions have changed the way we think of children and how to educate them (Elkind, 1995, 2000/2001).

Maturational Theory

The maturational theory of Arnold Gesell (1925) continues to affect what goes on in schools, particularly in early childhood classrooms in some parts of the United States. Gesell based his theory on three major assumptions: (1) development has a biological basis, (2) good and bad years alternate, and (3) body types (endomorph, ectomorph, mesomorph) are correlated with personality development (Thomas, 1992). Maturational theory strongly influenced the teaching of reading in the mid-1900s (Morphett & Washburne, 1931). Children were not thought to be ripe for reading until they had a mental age of $6\frac{1}{2}$. Consequently, readiness activities were developed for children who were not yet ready to read. Some of this nonsense still occurs in preschool, kindergarten, and even primary-level classrooms. Today, maturational theory is partially responsible for the existence of pre-kindergartens and pre–first grades aimed at children who supposedly need the "gift of time," because of immaturity or a late birthday. These classrooms tend to have a ratio of boys to girls of anywhere from 7:1 to 10:1.

Practitioners subscribing to maturational theory consider any difficulties a child experiences as being found *within* the child. This oversimplistic explanation for anything from reading problems to AD(H)D is extremely limiting to children and to those who work with them. If a problem lies within a child, then what value does a supportive (or, for that matter, a nonsupportive) environment have?

Behaviorist Theory

The behavioral theories of B. F. Skinner (1974) and S. W. Bijou (1989) also continue to influence what goes on in schools, especially for some special education programs. The mechanistic theory of behaviorism emphasizes the role of the environment on an individual's development. Preparing the environment for appropriate reinforcement is a major goal.

Two examples of Skinner's contribution to education include behavior modification and programmed learning. Both of these rely heavily on immediate reinforcement, in which a child has to exhibit the "right" behavior or produce the "correct" answer in order to be positively reinforced.

Teachers using behavioral theory will consider any difficulties a child has as being found within the environment. As with Gesell's overemphasis on nature, Skinner's overemphasis on nurture limits our understanding of children and their differences. Applications of this theory have resulted in an overemphasis on isolated skills and drill, as well as a heavy reliance on teacher-directed and teacher-reinforced activities. Consequently, teachers often ignore children's curiosity and prior knowledge.

Psychoanalytic Theory

Freud's psychoanalytic theory served as the theoretical basis for analysis of behavior disorders during the 1920s through the 1940s. "Behavior problems displayed by children were viewed as symbolic manifestations of unresolved conflict, often emanating from early caregiver-child interactions" (Hinshaw, 1994, p. 10). Problems with attention and activity levels were attributed to unconscious processes. Play therapy was the recommended form of intervention, with accompanying therapy for the child's parents. Psychodynamic models continue to have an effect on education and intervention for children with special needs.

One of the biggest problems with psychoanalytic theory is the inherent allocation of blame on parent-child interactions—more specifically, on the mother's actions. Fortunately, theoretical shifts have moved from a blame-the-parent model to more bidirectional, transactional, and interactional models of childhood differences.

Constructivist Theory

Although there are several "brands" of constructivism, Piaget's theory (1952) continues into the twenty-first century to affect what goes on in many classrooms. This theory relies heavily on logico-mathematical knowledge and universal invariant stages of development to the neglect of other forms of knowledge and the importance of context in a child's development. Even though knowledge is constructed from the "inside out" through interaction with the environment, the focus is more on the individual's coordination of relationships rather than on socially constructed knowledge.

Autonomy is the aim of education in constructivism (Kamii, 2000). Constructivist theory, however, has not adequately addressed either individual differences or cultural and contextual contributions to development and education (Delpit, 1988; Kessler & Swadener, 1992; Mallory & New, 1994). Thus, the needs of children who are different often are not met in constructivist classrooms.

The Sociohistorical Approach

The more cultural approach of Vygotsky (1978) affected learning and development through an emphasis on sociohistorical context, language and literacy learning, and the scaffolding of an adult or more able peer within a child's zone of proximal development. While Vygotsky emphasized the salience of culture and language, the zone of proximal development concept probably has had the biggest effect on education.

The zone of proximal development is the instructional level of a child, the area in which the child can most benefit from instruction with the help from an adult or more knowledgeable peer. According to Vygotsky (1978), that which a child can do today with help from a teacher (or more able peer), the child can do tomorrow by herself. Trying to figure out a child's zone of proximal development, however, is somewhat nebulous and difficult. Vygotsky did not expound on the nature of the child's zone of proximal development, how to determine it, or how to work with a child within that zone. For children exhibiting attention and activity-level difficulties, the zone of proximal development may be even more difficult to determine and utilize.

Ecological Systems Theory

Another theory used to guide education in the late twentieth century and early twenty-first century is Bronfenbrenner's (1989) ecological systems theory. Bronfenbrenner proposed that children are influenced by and influence the multiple systems in which they reside, either directly or peripherally. These systems include the microsystem, the mesosystem, the exosystem, and the macrosystem. Applications of this contextual theory focus on the seemingly endless variables within the child, and between the child and the numerous contexts affecting her. While few people would quarrel with the importance of these influences, trying to account for all of the endless interactions and variables affecting a child is exhausting and impractical. How would we ever have enough information about the child's temperament, activity levels, attentional states, or learning capacities as they relate to the microsystem, mesosystem, exosystem, and macrosystem?

Multiple Intelligences Theory

The multiple intelligences theory of Howard Gardner (1983) is a more recent influence on education. Traditional views of intelligence favored particular cognitive processes, including certain types of problem solving (mathematical-logical intelligence) and language abilities (linguistic intelligence). According to Gardner, however, these are just two types of intelligence. Five other intelligences—musical, visual spatial, bodily kinesthetic, interpersonal and intrapersonal—must be considered. Gardner has also added an eighth intelligence he calls the naturalist. A naturalist is someone who has the ability to recognize important distinctions in the natural world (Checkley, 1997).

Multiple intelligences theory shows promise in developing appropriate practices for children who do not fit the traditional mold or do not excel in the math or linguistic areas. Teachers can use children's types of intelligence(s) to assist in planning and teaching in areas in which they are not as gifted. Schools and teachers, however, are not usually equipped equally to deal with multiple intelligences. For example, children from lower socioeconomic areas may not have many opportunities to explore music or visual spatial intelligence(s), even if these are areas in which they might thrive. More efforts need to be made to fully understand multiple intelligences and to develop the resources necessary to support them.

Problems with Traditional Psychological Theories

All of the theories just mentioned are still influencing what happens in education today—some more than others. However, there are several issues with the psychological theories we have chosen to adopt as foundations for educating children and adolescents. Three of the most important are:

1. Most of our theories come from dead, white, Western men.
2. Discussions of our theories leave out significant details that, if known, would make us reconsider their usefulness.

3. The psychological theories we use to support our curriculum and instruction have neglected feminist, critical, and postmodern perspectives.

What Shall We Do with Dead, White, Western Men?

Why is it that over 95 percent of the individuals who take care of our children are women—many of them women of color—and yet over 95 percent of the people we use to inform our practice are dead, white, Western men? (Bee, 2000). Most of these men have never taught children. Even if they had, their conceptions of children were formed at another time, place, and context from the complex world in which we now live. Neither Gesell, Skinner, Freud, Piaget, nor Vygotsky have taught in a multicultural elementary or secondary school. None of them majored in education; most were psychologists or in professions related to psychology. Some made more money for an hour's lecture than child care workers or public school teachers make in two months. Have we really considered why we are using these men and their theories to inform how we teach in the twenty-first century? The issue here is not to throw the baby out with the bath water. That is, we don't have to dispose of everything we have learned from Piaget or Vygotsky or Freud. However, in light of their backgrounds and the current state of education, we need to be constantly questioning the relevance of their theories in a postmodern world. Further, if we subscribe to their theories, we need to look more closely at the details of their work that is often left out of textbook discussions.

What Did These Dead, White, Western Men Really Say?

Textbooks can be very dangerous things—often not because of what is said in them, but because of what is left out. An example of this is how G. Stanley Hall (1844–1924), the inventor of the term *adolescence* (Hall, 1899), has been recognized in human development and child development books as the "father of developmental psychology" (Turner & Helms, 1983, p. 19). However, what the authors fail to discuss are his views concerning women. He believed that girls should go to all-female schools where they could "metaphorically be turned out to grass and lie fallow so far as strenuous intellectual effort goes" (Hall, 1908, p. 589). He also pointed out that it was important for girls to "keep the purely mental back and by every method . . . bring the intuitions to the front" (Hall, 1899, p. 640). In discussing Hall's contributions to child development and education, authors have failed to point out his other ideas and the fact that his writing discriminates against women and limits their opportunities for full participation in education and society (Sadker & Sadker, 1994).

A second example of relevant omission is the work of Jean Piaget (1896–1980). Piaget believed in universal, invariant stages. In a series of interviews with Jean-Claude Bringuier, Piaget discusses these stages. Bringuier asks Piaget if all children go through the same stages in the same order. Piaget responds, "Yes, of course . . . Children in Martinique are in the French school system . . . They do get through, but in my studies of operations and conversations they are four years behind" (Bringuier, 1980, p. 34).

Bringuier was curious as to why this happens. Piaget tells him, "Their society, which is lazy. The father of one of these children had just built a house. When it was finished, he realized he had forgotten to put in the stairs" (Bringuier, 1980, p. 34).

Piaget does not take into account that many of the inhabitants of Martinique were brought there as slaves and did not intentionally adopt the French system. The French system was imposed on them. He does not consider that their ways of thinking and operating may be different from his white, upper-middle-class way of thinking. Very few texts adequately discuss this when discussing Piaget's universal, invariant stages.

A third example of glaring omission is in the work of Lawrence Kohlberg (1969). Kohlberg proposed a theory of moral development that was highlighted in virtually every child and human development text in the 1970s and 1980s. However, these sources failed to report that Kohlberg's original sample was male (see Turner & Helms, 1983; Vander Zanden, 1989).

During the past 30 years, theories have been proposed to counter many of the psychological theories used in education. These theories have included critical, postmodern, and feminist perspectives.

Critical Theory

Although critical theory is more a social or political theory than a developmental one, its influence on education has gained momentum over the past two decades. There are, in fact, many critical theories that have several things in common. Critical theories "examine the way in which philosophies and practices have determined what is taught in school and have served the 'state' to reproduce class lines and economic relationships" (Bloch, 1992, p. 6). Critical theories also "examine interrelationships among cultural, ideological, and economic relationships and race, class, and gender-related oppression" (p. 6).

Most critical theorists believe that certain forms of knowledge are valued over other forms. For example, when cutbacks occur in the schools, it is likely the arts will go, while the math and science curricula are likely to be increased. They further believe that school knowledge belongs to a certain group and that group remains in charge of school knowledge, often keeping it from other groups. The bottom line is that knowledge is unequally distributed and those in power use that knowledge to maintain their dominant position in society (Bloch, 1992).

Modern and Postmodern Theories

Perhaps one of the biggest and most recent shifts in our understanding of children took place with the advent of postmodernity. Elkind (1995) defines postmodernism as "not a revolt against the beliefs of modernity. Rather, it is perhaps best regarded as a set of attitudes and efforts designed to modify and correct modern ideas that have been perverted and modern beliefs that have proved to be too broad or too narrow" (p. 9). Table 4.2 shows a comparison of modern beliefs and practices versus postmodern beliefs and practices.

Both modernity and postmodernity currently exist simultaneously. Some families' beliefs and practices are more representative of the modern world. Others clearly live with postmodern values. It is not the purpose of this chapter to make a value judgment as to whether modernity or postmodernity is best. Clearly, both have their strengths and weaknesses. Because we currently live in both a modern and postmodern world, however, conflicting conceptions of children and schooling abound.

One example of this conflict can be seen in a conversation between a mother and daughter talking about the daughter's son who was recently diagnosed with AD(H)D. The grandmother said, "No wonder Mark has AD(H)D. You and his father work all the time. You never eat together as a family. Everyone is always going their own way. Since you hurry all the time and go here and there, I'm not surprised at all" (Aldridge, Eddowes & Kuby, 1998).

The daughter replied, "Mother, you don't understand. I work and go to school. Mark takes tennis and piano lessons. Although we are all busy, we are happy. It doesn't matter that we eat together. I take Mark to tennis and piano and his father or a sitter are with him when I have to work or go to class."

The mother and daughter have different ideas about what families should be like. The mother appears to have more modern values, while her daughter seems to subscribe to her own postmodern reality. As for Mark, while we do not know all the contributing factors to his diagnosed AD(H)D, we do know that he is being raised in a basically postmodern family. Anyone working with Mark and his family will need to take this into consideration.

Changing Curricular Practices

If we combine Heald-Taylor's (1996) description of curriculum models and Jungck and Marshall's (1992), we can formulate four basic models of teaching that are in practice today: (1) curriculum as transmission, (2) curriculum as transaction, (3) curriculum as inquiry, and (4) curriculum as transformation. While curricular practices are shifting from transmission toward transformation, all four models are very much in practice today. In fact, many would argue that curriculum as transmission is still the prevailing practice—especially in light of all the standardized testing.

Teaching as Transmission

In *teaching as transmission*, the curriculum is clearly prescribed by "experts" and measured as a commodity or product. This is traditional teaching. The teacher's

TABLE 4.2 A Comparison Between Modern and Postmodern Beliefs and Practices

Beliefs and Practices	Modernity	Postmodernity
1. General beliefs and practices	*Progress and Reason*—Humans are gradually improving *Universals*—Creative and rational thought can transcend social and historical boundaries in the arts and sciences *Regularity*—Humans value a search for natural laws that govern the physical and social worlds	*Ascendancy of language over reason*—Humans are embedded social, cultural and historical contexts *Particulars*—Humans are more concerned with specific cultural issues than with grand universals *Irregularity*—Humans value differences and irregularities in language, culture, science, the arts, industry, family & school
2. General beliefs about the family	*Romantic love*—There is only one person in the world who is your other half *Maternal love*—Mothers instinctively love and care for their children *Togetherness*—Family is placed before self (family eats together at mealtime)	*Consensual love*—One person cannot fulfill all your needs; divorce is a real possibility *Shared parenting*—Mothers, fathers, extended family and other caregivers share responsibility for children *Autonomy*—Self is placed before family (family does not eat together, each person is "doing own thing," i.e., soccer practice, etc.)
3. General beliefs about school and children	Education for progress, universality and regularity Personal adjustment Childhood innocence and adolescent maturity	Education for diversity, pluralism, and autonomy Self-esteem The competent child

Adapted from D. Elkind (1995). School and family in the postmodern world. *Phi Delta Kappan*, September 1995, 8–14.

role is as a technician who utilizes the prescribed curriculum, such as basal readers or curriculum guides, and makes few real decisions. She simply follows the preformed lesson plans. Students work individually to complete the same tasks. Usually, this task involves getting the correct answer. Decisions are made by outside experts and all meaning resides in either the materials or the experts (Heald-Taylor, 1996).

Curriculum as Transaction

Curriculum as transaction is different from teaching as transmission. In transaction, "knowledge is seen as constructed and reconstructed by those participating in the teaching-learning act" (Jungck & Marshall, 1992, p. 94). While teachers still use curriculum guides, they make decisions about selections and activities for students. Although students usually study the prescribed curriculum, they work in groups. Activities are more open-ended and promote higher-level thinking. Students can choose among various ways to represent what they have learned. Decisions still are made primarily by the teacher, with student input, while meaning is guided by the teacher, but constructed by the students (Heald-Taylor, 1996).

Curriculum as Inquiry

A third model is *curriculum as inquiry*. Just as with curriculum as transaction, inquiry classrooms encourage considerable student interaction in groups. The same group skills a teacher would encourage and develop in transaction classrooms are taught in inquiry classes.

Curriculum as inquiry has been used more and more over the past 25 years—particularly in whole language, developmentally appropriate, early childhood classrooms. Teachers in this type of curriculum create an inquiring environment that encourages children to explore and learn. The students play an active role in determining what the class, in general, and what they, in particular, will study. If the teacher has exposed the children to several authors of good literature, for example, the children may be the ones to decide which one will be the subject of an author study. If a tornado recently hit the community, the students may express an interest in learning more about tornadoes, and so it becomes the focus of the theme or unit of study. Many such decisions are made by the students, who are encouraged to construct their own meaning. Meaning in these classrooms does not rest with some outside expert.

General management of an inquiry classroom takes a tremendously resourceful and skilled teacher. Any instructor who does not have such abilities will surely risk havoc in the classroom from students who are inattentive or overactive. In inquiry classrooms, the curriculum is less crucial than the teacher's ability to be a good manager. When instructors have the skill and resources to

GOVERNORS STATE UNIVERSITY
UNIVERSITY PARK
IL 60466

effectively run an inquiry class, children who would otherwise be inattentive or overactive may actually thrive.

Curriculum as Transformation

A fourth model, *curriculum as transformation*, appears at first glance to be identical to the curriculum as inquiry model. There is, however, one important difference. In transformation classrooms, the curriculum is designed to study how people or other living creatures make a difference in the world. In an inquiry classroom, if students express an interest in studying insects, a unit on insects is developed. In transformation classrooms, however, this study of insects would go a step further. Students' interest in insects would lead to a study of how insects make a difference in the world. What insects are helpful? How can humans work with insects to maintain an appropriate ecological balance? In these classrooms, curriculum takes on a whole new meaning. We study things so that we can make a difference on the planet (Jungck & Marshall, 1992).

In terms of management, the same things can be said about transformation classrooms as can be said for inquiry programs. A skillful and resourceful teacher will make all the difference in the world.

Conclusions

In this chapter, we have seen the shifts that have occurred and are occurring in our current understanding of children. We have moved through organismic and mechanistic paradigms to a new era of developmental contextualism, in which the child and context are seen as much more complex and interactive than originally conceived. Theories that inform our educational practices are also changing. Those that relied too heavily on the child's nature (Gesell, 1925) or on environment (Skinner, 1974) are giving way to more interactive theories, such as Bronfenbrenner's ecological systems theory (1989) and Vygotsky's sociohistorical approach (1978). The theories of dead, white, Western men have been questioned and critical pedagogy may help us consider the social, political, and economic ways in which we view children.

In many ways, we live in both a modern and postmodern world. We have one foot in modernity while the other foot is in postmodernity. This is sometimes a very painful and uncertain place to be, as many people are not completely sure of their own beliefs about children, families, schools, and society.

Curricular practices are also changing. While many teachers still subscribe to teaching as transmission, others have moved on to teaching as transaction, inquiry, or transformation. Whatever the future brings, it is certain that we must continue to examine the theories that guide us and decide whether we will resist or move with the theoretical shifts that are currently shaping our understanding of children.

REFERENCES

Aldridge, J., Eddowes, E. A., & Kuby, P. (1998). *No easy answers: Helping children with attention and activity level differences.* Olney, MD: Association for Childhood Education International.

Aldridge, J., Kuby, P., & Strevy, D. (1992). Developing a metatheory of education. *Psychological Reports, 70,* 683–687.

Bee, H. (2000). *The developing child* (9th ed.). Boston: Allyn & Bacon.

Bijou, S. W. (1989). Behaviorism. In R. Vasta (Ed.), *Annals of child development* (pp. 61–83). Greenwich, CT: JAI Press.

Bloch, M. (1992). Critical perspectives on the historical relationship between child development and early childhood education research. In S. Kessler & B. B. Swadener (Eds.), *Reconceptualizing the early childhood curriculum: Beginning the dialogue* (pp. 3–20). New York: Teachers College Press.

Bringuier, J. (1980). *Conversations with Piaget.* Chicago: University of Chicago Press.

Bronfenbrenner, U. (1989). Ecological systems theory. In R. Vasta (Ed.), *Annals of child development,* (Vol. 6) (pp. 187–250). Greenwich, CT: JAI Press.

Checkley, K. (1997). The first seven . . . and the eighth: A conversation with Howard Gardner. *Educational Leadership, 55*(1), 8–13.

Delpit, L. (1988). The silenced dialogue: Power and pedagogy in educating other people's children. *Harvard Educational Review, 58*(3), 280–298.

Elkind, D. (1995). School and family in the postmodern world. *Phi Delta Kappan, 76,* 8–14.

Elkind, D. (2000/01). The cosmopolitan school. *Educational Leadership, 58*(4), 12–17.

Ford, D. H., & Lerner, R. M. (1992). *Developmental systems theory.* Newbury Park, CA: Sage.

Freud, S. (1935). *New introductory lectures on psychoanalysis.* New York: Norton.

Gardner, H. (1983). *Frames of mind: The theory of multiple intelligences.* New York: Basic Books.

Gesell, A. (1925). *The mental growth of the pre school child.* New York: Macmillan.

Hall, G. S. (1899). *Adolescence.* New York: Appleton.

Hall, G. S. (1908). The question of coeducation, *Muncey's Magazine, 35,* 589.

Heald-Taylor, B. G. (1996). Three paradigms for literature instruction in grades 3 to 6. *Reading Teacher, 49*(6), 456–466.

Hinshaw, S. P. (1994). *Attention deficit hyperactivity in children.* Thousand Oaks, CA: Sage.

Jungck, S., & Marshall, J. D. (1992). Curricular perspectives on one great debate. In S. Kessler & B. B. Swadener (Eds.), *Reconceptualizing the early childhood curriculum: Beginning the dialogue* (pp. 19–37). New York: Teachers College Press.

Kamii, C. (2000). *Young children reinvent arithmetic: Implications of Piaget's theory* (2nd ed.). New York: Teachers College Press.

Kessler, S., & Swadener, B. B. (Eds.). (1992). *Reconceptualizing the early childhood curriculum: Beginning the dialogue.* New York: Teachers College Press.

Kohlberg, L. (1969). Stage and sequence: The cognitive-developmental approach to socialization. In D. A. Goslin (Ed.), *Handbook of socialization theory and research.* Chicago: Rand McNally.

Kuhn, T. S. (1970). *The structure of scientific revolutions* (2nd ed.). Chicago: University of Chicago Press.

Lerner, R. M. (1986). *Concepts and theories of human development* (2nd ed.). New York: Random House.

Mallory, B. L., & New, R. S. (Eds.). (1994). *Diversity and developmentally appropriate practice: Challenges for early childhood education.* New York: Teachers College Press.

Miller, P. (1993). *Theories of developmental psychology* (3rd ed.). San Francisco: W. H. Freeman.

Morphett, M. V., & Washburne, C. (1931). When should children begin to read? *Elementary School Journal, 31,* 496–503.

Pelligrini, A. D., & Horvat, M. (1995). A developmental contextualist critique of attention deficit hyperactivity disorder. *Educational Research, 24*(1), 13–19.

Pepper, S. C. (1942). *World hypotheses: A study in evidence.* Berkeley, CA: University of California Press.

Piaget, J. (1952). *The child's conception of number*. London: Routledge & Kegan Paul.

Sadker, M., & Sadker, D. (1994). *Failing at fairness: How our schools cheat girls*. New York: Houghton Mifflin.

Skinner, B. F. (1974). *About behaviorism*. New York: Knopf.

Thomas, R. M. (1992). *Comparing theories of child development* (3rd ed.). Belmont, CA: Wadsworth.

Thomas, R. M. (1999). *Human development theories: Windows on culture*. Thousand Oaks, CA: Sage.

Turner, J. S., & Helms, D. B. (1983). *Lifespan human development* (2nd ed.). New York: Holt, Rinehart and Winston.

Vander Zanden, J. W. (1989). *Human development* (4th ed.). New York: Random House.

Vygotsky, L. S. (1978). *Mind in society: The development of higher psychological processes*. Cambridge, MA: Harvard University Press.

CHAPTER

5   The Controversy over Brain Research

NINA KING

The past decade has seen a tremendous increase in our ability to understand the brain. This chapter will begin by looking at what we know about the brain, discuss elements that promote or diminish brain functioning, and describe the processes of attention and memory necessary for learning. The most recent neurological discoveries will be shared, as will how intelligence, teaching, and learning are implicated in the findings, and practical recommendations for teachers, parents, and caregivers will be offered. A brief examination of the status of early care and education in the United States will be made, indicating the need for proactive change in order to utilize these latest revelations.

Technology and the Study of the Brain

What a wonder the human brain is—a three-pound mass of tissue capable of contemplating the universe as well as pondering its own existence. It can create, dream, and imagine what is not, while at the same time wonder "*Why* not?" While the human race has probably always been fascinated by the mind, the modern study of the brain began about 30 years ago with research on the left and right hemispheres (Shore, 1997). Information gathered in the last five years, however, has sparked renewed interest, particularly within the education community.

    Teachers have always been brain researchers of a sort since they are challenged daily to discover better ways to stimulate memory and learning in the minds of students. For example, teachers perceive how long a lesson should be in order to maximize interest, know that young children can learn a second language more easily than adults can, and understand that play is a vital ingredient for the physical as well as mental development of early learners (Bredekamp & Copple, 1997; Johnson, Christie & Yawkey, 1999). New scientific tools for exploring the human brain are helping to explain many of these and similar observations.

    According to Bucko (1997), it is with the recent technological development of neural imaging, molecular biology, and computers that the interrelationship of various areas of the brain has been revealed. Neural imaging in the form of Positron Emission Tomography (PET) scans provides an astounding view of which areas of the brain are stimulated by certain pictures or objects. In this process, a person is injected with tracer chemicals that mimic glucose, the brain's energy source. When the brain tries to use it as fuel, the chemical emits particles called positrons (Shore, 1997). Colored lights corresponding to exact locations being aroused in the brain flash on an imagery screen. Through this technology it has been found that bilingual persons process their native language in different areas of the brain than those areas accessed by the second language (Bucko, 1997). Also, emotions such as happiness and sadness are not handled in the same area of the brain, hence, one is able to experience mixed emotions (Bucko, 1997). A person synthesizes a red ball rolling along a table in four different areas of the brain (Sylwester, 1993–94).

Another advancement that has assisted in the understanding of the brain is molecular biology. Eric Kandel, from Columbia University, discovered a short string of chemical molecules he labeled CREB that seems to be necessary in turning short-term memory into long-term memory. Since CREB is less abundant in older persons, it may help explain some memory loss occurring with age (Bucko, 1997). Finally, while using the metaphor of the computer to describe brain functioning has been refuted as incomplete (Sylwester, 1993–94), computer technology has aided in understanding the complexities of processing. Through these scientific innovations, more has been learned about the brain in the last few years than in the previous 100. In fact, according to Wolfe and Brandt (1998), close to 90 percent of all neuroscientists who have ever lived are alive today.

The Brain

The human brain is comprised of three major regions. The innermost area has been termed the primitive, reptilian, or lizard brain (Howard, 1994). This core section, which includes the brainstem, coordinates the survival functions of the body—reproduction, respiration, circulation, and digestion. The cerebellum sits behind the upper brainstem and controls coordination of complex movement (Giuffre & DiGeronimo, 1999). The middle region of the brain, the limbic system, controls the fight-or-flight impulse and is associated with stress, sleep, and depression. Within this section lies the hippocampus, amygdala, and other structures that are important in governing emotion and that play a role in memory and learning (Brierley, 1994; Shore, 1997). The outer area of the brain, the cortex, is associated with creativity, learning, thinking, planning, remembering, and using language and numbers (Howard, 1994; Shore, 1997).

A critical and interesting component is found at the top of the brainstem—the reticular activating system (RAS), described by Howard (1994) as a kind of "toggle switch" whose job it is to react to sudden threat of safety by allowing either the limbic system or the cortex to take over. When we are experiencing a stressful situation, the RAS activates the limbic system's fight or-flight response. When the danger or threat is removed, the more creative cortex may once again take over (Howard, 1994). Improper RAS functioning has been found responsible for rage behavior in some individuals, the presence of a tumor causing sustained limbic arousal (Howard, 1994; Joseph, 1992).

Left and Right Hemispheres of the Brain

The wrinkled cortex, about 2,000 square centimeters in area (Brierley, 1994) is divided into two hemispheres connected by the corpus callosum. This bridgelike structure acts as a kind of relay center allowing for communication between the two larger regions. Each hemisphere is arranged into four different lobes termed the occipital, temporal, parietal, and frontal. In the back of the cortex is the occipital lobe, which processes visual input. At the sides of the cortex near the ears are located the temporal lobes, which deal with auditory stimuli. Also on the sides but more toward the back of the brain lie the parietal lobes, where interpreting and harmonizing of sensory input occurs. The frontal lobes are located just behind the forehead and are associated with planning, problem solving, and higher-level thinking (D'Arcangelo, 1998).

   Generally, each hemisphere is considered to have somewhat different emphases. The left side of the brain is believed to be associated with analytical concepts, cause and effect, and language and symbols, while the right side is linked primarily with feelings, intuitive thoughts, form, distance, and space (McCarthy, 1997). Furthermore, the brain is cross-wired, with the right hemisphere controlling the left side of the body, and the left hemisphere controlling the right side (Ramachandran & Blakeslee, 1998).

   It would be incorrect, however, to assume that the left and right hemispheres, or even areas within each hemisphere, are totally independent. On the contrary, each hemisphere depends heavily upon the other. In fact, one discovery of modern brain research has been the interrelationship among different sectors of the brain. This is due, in part, to the complex connections between neurons—the building blocks of the brain.

Brain Cells

There are two kinds of brain cells—glial cells and neurons. The glial cells are elongated, supporting cells, almost like scaffolding, that help neurons reach their proper position during brain formation (Shore, 1997). We are born with approximately one hundred billion neurons, our having lost one-third to one-half of them before birth (Wolfe & Brandt, 1998; Shore, 1997). This neural pruning continues at a slower rate throughout life, the human brain losing up to 100,000 cells daily.

One way of visualizing the number of neurons in the average brain is to imagine a number greater than all of the trees in all of the forests on the whole surface of the earth (Abbott, 1997). Ramachandran and Blakeslee (1998) report that a piece of cortex the size of a grain of sand would contain about 100,000 neurons.

Neurons differ in kind and size, but each has a nucleus, usually only one axon, and many dendrites (Brierly, 1994; Shore, 1997). The axon is an output strand that sends electric nerve signals to other neurons. Dendrites, shorter branchlike fibers, are more numerous and are designed to connect with axons of other cells to receive incoming messages. The point at which an axon and a dendrite meet is called the synaptic gap because the two do not actually touch. An electric signal from one cell must jump this tiny space in order for the message to be received. The pulse of electricity causes a release of chemicals, called neurotransmitters, which facilitate this leap. When this happens, a connection is made, and eventually "dendrite trees" are formed that can receive messages from many other neurons. Large neurons may have as many as 20,000 dendrites, while smaller ones may have only 2,000 (Shore, 1997). When a nerve pathway is frequently used, the threshold of the synaptic gap falls, so that it travels more easily the next time (Brierley, 1994). In fact, a level of neurotransmitters released can be reached at which the connection can never be lost—the pathway becomes exempt from elimination (Shore, 1997). Abbott (1997) estimates the length of this "wiring" between neurons to be about 100,000 kilometers or 62,150 miles.

Neurons respond to the environment by growing and forming new connections or by atrophying from lack of use. The implications for education are profound and will be discussed in later sections of this chapter.

Factors Affecting Brain Functioning

Neurotransmitters

It is important to understand the workings of a few of the brain's neurotransmitters, because a knowledge of how they function will be helpful in understanding body-brain responses to certain elements in the environment. Neurotransmitters are chemicals released at the synaptic gap and are associated with the health of the synapses and neurons. The levels of neurotransmitters released cause the activation or inhibition of certain behavioral and physiological responses of the body. For example, children who play an exciting game and then attempt to settle down for nap time will have a difficult time getting to sleep since the excitement of the game would cause an increase in acetylcholine, which boosts alertness. The following list describes six of the body's many neurotransmitters and gives a short explanation of their functions:

> *Acetylcholine*—important in maintaining the plasticity of the neuron wall, in learning and memory, and in alertness; also necessary in activating REM sleep

Calpain—acts as a cleaner of the synaptic gap

Dopamine—associated with mood and movement

Endorphins—cause a pleasurable sensation when triggered by laughter, pain, and aerobic exercise; sometimes called the body's morphine

Epinephrine (or *Adrenaline*)—associated with arousal and alertness

Melatonin—production is suppressed by natural light; essential to setting the body's internal clock and in the onset of sleep

Norepinephrine (or *noradrenaline*)—establishes long-term memory and aids in forming new synapses connected with memory; released during fight-or-flight arousal

Serotonin—depletion causes depression, overproduction causes aggression, and balanced amounts evoke relaxation and sleep (Howard, 1994).

Kenneth Giuffre and T. F. DiGeronimo (1999) give an excellent and complete description of food and other factors that affect the functioning of the brain in their book, *The Care and Feeding of Your Brain: How Diet and Environment Affect What You Think and Feel* (1999). Much of the following information will paraphrase their descriptions of a few of what they term brain "boosters" and "zappers" and what here will be called *promoters* and *inhibitors*.

Inhibitors

Caffeine. While caffeine may give you a quick lift, it is actually accelerating memory loss. Caffeine affects brain cells by causing the production of a compound called cyclic AMP that acts like the neurotransmitter norepinephrine in alerting the body during stress. However, with sustained AMP production the body is seemingly responding in hyperalert status, such as during a stressful situation, and will eventually be depleted of this needed chemical. When this occurs, the body will be unprotected against the next wave of stress (Giuffre & DiGeronimo, 1999). Children who are allowed frequent caffeinated beverages are being set up for a big letdown.

Nicotine. Most people already know many negative affects of smoking. Like caffeine, smoking produces an initial lift. Also, like caffeine, nicotine promotes memory loss. It causes the deterioration of blood vessels, limits the flow of blood to the brain, increases the chance of stroke, and affects the ability to remember and think. Smoking also mimics the stress reaction, kills brain cells, and increases the possibility of Alzheimer's disease (Giuffre & DiGeronimo, 1999). It is also important to know that smoking around children carries a high risk of causing behavior problems as well as mental dysfunction (Howard, 1994).

Adults who smoke are providing role models for adolescents. The United States Department of Health and Human Services' publication *Child Health*

U.S.A. 1998 reports a substantial increase in adolescent smoking in the previous eight years. It is interesting to note that while the larger numbers showed across all sociodemographic groups, it was found that respondents with no future college plans were more likely to smoke.

Alcohol.   Short-term use of alcohol causes a reaction similar to that of sedatives in prohibiting the retention of memories. Alcohol also causes some nutritional deficiencies such as the depletion of the vitamin thiamin. A thiamin deficiency can cause permanent damage to the thalamus, a structure connected to the hippocampus, which is related to long-term memory processing (Giuffre & Di Geronimo, 1999).

Marijuana.   The active ingredient in marijuana, THC, affects the hippocampus by interfering with the system that creates long-term memories. Studies have shown that even after giving up marijuana, former users were not able to regain all of the abilities to focus and attend. It is as if they had an *acquired attention deficit disorder* (Giuffre & DiGeronimo, 1999). The U.S. Department of Health and Human Services (1998) noted that the number of adolescents who had reported using marijuana in the past month increased from 7.1 percent in 1996 to 9.4 percent in 1997, with fewer numbers even viewing marijuana as risky.

Artificial Sweeteners.   Artificial sweeteners such as aspartame increase general brain stimulation and arouse the stress response. With long-term use, they may deplete seratonin levels, resulting in depression (Giuffre & DiGeronimo, 1999).

Fats and Proteins.   While some fat is necessary for optimum brain functioning (see Promoters), excessive intake of fats and proteins has a negative effect on the body by promoting the production of free radicals and by causing plaque to form in arteries. Free radicals are the waste products generated when the body burns its fuel for energy, or when specific substances are broken down, such as a burned steak or fat-filled processed cakes (Giuffre & DiGeronimo, 1999). Through a complicated process, free radicals can cause damage to brain cell walls, or even lead to cell death. Plaque deposits can cause arteriosclerosis, which restricts blood flow to the brain, affecting memory retrieval and storage. The popular fat-laden, fast-food lifestyle maintained by many families is anything but intelligent.

Stress.   It is well documented that stress can affect the physical health of an individual, causing ulcers, hypertension, skin ailments, and headaches. During sustained stress, the immune system can be impaired, resulting in more serious problems such as stroke, diabetes, kidney disease, heart disease, and cancer (Howard, 1994). Within the brain, stress causes the limbic system to take over, reducing the chance that the cortex will function as well in focusing or in memory retrieval. Howard (1994) explains that three reactions occur as a result of stress—freeze, fight, or flee. Some people may experience a kind of paralysis during stress, not being able to perform normally routine tasks—in essence, freezing. Others may exhibit a tendency toward greater aggression or rage—the urge to fight. If something at work is causing the stress, the reaction might be flight—missed meetings, forgotten appointments, or disorganization of paperwork. If the stress is school-related, a child may forget homework, projects, or become distracted and disoriented. Sylwester and Cho (1993–94) suggest that one might flee the stress by intensely focusing on an insignificant task rather than facing the problem. The limbic system is in charge at this level, and the thinking, reasoning cortex is no longer in control. The brain is running on automatic pilot, essentially downshifting (Abbott, 1997; Pool, 1997). As a psychological response to a threatening or highly stressful situation, downshifting is often accompanied by a sense of helplessness, fatigue, anxiety, and/or fear. Mounting evidence suggests that downshifting is occurring in schools everywhere (Pool, 1997).

Promoters

Fat.   The body needs a moderate amount of fat in the diet for maintaining brain cell wall elasticity. Thirty percent of fat in a normal diet is acceptable if one is careful not to use too much saturated fat. Children should not be encouraged to adhere to a no-fat diet, nor should even adults totally eliminate fat from the foods they eat.

Calcium.   Calcium is needed in the diet for healthy bodies and clear thinking. Similar to the terminals on a car battery, synapses can develop a protein build-up that can inhibit nerve signals' leap across the synaptic gap. Calpain, derived from calcium, is the body's neurotransmitter for taking care of this problem (Howard, 1994). A deficiency of calcium in the body inhibits the formation of calpain. A moderate amount of milk and calcium-rich foods such as green, leafy vegetables should be included in a healthy diet for adults as well as children.

Exercise.   Exercise is known to have many physiological benefits. The increased blood flow that accompanies exercise aids brain functioning by bringing in oxygen and by clearing the brain of free radicals (Guiffre & DiGeronimo, 1999). Other benefits include raising serotonin levels, thereby improving sleep and decreasing depression.

Sleep.   Sleep is the night shift for the brain's clean-up crew. During sleep, the brain takes back serotonin and norepinephrine from synapses in preparation for awakening (Guiffre & DiGeronimo, 1999). Inadequate sleep interrupts this process, and a lack of these neurotransmitters is associated with all the symptoms of chronic stress including "paranoia, inability to concentrate, loss of memory, and loss of general cognitive function" (Guiffre & DiGeronimo, 1999, p. 43).

Over time, this can cause brain cell death. Sleep deprivation also interferes with the brain's ability to turn short-term memory into long-term memory. Guiffre states that it is only with deep, prolonged sleep that this action can fully take place. Furthermore, Howard (1994) reports that "people who nap consistently live longer and show a 30 percent lower incidence of heart disease" (p. 99). Are children getting enough sleep? Look in any classroom and it is evident that not all our youth are. Getting sustained and regular sleep is a critical component in brain growth.

Environment.   Howard (1994) reports that for alertness, warmer temperatures within the comfort zone are best. Cooler temperatures cause the brain to be more relaxed, thereby less alert. According to this information, the former belief that keeping classrooms cool stimulates the brain was inaccurate. Extremes on either end of the scale will cause discomfort or lack of concentration for some students. Keep the environment pleasant, calm, and comfortable.

Music.   In January 1998, Georgia's governor at that time, Zel Miller, asked his state legislature to approve $105,000 in his 1999 budget to provide every new-born in Georgia a compact disc of classical music (Stanley, 1998). Miller was possibly responding to the research findings of Gordon Shaw's studies into the relationship between music and spatial intelligence. Shaw, with Frances Rauscher (1997), conducted a two-year investigation involving three groups of preschool-ers, one group receiving private keyboard and singing lessons, one group getting individual computer instructions, and a third group receiving no specialized training. The group that received music lessons scored 34 percent higher on tests measuring spatial and temporal ability than the others.

In a later study, Rauscher (reported in Verrengia, 1998) conducted an experiment in which she exposed one group of lab rats to music by Mozart 12 hours a day for the first 60 days of their lives, another group to white noise, and a third to minimalist composer Philip Glass. When the rats were timed running a maze, those exposed to Mozart ran the course in the shortest time, 35 seconds; rats that listened to white noise came next at 44 seconds, and the Philip Glass rats ran the maze in the longest time, 55 seconds. Rauscher believes that music may stimulate a specific area in the brain, perhaps reorganizing cells in that area. She is hoping to discover additional neural growth in the rats that listened to Mozart (Verrengia, 1998). It is interesting to note that in the former study, the children who scored highest on spatial/temporal tests had not merely been exposed to music, but had actually been given music lessons.

Some researchers agree that there is a connection between spatial intelli-gence and music exposure. Consider the fact presented by James Pointer (1999) in the *National Association of Secondary School Principals Bulletin*. According to this report, in a 1988 test of educational achievement, the United States ranked four-teenth among seventeen countries International Association for the Evaluation of Educational Achievement (IAEEA). The interesting fact is that in every nation scoring above the United States on that test, music is a primary focus of the curriculum. The report goes on to cite many persons of high intelligence who also happen to be musicians. The determination of whether a music-mind connection is valid or not will need further investigation. In the United States, however, the arts take a back seat to all other programs in most schools. Frequently, schools have music or art classes only once or twice a week, and these programs are the first to be cut during financial difficulties.

Memory

Memory exists in many areas of the brain (Abbott, 1997). There are two basic types of memory—short-term and long-term. When one takes in an experience, the area of the brain just behind the forehead holds the information for a short time, determining in a few moments whether to store it in long-term memory or to move on to something else (Bucko, 1997; Sylwester & Cho, 1993–1994). An overwhelming number of stimuli bombard the brain simultaneously during the waking hours, forcing it to make numerous snap decisions. If one is putting away the car keys while making a doctor's appointment on the telephone, which is more important to remember? The brain must decide in a few seconds. Later, the doctor's appointment may be remembered, but not where the keys were put.

In making a memory, connections between neurons are established. If the neural connections are repeated over and over, the memory is strengthened. A great part of maintaining and updating long-term memory involves what Sylwester and Cho (1993–1994) call "external-internal shift." The brain is constantly shifting between new stimuli (external events) and searching through prior knowledge or interests (internal memories) for connections. This continuous search for links between new stimuli and old memories builds new synapses, resulting in learning. Recalling and retelling memories make the neural pathways that process and contain them stronger (Sylwester & Cho, 1993–94).

Some facts seem easy to forget, while others remain longer. There are two kinds of input—"what" and "how to." "What" facts include faces, names, and dates. "How to" data involves skills like reading, writing, and sewing. The "how to" information is more easily retained since it is associated with more areas of the brain. For example, writing involves the sense of touch in holding the pencil, vision in seeing the marks made on the paper, and perhaps even sounds associated with the activity. The more neurons that are connected, the stronger the memory and the less likely it will be forgotten. The "what" facts—names and dates, for example—are more easily lost, since they are not scaffolded by as many other pathways. Association, repetition, and imagery are good ways to strengthen the neural connections making memories. It is clear that this information reinforces a discovery or hands-on curriculum that emphasizes activities involving the whole child rather than just presenting facts (Bredekamp & Copple, 1997).

Attention

Closely related to memory and critical to learning is the ability to attend or concentrate. According to Sylwester and Cho (1993–1994), a good attentional system must be able to do four things. First, it must sift through, identify, and focus on the most crucial item in a busy environment. Second, it must keep its focus while still observing, monitoring, or ignoring other sensory input. Third, it must be able to retrieve memories that could be connected to the present focus. Last, the attentional system must be able to change its focus if more important data is observed. Very young children, however, have not developed the ability to pay attention to more than one thing.

Children who exhibit dysfunction in attention may suffer from chemical imbalances resulting in attention deficit hyperactivity disorder or other concentration-related disorders such as schizophrenia and retardation. Some stimulant drugs, properly prescribed, increase the availability of the brain's neurotransmitters associated with attention and seem to inhibit distracting stimuli, thereby increasing the child's ability to attend appropriately (Sylwester & Cho, 1993–1994).

A difficulty with the normal attentional system, however, is that it is designed to respond quickly to radical changes in the environment and to react passively to the mundane. This spells trouble for many students because the usual low-level, routine tasks in schools do not inspire the brain to remember. Sylwester and Cho (1993–1994) call this the brain's "built-in bias" to the conventional, low-contrast curriculum. Since the brain attends more easily to data that it can connect to previous memories and that evoke a strong sensory response, it is vital that teachers use this knowledge to plan more effectively.

A problem that may be just as difficult to address is the brain's tendency toward *habituation*, a term Howard (1994) describes as the psychological word for "enough is enough." As explained earlier, the brain responds to unique stimuli, not to routine. However, if the arousing event is maintained without change, the brain becomes accustomed to it (habituated) and reduces its attentiveness toward it. One may "tune out" background noise or let the mind wander during a long, monotonous speech. How much more "turned off" the brain becomes if the curriculum has *no* such stimulating experiences to offer!

Critical/Sensitive Periods and Learning

Howard (1994) defines learning as the establishment of new synapses. In the first 8 to 10 years of life, the human brain experiences an explosion of growth in dendrite formation (D'Arcangelo, 1998). The speed of synaptic formation can proceed at a rate of up to three billion per second (Wolfe & Brandt, 1998). A young child's brain at age 2 has about twice as many synapses as the child's pediatrician's, and by age 3 is about two and a half times more active (Shore, 1997). In the first three years of life, establishment of synapses outpaces pruning. During the next seven years, elimination and production of neurons are about equal; and from early adolescence on, the eradication of cells outnumbers growth (Shore, 1997).

The first few years are crucial times for learning specific skills such as language (Education Commission of the States, 1998). Everyone is born with the capability to learn any language on earth. However, only those neurons associated with vocalizations being heard in the environment will be connected, strengthening those pathways through repetition. Neurons not accessed by the native language may atrophy or die through lack of use. This is why it is much easier for a young child to learn to speak a second language fluently than for an adult. Furthermore, this early brain plasticity allows for enormous reorganization under severe conditions. For example, language ability lost due to damage to the brain may be regained if the accident occurs in early life (Brierley, 1994).

These findings have caused some to declare the first ten years of life a critical period in brain growth. However, that may be too grim a conclusion, causing some to believe it fruitless to attempt learning difficult tasks past puberty. Wolfe and Brandt (1998) have chosen instead to call this a sensitive period—a "window of opportunity" for parents, caregivers, and teachers.

Schools and Teaching

Memories and skills are made stronger by the brain's natural tendency of parallel processing, the complex thinking that involves many areas of the brain, such as sensory memories, concept identification, and speech. Pool (1997) states that children learn best through "orchestrated immersion," involvement in complex experiences that evoke connections to real life. Children perform better in a state of mind he calls "relaxed alertness," a low-threat/high challenge mental attitude.

Unfortunately, traditional methods of teaching in America do not match the way the brain learns best. Many schools impede higher-order thinking with their emphases on the teacher as the supplier of knowledge. According to Pool (1997), new brain-based teaching promotes collaboration, mutual responsibility, and both teacher and student as learners. Since the brain likes repetition, however, even educators find it difficult to change their methodologies after decades of teaching the same way. As Howard Gardner states in *The Unschooled Mind* (1991), "Much if not most of what happens in schools happens because that is the way it was done in earlier generations, not because we have a convincing rationale for maintaining it today" (p. 202).

The way a person discerns reality and responds to it forms a pattern over time (McCarthy, 1997). These patterns become the brain's routine ways of dealing with life—its modes of learning. In recent years, many educators have attempted to identify styles of learning so as to facilitate individual cognitive growth. Gardner (1999) describes eight intelligences or ways of learning. According to this theory, humans possess the potential for accomplishment in one or more areas of linguistic, musical, logical-mathematical, naturalist, spatial, bodily-kinesthetic, interpersonal, and intrapersonal intelligences. Inspired by Gardner's ideas, many activities have been recommended for accessing students' preferred learning styles, as well as for inspiring development of less discernible areas.

Some warn not to take the eight intelligences theory to an inappropriate level, however. Thomas Hatch suggests that instead of asking how many intelligences a child has, one should ask, "In what ways does the child demonstrate intelligences?" (1997, p. 27). Pool (1997) also counsels educators to be careful when implementing a limited knowledge of Gardner's theory, not to provide mere variations on the traditional curriculum, but to provide complex learning experiences that encourage neural branching.

Other educators have examined how individual students learn best, while cautioning against labeling children. McCarthy (1997) describes four learning modalities. Type 1 learners favor feeling and reflecting; learn by talking, listening, and asking questions; and need to connect mathematical concepts to real life. Type 2 learners enjoy working independently and reading; and favor lectures and the exchange of ideas. Type 3 learners are depicted as commonsense students who prefer tasks, deadlines, and physical activity; and who are uncomfortable with reading used as the only way to learn. Type 4 learners are described as risk takers, questioners, explorers, and haters of routine. McCarthy's 4MAT Framework promotes giving all students experience in every style, proceeding through a cycle that includes building lessons around the following questions:

1. *Why* do I need to know this? (the personal meaning important to Type 1 learners)
2. *What* exactly is this concept or skill? (the conceptual understanding critical to Type 2 learners)
3. *How* will I use this in my life? (the real-life skills crucial to Type 3 learners)
4. If I do use this, *what possibilities* will it create? (the unique adaptations necessary for Type 4 learners) (McCarthy, 1997, p. 49)

By accessing the thinking and feeling aspects of students' brains, as well as spatial and other domains, McCarthy states that higher-order thinking will occur, resulting in greater learning.

Similarly, Sternberg (1997) suggests that teachers plan lessons that ask all students to (1) recall facts; (2) analyze, compare, evaluate, judge, or assess; (3) create, invent, imagine, or design; and (4) use, put into practice, or implement. By addressing the whole child in this manner, Sternberg maintains that schools may find thousands of children to be smarter than once thought.

Cardellichio and Field (1997) suggest the following seven ways teachers can promote neural branching just by getting students to look at things in a different way than they normally would:

1. Hypothetical thinking ("What if this had happened instead of that?")
2. Reversal ("How would things change if I turn this idea, event, or problem around?")

3. Application of different symbol systems ("Can I represent this in a totally different way than is commonly used?")
4. Analogy ("How is this like that?")
5. Analysis of point of view ("What other ways of looking at this can be found? Who might think of this differently?")
6. Completion (supply the missing piece)
7. Web analysis (diagram related ideas or effects of a concept or event)

Teaching Strategies for an Enriched Curriculum

These additional suggestions are proposed to assist teachers in forging the type of curriculum and environment advantageous for cognitive growth.

1. Create a calm, clean, stress-free, and comfortable classroom climate (Shore, 1997). *The brain's cortex functions most fully under stress-free conditions.*
2. Do not label students, but do provide a variety of activities accessing all learning modalities (McCarthy, 1997). *The brain remembers best by accessing familiar pathways and by stimulating many areas through novel experiences.*
3. Utilize cooperative learning in the form of dyads, small groups, debates, and role playing; allow students to discuss out loud and to collaborate (Sylwester & Cho, 1993–1994); Wolfe & Brandt, 1998). *Exchanging ideas and brainstorming solutions to problems stimulate thinking in different ways, which in turn promotes neural growth.*
4. Connect new information to something the student already knows (Lowery, 1998). *The brain likes to look for relationships. Matching new facts or skills to prior knowledge will strengthen neural paths and create new ones.*
5. Use storytelling as a teaching and learning tool. *Mental imagery is associated with creative thinking, which promotes the strengthening of pathways.*
6. Play games and provide hands-on activities. *Long-term memory is formed by repetition and by accessing many areas of the brain through complex experiences.*
7. Include music and art frequently. *While the jury is still out on the connection between music instruction and spatial intelligence, the arts seem to have a positive effect on brain functioning by adding, at the very least, a complexity and richness to the environment.*
8. Encourage in-depth projects and longer time allowances for exploration. *More time spent on related topics increases synaptic formation through developing a network of concepts.*
9. Use the classroom as a laboratory, allowing students to solve problems in their immediate world (Sylwester & Cho, 1993–1994). *The brain is constantly searching for meaning. Allowing children to look for their own solutions will effect dendrite growth.*
10. Tap into your creativity and teach with imagination (Pool, 1997). *Attention is held and long-term memory formed through experiencing unique events.*

11. Form "process groups" of teachers who get together to share ideas (Pool, 1997). *Teachers need time to collaborate and seek solutions to common problems. This will encourage neural growth in the brains of teachers, as well.*
12. Match forms of assessment with appropriate learning styles; try portfolios; record and pass on information about a child's strengths (Hatch, 1997). *Most tests evaluate only one kind of learning. Authentic assessment and the use of portfolios more accurately reflect what a student knows, and sharing this information saves time for the next teacher in getting to know the child's preferred style of learning.*

Parents and Young Children

Brain research has affirmed the importance of family and quality child care for infants and young children. One study with preemies showed that babies who were touched more often gained twice the weight as those receiving less contact. Furthermore, preemies regularly visited by parents vocalized twice as much in the third week as those visited infrequently (Wolfe & Brandt, 1998). Warm, consistent care of infants and toddlers encourages secure attachments to those who care for them (Shore, 1997).

Early childhood educators have always recognized the importance of the first years of life. With confirmation from brain research, the Southern Early Childhood Association (1997) recommends the following practices:

1. Read to children daily.
2. Follow their moods. (Know when to feed, change, and put them to sleep.)
3. Plan activities matching ages and development.
4. Communicate verbally with babies as well as young children.
5. Choose warm, responsive caregivers.
6. Enjoy activities involving the senses.

Parents are cautioned, however, to be careful in applying the new skills-developing activities. Parents should not engage in inappropriate activities such as using flashcards with infants, or forcing small hands to work at paper and pencil tasks. Caregivers also should not be concerned about skill development by certain dates. If provided with loving, responsive nurturers, a pleasant, and sensory-rich environment, and time to explore and play, most children will develop just fine.

Conclusions

Many things threaten learning in the lives of children today. From child abuse, malnourishment, and family and community violence to alcohol, drug abuse, and smoking, children in the United States face serious obstacles to physical and cognitive development. The figures are staggering. Although the number of children under age 18 living in poverty fell by approximately 200,000 from 1995 to the present, it still represents 2.7 million more children than were reported living in poverty in 1980. The numbers of abused children are also disturbing. In 1996 it was reported that 968,748 children were victims of substantiated or indicated child abuse or neglect. About 90 percent of perpetrators were adjudged to be parents, relatives, or persons in caretaking roles (U.S. Department of Health and Human Services, 1998).

Even good child care programs have problems that cannot help affecting the cognitive growth of young children. Low salaries of caregivers contribute to high staff turnover, which is detrimental to attachment formation in young children. Inconsistency of personal care places infants and toddlers under stress. When the brain is under stress, the fight or flight response takes over and, if sustained, brain cell death occurs.

Information about schools is not much better. First, the Education Commission of the States' *Executive Summary of the Progress of Education Report 1998* noted that although many states have implemented policies to improve the quality of teaching, there continues to be a gap in what is known to be good teaching and what actually goes on in schools. Educators apparently know what is right but do not practice it, or are inhibited by inflexible administrative policy or other factors beyond their control. Second, while academic standards have been established in most states, and many assessment policies are being reformed, they are insufficient to guarantee improved learning. Could this be a case of too little, too late? Third, the presence of technology in the schools has grown rapidly—about five billion dollars a year spent nationally—but the effect on learning varies widely, depending on how it is used. Merely having a computer in the classroom does not mean children are benefiting from the technology. Fortunately, the current interest in neuroscience and its connection to early childhood has led many states to initiate new programs promoting the health and care of infants, toddlers, and young children. Some states are spending money for intervention services or even expanding special services to all young children. However, it is questionable whether these initiatives will be sustainable over the course of time.

The discoveries in neuroscience discussed in this chapter have confirmed what early childhood advocates have always advanced as quality care and education. The first ten years of brain development lay the foundation of all future learning. All children deserve to receive appropriate, enriching experiences provided by caring adults in a relaxed, safe environment. Child care centers as well as schools can and must do better. Abbott (1997) recommends that not only schools but also whole communities change the ways they think and work.

Neuroscience will continue to unlock mysteries of the human brain, providing even more information for a curious world. Parents, educators, and other advocates of young children must use this new information wisely.

REFERENCES

Abbott, J. (1997). To be intelligent. *Educational Leadership, 54*, 6–10.

Brain research and education: Neuroscience research has impact for education policy. (1998). Denver, CO: Education Commission of the States (ECS).

Bredekamp, S., & Copple, C. (Eds.) (1997). *Developmentally appropriate practice in early childhood programs* (rev. ed.). Washington, DC: National Association for the Education of Young Children.

Brierley, J. (1994). *Give me a child until he is seven: Brain studies and early childhood education* (2nd ed.). London and Washington, DC: The Falmer Press.

Bucko, R. L. (1997). Brain basics: Cognitive psychology and its implications for education. *ERS Spectrum, 15*, 20–25.

Cardellichio, T., & Field, W. (1997). Seven strategies that encourage neural branching. *Educational Leadership, 54*, 33–36.

D'Arcangelo, M. (1998). The brains behind the brain. *Educational Research, 56*, 20–25.

Education Commission of the States (ECS). (1998). *Progress of Education reform 1998—Executive summary* [On-line]. Available: http://www.ecs.org/ecs/essweb

Education Summary of the Progress of Education Report 1998. Washington, DC: Author.

Gardner, H. (1991). *The unschooled mind.* New York: Basic Books.

Gardner, H. (1999). *The disciplined mind: What all students should understand.* New York: Simon & Schuster.

Giuffre, K., with DiGeronimo, T. F. (1999). *The care and feeding of your brain: How diet and environment affect what you think and feel.* Franklin Lakes, NJ: Career Press.

Hatch, T. (1997). Getting specific about multiple intelligences. *Educational Leadership, 54*, 26–29.

Howard, P. J. (1994). *The owner's manual for the brain: Everyday applications from mind-brain research.* Austin, TX: Leornian Press.

Johnson, J. E., Christie, J. F., & Yawkey, T. (1999). *Play and early childhood development* (2nd ed.). New York: Longman.

Joseph, R. (1992). *The right brain and the unconscious.* New York: Plenum Press.

Lowery, L. (1998). How new science curriculums reflect brain research. *Educational Leadership, 56*, 26–30.

McCarthy, B. (1997). A tale of four learners: 4MAT's learning styles. *Educational Leadership, 54*, 46–51.

Pointer, J. R. (1999). Academic achievement and the need for a comprehensive, development music curriculum. *National Association of Secondary School Principals Bulletin, 83*, 108–111.

Pool, C. R. (1997). Maximizing learning: A conversation with Renate Nummela Caine. *Educational Leadership, 54*, 11–15.

Ramachandran, V. S., & Blakeslee, S. (1998). *Phantoms in the brain.* New York: William Morrow.

Shaw, M., & Rauscher, F. (1997). Music beats computers at enhancing early childhood development (1997). *Teaching Music, 4*, 42–43.

Shore, R. (1997). *Rethinking the brain: New insights into early development.* New York: Families and Work Institute.

Southern Early Childhood Association. (1997). Position statement on brain development. Little Rock, AR: SECA.

Stanley, E. (1998, January 22). Classical music is key to governor's goal of sharp babies at rest. *The Los Angeles Times*, p. 5.

Sternberg, R. J. (1997). What does it mean to be smart? *Educational Leadership, 54*, 20–24.

Sylwester, R. (1993–1994). What the biology of the brain tells us about learning. *Educational Leadership, 51*, 46–51.

Sylwester, R., & Cho, J.-Y. (1993–1994). What brain research says about paying attention. *Educational Leadership, 50*, 71–75.

U.S. Department of Health and Human Services (1998). Child health U.S.A. 1998. Washington, DC: Author.

Verrengia, J. B. (1998, November 8). Lab rats listen to Mozart, become maze-busters. The *Los Angeles Times*, p. 26.

What new research on the brain tells us about our youngest children: Summary on the White House conference on early childhood. (1997). *Dimensions of Early Childhood*, *25*(2), special insert.

Wolfe, P., & Brandt, R. (1998). What do we know from brain research? *Educational Leadership*, *56*, 8–18.

CHAPTER

6 Developmentally Appropriate Practice

Every day Ms. Latham's third graders are expected to sit quietly at their desks from 8:30–11:00, completing worksheets and workbook pages. No talking is allowed. If children need assistance, they are expected to raise their hands and wait patiently until Ms. Latham calls them to her desk. Expectations are similar in the afternoon as well. The students complete math problems that have been written on the blackboard. Then Ms. Latham lectures the whole class in either a social studies or a science lesson. Ms. Latham uses a reinforcement system in which students who have successfully completed all their work at the end of the week receive a prize.

Down the hall Mr. Brunson's fourth-grade class is quite different. Students are actively engaged all morning in collaborative groups. Each group of four students is discussing the subtopic that they have chosen from the theme "Elections in a Democratic Society." In fact, students work in groups or individually most of the day. Mr. Brunson has established learning stations in which students experience hands-on learning. Mr. Brunson expects students to feel passionate about their work since they have helped select the topics they will study. Rewards are rarely given because learning should be its own reward.

The above examples indicate two teachers with vastly different philosophies. Is one teacher involved in more developmentally appropriate practice or is it just a difference of styles? Just what is *developmentally appropriate practice*? This chapter is designed to answer six important questions. What is developmentally appropriate practice? What is the history of developmentally appropriate practice? What is the research base for developmentally appropriate practice? How has developmentally appropriate practice influenced educational practice? What are the criticisms of developmentally appropriate practice? What is the future of developmentally appropriate practice?

What Is Developmentally Appropriate Practice?

The original developmentally appropriate practice guidelines, published in 1986 and 1987 by the National Association for the Education of Young Children, were written "to provide guidance to program personnel seeking accreditation; the accreditation criteria call for developmentally appropriate activities, materials, and expectations" (Bredekamp, 1997, p. 35). A second purpose was to respond to the trend of pushing academic learning further and further down into the preschool level. The original guidelines had two dimensions that included both age appropriateness, and individual appropriateness (Bredekamp, 1987).

In 1997, the guidelines were revised to emphasize the teacher as a reflective decision maker, planning for children based on three important dimensions. These included (1) what is known about child development and learning, (2) what is known about the individual child in the group, and (3) what is known about the cultural and social contexts of the students we teach (Bredekamp & Copple, 1997; Bredekamp, 1997). Essentially, the revised guidelines added *culturally appropriate practice* to the existing *age appropriate practice* and *individually appropriate practice*.

But what about older children? Extending the trend of developmentally appropriate practice upward, the Association for Childhood Education International (ACEI) published *Developmentally Appropriate Middle Level Schools* (Manning, 1993). Recognizing early adolescence as a legitimate developmental period between childhood and adolescence, these guidelines were provided to specifically address preadolescence or children from roughly 10–14 years of age. Developmentally appropriate practice for preadolescents can be defined as both organizational and curricular provisions "designed to meet 10- to 14-year-olds' developmental needs while acknowledging their tremendous diversity" (p. 7).

But what about high school? Interestingly enough, the older a child becomes, the less we talk about developmentally appropriate practice. In fact, there are no specific guidelines endorsed by a professional organization that directly address developmentally appropriate practice for students above 14 years old. An important question is, should there be developmentally appropriate practice guidelines for high school students? What would that mean? We will explore these questions later.

What Is the History of Developmentally Appropriate Practice?

The roots for developmentally appropriate practice extend back to the early 1900s when the International Kindergarten Union appointed a panel of 19 experts to determine how children should be taught in kindergarten. From this group three separate reports were issued—one advocating highly structured, teacher-directed instruction, another a play-based, child-initiated emphasis, and a third that was a compromise of the other two (Bredekamp, 1997). In the mid-1920s the National Association for Nursery Education (NANE), which later became the National Association for the Education of Young Children (NAEYC), published *Minimum Essentials for Nursery School Education* (*NANE*,

1930). By the 1980s there were a large number of day care programs that were unregulated, with a staggering number of untrained workers. The NAEYC once again began to develop criteria for high-quality preschools and early childhood programs by developing a national voluntary accreditation system in 1985 (Bredekamp & Glowacki, 1996). This resulted in the publishing of the 1986 and 1987 versions of developmentally appropriate practice (Charlesworth, 1998). During the next decade, criticisms and concerns of the document were published (see Bloch, 1991; Delpit, 1988; Katz, 1996; Kessler & Swadener, 1992; Mallory & New, 1994).

The roots of developmentally appropriate practice for middle school students also goes back 100 years. In 1899 G. Stanley Hall published a two-volume source entitled *Adolescence*, coining the term *adolescence*. By 1944 preadolescence was proposed as a developmental stage (Redl, 1944), and by 1951 a text on the psychology of the preadolescent was available (Blair & Burton, 1951). During the next 50 years numerous sources described the development and needs of preadolescents (see Dorman, 1984; Eichhorn, 1966; Havighurst, 1968; Kagan & Coles, 1972; Lipsitz, 1984), and the *Journal of Early Adolescence* was founded by Thornburg in 1981 (Manning, 1993). Organizations such as the Association for Childhood Education International (ACEI) began publishing articles focusing on preadolescence. In fact, ACEI began a new publication known as *Focus on Later Childhood/Adolescence*.

What Is the Research Base for Developmentally Appropriate Practice?

Not surprisingly, developmentally appropriate practice (DAP) spurred numerous research agendas, many of them originating at Louisiana State University (Charlesworth, Hart, Burts, Mosley & Fleege, 1993; Charlesworth, 1998). A summary of some of the findings, related to early childhood education, are described below:

■ Children in less developmentally appropriate classrooms exhibit almost twice the levels of stress behaviors as compared to children in developmentally appropriate practice programs. (Burts et al., 1992; Love, Ryer & Faddis, 1992)

■ Students in inappropriate preschool programs have poorer academic achievement once they get to elementary school. (Bryant, Burchinal, Lau & Sparling, 1994)

■ Children in developmentally appropriate classrooms rank higher on behavioral evaluations. (Marcon, 1994)

■ Students in developmentally appropriate programs score higher on measures of work-study habits. (Marcon, 1992)

- Students in developmentally inappropriate classrooms are more distractible. (Charlesworth, 1998)
- Children in developmentally appropriate programs are more prosocial during the early elementary years. (Charlesworth, 1998)
- Males, children from low socioeconomic status homes, and African Americans are the most "adversely affected by [developmentally inappropriate practice] DIP programs." (Charlesworth, 1998, p. 276)
- Children in [Developmentally Appropriate Practice] DAP classrooms do better than those in DIP classrooms on the California Achievement Test. (Charlesworth, 1998)

Few studies have directly addressed developmentally appropriate practice in middle schools (Manning, 1993). Again, interest and research on developmentally appropriate practice appear to be centered in early childhood education.

How Has Developmentally Appropriate Practice Influenced Educational Practice?

Developmentally appropriate practice has influenced education in a number of ways. Listed here are ten examples of how developmentally appropriate practice has made an impact on educational philosophy and practice.

Accreditation

The development of standards for accreditation have been remarkably influenced by developmentally appropriate practice. The National Association for the Education of Young Children launched an accreditation system in 1985. Today, early childhood programs which are accredited by NAEYC have followed developmentally appropriate practice guidelines (Bredekamp, 1997; Bredekamp & Glowacki, 1996). Furthermore, NAEYC is one of the largest professional education organizations in the world, with over 100,000 members (Gestwicki, 1999). Many of the members have been involved in accreditation and have subscribed to many of the tenets of DAP (Bredekamp, 1997).

An Emphasis on the Whole Child

Most teachers who subscribe to developmentally appropriate practice believe that physical, social, emotional, and cognitive development are closely related, interact, and strongly influence one another. "All learning experiences are recognized as integrated opportunities for growth, instead of separate skill or content entities" (Gestwicki, 1999, p. 9). The use of integrated teaching using thematic units and projects that cut across developmental domains has been employed more because of developmentally appropriate practice.

Individualized Instruction

All children learn at varying rates in different areas of development. There are interindividual differences, or differences *among* children, and intraindividual differences or differences *within* the same child in areas of development. Teachers who recognize these differences are more likely to individualize instruction to the unique needs of each child (Charlesworth, 1998).

The Acceptance and Use of Children's Prior Knowledge

All education builds on previous experiences. The developers of developmentally appropriate practice guidelines encourage teachers to take into consideration children's previous experiences when planning instruction. Learning is influenced by multiple cultural and social contexts. All children develop in these multiple contexts. These contexts should be valued and used in instruction, rather than ignored (Gestwicki, 1999).

Active Learning

Particularly with younger children, hands-on materials and movement are necessary for optimal learning and development. Children construct knowledge through interaction with the environment. Knowledge, whether it is physical, social, or mathematical, is constructed from inside the child through activity (Kamii, 2000). Developmentally appropriate practice supports a constructivist approach to education (Kamii, 2000; Manning, 1993).

More In-Depth Study of a Topic

Children learn more when their day in school is less fragmented and they have opportunities to study fewer topics but study these in greater depth (Chard, 1997; Katz & Chard, 1989; Manning & Manning, 1981). Just as constructivism has been encouraged by developmentally appropriate practice advocates, so has the project approach (Katz & Chard, 1989; Chard, 1997).

The Importance of Play

Play is an important way children learn. It strongly affects not only cognitive development, but also social, emotional, and language development. According to Gestwicki (1999), "teacher-supported play is an essential component of developmentally appropriate practice" (p. 10). Teachers who use DAP guidelines incorporate play as an integral part of the curriculum.

Multiage Grouping

The implementation of multiage classrooms has increased due to DAP guidelines (Gestwicki, 1999). Traditional same-age-group classrooms do not go well with developmentally appropriate practice, nor does retention. Children learn from others, both younger and older. The use of multiage classrooms has increased in the past ten years, partly due to developmentally appropriate practice (Gestwicki, 1999).

The Teacher as Reflective Decision Maker

A strong addition to the revised developmentally appropriate practice text (Bredekamp & Copple, 1997) was an emphasis on teachers making informed decisions and on their becoming reflective practitioners. Bredekamp and Copple acknowledged that while guidelines can inform teachers, they must use their knowledge of children and the multiple contexts in which both teachers and children operate to make informed decisions.

Parent Involvement

A major component of developmentally appropriate practice is working in concert with families. Parents and guardians are encouraged to be active participants and co-operators in developing the best education for their children. The increase in parent involvement in schools can be partially attributed to DAP (Wien, 1995).

What Are the Criticisms of Developmentally Appropriate Practice?

In the past 15 years numerous criticisms have been wielded at developmentally appropriate practice. These criticisms can be divided into three major categories that include (1) problems related to children with disabilities, (2) criticisms related to context, and (3) issues related to theory.

Problems Related to Children with Disabilities

Some special educators have suggested that developmentally appropriate practice can be equally beneficial for children with disabilities (Charlesworth, 1998), but others have called into question the applicability of DAP guidelines to children with special needs (Jipson, 1991). Some have even suggested that developmentally appropriate practice is necessary for children with special needs but not sufficient. Donna Dugger-Wadsworth (1997) sees limited problems in using DAP with children with disabilities. Charlesworth (1998) agrees. She suggests, ". . . teachers need to learn how to modify materials and activities so that special needs children can be included in regular classroom activities" (p. 280). Still, children with special needs may need more direct instruction and intensive one-on-one attention to achieve their full potential. Bredekamp and Copple (1997) see no problem in using DAP with children with diverse abilities because the teacher is expected to be a reflective decision maker. However, Lubeck (1998) questions the use of DAP guidelines with not only children with special needs, but children from various backgrounds.

Criticisms Related to Context

One of the biggest problems with DAP, according to the critics, is the fact that it does not work in certain contexts. There are problems in implementing DAP with African American children (see Phillips, 1994), Native American individuals (see Williams, 1994), children in school who use English as a second language (see Genishi, Dyson & Fassler, 1994) and children from other cultural contexts, including those from a lower socioeconomic environment (see Bowman & Stott, 1994).

Developmentally appropriate practice reflects liberal middle-class values and is often very different from the real-world practice, beliefs, and prior experiences of parents and teachers who do not share these assumptions. In subtle ways, those who do not subscribe to DAP are often seen as uncaring people who do not attempt educational practices that are in the best interest of children. For example, Meredith, who is a teacher of young children, does not subscribe to DAP guidelines. She is currently taking a child development class in which developmentally appropriate practice assumptions guide class discussions. In her reflections, she is questioning her own beliefs as well as the DAP guidelines. Here she writes about her ideas on the hurried child.

> This issue has brought to my attention some important factors that pertain to my daily life; as a teacher, and as a parent. Every day in my classroom, my students do many of the things that the experts warn against. We do many pencil and paper tasks, we have interactive Bible lessons, which last at least 30 minutes, we have homogeneous reading groups, and the children memorize many things such as the Lord's Prayer and A–Z in Bible verses. All of these things are taboo according to developmentally appropriate practice.
>
> I have to say there have been times when I have asked the questions, "Is this really the best program for the children? Was it better when I was in kindergarten and all we did was socialize, play, and do hands-on activities?" My opinions are still uncertain. I have been teaching this same curriculum for two years now and it seems to have worked well for the majority of the children. None of the students seem to be experiencing high stress. In fact, they cannot wait to return to school from day to day. My own daughter is in my class and she loves it. She is a normal

five-year-old who enjoys being a child like any other. I also try to help the children understand everything they are learning. I am the kind of teacher, though, who allows much time for socialization, imaginative play, experimental learning, and just being a kid. I use reflective teaching in my class and am constantly aware of what is and what is not working with the children. If things do not seem to be going well, I change to find a more suitable method for the setting.

On the other hand, I do worry about the children in today's society growing up too quickly. I also understand the fact that by fourth grade, you cannot determine those children who went to preschool or those who entered school in first grade. As a parent, it is very important that my child does not grow up too quickly.

My main goal right now, as a parent and as a kindergarten teacher, is to provide children with a strong foundation that will give them a love and hunger for learning that will last a lifetime. It is my personal belief that I cannot do this on my own. I want to make positive, lasting impressions on those around me that will show them love and lead them down the right path. I hope what I am doing is giving the children the best of both worlds by allowing them to gain self-esteem, create lasting childhood memories, and ignite a passion for learning success.

Meredith lives, works, and rears her daughter in a community that does not generally support developmentally appropriate practice. Does Meredith exhibit developmentally appropriate practice in her classroom? Some would say yes. In fact, Sue Bredekamp and Carol Copple (1997) would probably say yes. Meredith is a reflective practitioner. She thoughtfully prepares her teaching and tries to balance teacher directed with child initiated activities. However, she does use worksheets, memorization, has children sit and listen for long periods of time, and utilizes homogeneous grouping—all of which are not recommended as developmentally appropriate practice.

Another student in the child development class believes she did not experience developmentally appropriate practice when she was a young child but believes her learning experiences were good for her, even though they may not be classified as DAP. Lakennia writes,

I was placed in a preschool at the age of two. I was introduced to a lot of new things and places at a very young age. I believe I was in a rushed environment because I was expected to do many things that my mother did not require of me at such a young age. I was told to clean up after myself, write my name and trace things. I was also taught to tie my own shoe laces and many other difficult tasks. The more of these tasks that I could accomplish the more pleased I was and this encouraged me to learn more. I enjoyed the attention given by my parents when I could do something other children who stayed at home could not do. I enjoyed the feeling of success when I finally learned how to do something that the others in my class could do. I was hurried but some of it was of my own doing and it has made me into the self-assertive person I am today.

Lakennia, like Meredith, is questioning developmentally appropriate practice. The waters of developmentally appropriate practice have been muddied even more since the revised edition was published (see Bredekamp & Copple, 1997). With the addition of an entire chapter devoted to the teacher as reflective decision maker, and the incorporation of context and culture as being important considerations in developmentally appropriate practice, practitioners are less certain of exactly what developmentally appropriate practice is. Sally Lubeck (1998) suggests that by including voices critical of DAP, the guidelines have become an attempt to be all things to all people. But Lubeck believes there are multiple points of view and that DAP is based on specific assumptions and a highly selective theoretical background that cannot absorb many dissenting voices.

Issues Related to Theory

Developmentally appropriate practice is clearly based on the theories of Piaget, Vygotsky, and Erikson (see Bredekamp & Rosegrant, 1992). In defense of Piaget, Vygotsky, and Erikson, it should be noted that these three theorists were not really interested in their work shaping educational practice. They wanted, instead, to contribute to other fields, especially psychology.

While other theorists are mentioned, virtually all of them are modern (as opposed to postmodern) theorists who are also dead, white, Western men (Hsue & Aldridge, 1995). All of the theories on which DAP guidelines are based are Euro-American, masculine, psychologically based theories, yet the majority of the people who teach are women—many of them women of color. While this might seem amusing but not important at first glance, let's take a look at some of the statements these men have made about women and minorities.

As pointed out in Chapter 4, G. Stanley Hall, the father of developmental psychology, indicated that women should not go to college with men but to a separate college where they can rest their brains and use their intuition (Sadker & Sadker, 1994). Piaget indicated that the children of Martinique were four years behind in their progression through the stages of cognitive development because their families were lazy (see Bringuier, 1980). He did not seem to take into consideration the fact that the children who were tested using his theory in France, Switzerland, or French Canada were white, upper-middle-class children whose families chose to be a part of the French education system. The children of Martinique were children of color whose families were taken against their will as slaves. Their historical ways of thinking and educational system were quite different from the one imposed on them by the French. Kohlberg, a follower of Piaget, based his theory of moral development on a male sample, yet the child development texts of the 1970s and 1980s rarely reported this important fact (see Turner & Helms, 1983; Vander Zanden, 1989).

Another issue is the fact that DAP guidelines have virtually ignored postmodern, critical, and feminist thinking. There is probably a good reason for this. Developmentally appropriate practice is based on universal principles of child development, while postmodern and critical theories focus on the context, the particular, and refrain from the belief of universal ideas constructed by dead, white, Western males. With the decidedly biased framework, what will become of developmentally appropriate practice?

What Is the Future of Developmentally Appropriate Practice?

Just as occurred at the turn of the 20th century, at the beginning of the 21st century we cannot accurately predict what will happen with regard to educational issues in the next 100 years. That doesn't keep us from asking, "What is the future of developmentally appropriate practice?" Aldridge (1996) suggests five questions that need to be addressed in order to predict the future of DAP:

1. Is DAP a dynamic, ever-changing construct, or is the document considered the bible for educational practice?
2. Can DAP incorporate critics' voices?
3. Can DAP support a more family-centered focus with regard to very young children?
4. Can DAP be more culturally sensitive?
5. Will DAP advocates become more politically active in working for the rights of children and minorities?

Developmentally appropriate practice will always be an issue in education because the notion of DAP takes a particular perspective, which is not shared by everyone. Developmentally appropriate practice guidelines rely heavily on universal principles, which reflect modern values that are not embraced by most postmodern thinkers. According to Lubeck (1998) modern ideas "must be tempered with a postmodern appreciation for the oral, particular, local and timely—the practical concerns of people in specific situations" (p. 287).

REFERENCES

Aldridge, J. (1996). Is developmentally appropriate practice for everyone? *ACEI Focus on Infancy*, *9*(1), 1–2.

Blair, A. W., & Burton, W. H. (1951). *Growth and development of the preadolescent*. New York: Appleton-Century-Crofts.

Bloch, M. (1991). Critical science and the history of child development's influence on early education research. *Early Education and Development*, *2*(2), 95–108.

Bowman, B., & Stott, F. (1994). Understanding development in a cultural context: The challenge for teachers. In B. L. Mallory & R. S. New (Eds.), *Diversity and developmentally appropriate practice: Challenges for early childhood education* (pp. 119–134). New York: Teachers College Press.

Bredekamp, S. (1997). NAEYC issues revised position statement on developmentally appropriate practice in early childhood programs. *Young Children*, *52*(2), 34–40.

Bredekamp, S. (Ed.). (1987). *Developmentally appropriate practice in early childhood programs serving children from birth through age 8*. (Exp. ed.) Washington, DC: NAEYC.

Bredekamp, S., & Copple (Eds.). (1997). *Developmentally appropriate practice in early childhood programs*. (Rev. ed.) Washington, DC: NAEYC.

Bredekamp, S., & Glowacki, G. (1996). The first decade of NAEYC accreditation: Growth and impact on the field. In *NAEYC accreditation: A decade of learning and the years ahead*, S. Bredekamp & B. Willer (Eds.), (pp. 1–10). Washington, DC: NAEYC.

Bredekamp, S., & Rosegrant, T. (Eds.). (1992). *Reaching potentials: Appropriate curriculum and assessment for young children* (Vol. 1). Washington, DC: NAEYC.

Bringuier, J. (1980). *Conversations with Piaget*. Chicago: University of Chicago Press.

Bryant, D. M., Burchinal, M., Lau, L. B., & Sparling, J. J. (1994). Family and classroom correlates of Head Start children's developmental outcomes. *Early Childhood Research Quarterly, 9*, 289–309.

Burts, D. C., Hart, C. H., Charlesworth, R., Fleege, P. O., Mosley, J., & Thomasson, R. H. (1992). Observed activities and stress behaviors of children in developmentally appropriate and inappropriate kindergarten classrooms. *Early Childhood Research Quarterly, 7*, 297–318.

Chard, S. (1997). *The project approach*. New York: Scholastic.

Charlesworth, R. (1998). Developmentally appropriate practice is for everyone. *Childhood Education, 74*(5), 274–282.

Charlesworth, R., Hart, C. H., Burts, D. C., Mosley, J., & Fleege, P. O. (1993). Measuring the developmental appropriateness of kindergarten teachers' beliefs and practices. *Early Childhood Research Quarterly, 8*, 255–276.

Delpit, L. (1988). The silenced dialogue: Power and pedagogy in educating other people's children. *Harvard Educational Review, 58*(3), 280–298.

Dorman, G. (1984). *Middle grades assessment program*. Chapel Hill, NC: Center for Early Adolescence, UNC.

Dugger-Wadsworth, D. (1997). The integrated curriculum and students with disabilities. In C. H. Hart, D. C. Burts & R. Charlesworth (Eds.), *Integrated curriculum and developmentally appropriate practice: Birth to age eight* (pp. 335–362). Albany, NY: SUNY Press.

Eichhorn, D. (1966). *The middle school*. New York: Center for Applied Research in Education.

Genishi, C., Dyson, A., & Fassler, R. (1994). Language and diversity in early childhood: Whose voices are appropriate? In B. L. Mallory & R. S. New (Eds.), *Diversity and developmentally appropriate practice* (pp. 250–268). New York: Teachers College Press.

Gestwicki, C. (1999). *Developmentally appropriate practice: Curriculum and development in early education* (2nd ed.). Albany, NY: Delmar Publishers.

Hall, G. S. (1899). *Adolescence*. New York: Appleton.

Havighurst, R. J. (1968). The middle school child in contemporary society. *Theory into Practice, 7*, 120–122.

Hsue, Y., & Aldridge, J. (1995). Developmentally appropriate practice and traditional Taiwanese culture. *Journal of Instructional Psychology, 22*(4), 320–323.

Jipson, J. (1991). Developmentally appropriate practice: Culture, curriculum, connections. *Early Education and Development, 2*, 120–136.

Kagan, J., & Coles, R. (Eds.). (1972). *Twelve to sixteen: Early adolescence*. New York: Norton.

Kamii, C. (2000). *Young children reinvent arithmetic: Implications of Piaget's theory* (2nd ed.). New York: Teachers College Press.

Katz, L. (1996). Child development knowledge and teacher preparation: Confronting assumptions. *Early Childhood Research Quarterly, 11*(2), 135–146.

Katz, L. G., & Chard, S. C. (1989). *Engaging children's minds: The project approach*. Norwood, NJ: Ablex.

Kessler, S., & Swadener, B. (Eds.). (1992). Introduction *Reconceptualizing the early childhood curriculum: Beginning the dialogue* (pp. xiii–xxviii). New York: Teachers College Press.

Lipsitz, J. (1984). *Successful schools for young adolescents*. New Brunswick, NJ: Transaction.

Love, J., Ryer, P., & Faddis, B. (1992). Caring environments: Program quality in California's publicly funded child development programs. Portsmouth, NH: RMC Research.

Lubeck, S. (1998). Is developmentally appropriate practice for everyone? *Childhood Education, 74*(5), 283–292.

Mallory, B. L., & New, R. S. (Eds.). (1994). *Diversity and developmentally appropriate practices: Challenges for early childhood education.* New York: Teachers College Press.

Manning, M. L. (1993). *Developmentally appropriate middle level schools.* Olney, MD: ACEI.

Manning, M., & Manning, G. (1981). The school's assault on childhood. *Childhood Education, 58*(2), 84–87.

Marcon, R. A. (1992). Differential effects of three preschool models on inner-city 4-year-olds. *Early Childhood Research Quarterly, 7,* 517–530.

Marcon, R. A. (1994). Doing the right thing for children: Linking research and policy reform in the District of Columbia public schools. *Young Children, 50*(8), 8.

NANE (National Association for Nursery Education). (1930). *Minimum essentials of nursery school education.* Washington, DC: Author.

Phillips, C. B. (1994). The movement of African-American children through sociocultural contexts: A case of conflict resolution. In B. L. Mallory and R. S. New (Eds.), *Diversity and developmentally appropriate practice: Challenges for early childhood education* (pp. 137–154). New York: Teachers College Press.

Redl, F. (1944). Preadolescents: What makes them tick? *Child Study, 21,* 44–48.

Sadker, M., & Sadker, D. (1994). *Failing at fairness: How schools shortchange girls.* New York: Houghton Mifflin.

Turner, J. S., & Helms, D. B. (1983). *Lifespan human development* (2nd ed.). New York: Holt, Rinehart and Winston.

Vander Zanden, J. W. (1989). *Human development* (4th ed.). New York: Random House.

Wien, C. A. (1995). *Developmentally appropriate practice in real life. Stories of teacher practical knowledge.* New York: Teachers College Press.

Williams, L. (1994). Developmentally appropriate practice and cultural values: A case in point. In B. L. Mallory, & R. S. New (Eds.), *Diversity and developmentally appropriate practice: Challenges for early childhood education* (pp. 155–165). New York: Teachers College Press.

Progressive Education in the Twenty-First Century

SHELLY HURT-CHUMLEY

In 1896 a grand experiment in education began. John Dewey, an aspiring educational philosopher, opened a school in Hyde Park, Chicago, in which he was determined to test his ideas about education. Unbeknownst to Dewey at the time, the progressive movement in American education had begun (Edwards, Lindsay, Stainburn & Rodman, 2000). Reaching its height in the 1920s, progressive education has mutated and changed over the last century, with many instructional approaches emerging that appear to be pedagogically progressive. While some claim that progressive education is essentially a thing of the past, proponents of progressive education claim that it is alive, although in serious danger due to the fact that most states have adopted reforms that set standards for a prescribed curriculum (Edwards et al., 2000). Governing officials and citizens who know little about thinking and learning have successfully lobbied for accountability in education, high-stakes testing, educational outcomes, and a return to "the basics," provoking the question, "Is progressive education doomed to extinction?"

The purpose of this chapter is to examine three progressive approaches—*the project approach*, *theme immersion*, and *the developmental-interaction approach*. Current criticisms of progressive education will also be described. Finally, I will explore the reality that it is increasingly difficult to be a progressive educator in the public schools of today.

The Project Approach

The project approach evolved from the ideas of many educational pioneers, including Friedrich Froebel, William James, G. Stanley Hall, Francis Parker, John Dewey, Lucy Sprague Mitchell, and William Kilpatrick (DuCharme, 1993). Dewey believed that education was not preparation for life, but was life itself (Peterson, 1986). Thus, in-depth investigations of real topics and issues have long been associated with progressive education. Dewey actively engaged students in such study. However, it was William Kilpatrick who, at the height of the progressive era, first called this approach the "project method" (Katz & Chard, 2000; Kilpatrick, 1918).

The current understanding of the project method is the result of the work of Lilian Katz and Sylvia Chard (DuCharme, 1993). The two prefer the word *approach* as a descriptor, as they believe that engaging projects is one salient feature of early childhood education curriculum (Chard, 1998; Helm & Katz, 2001; Katz & Chard, 1989, 2000). They also suggest that this approach is ideally intended to complement the learning experiences of children from 3 to 8 years of age. While in-depth studies of topics that are of interest to young children are superior to rote learning, why Katz and Chard were compelled to specify a range of ages that would benefit from this approach is somewhat puzzling. If Dewey were correct in his thinking, and the young learn best by actively engaging in the learning process, would that theory not hold true for learners of all ages? Dewey (1916) believed that once communication has been cast in a mold and repeated in routine ways, it loses its educative power. Unfortunately, it seems as though children in the upper elementary and secondary grades are doomed to such monotony until prominent researchers in early childhood education see the implications of their work for all children, not just the very young.

Within the project approach, a topic can be examined in several ways. Usually an entire classroom community together will engage in an in-depth study of a topic. Project selections are based on the interests of the children. Sometimes this is expressed interest, and at other times it is assumed (Katz & Chard, 1989). While Katz and Chard (2000) do not recommend that adults force children to engage in studies that are artificial, they do encourage teachers to plant seeds of interest, in the hope of cultivating them. Once a topic is agreed upon, the students generally break into smaller focus groups based on a shared interest in a particular aspect of the topic. Questions, generated by the group, guide the study. Students then research the answers to the questions asked and prepare numerous artifacts to express what they have learned (Helm & Katz, 2001; Katz & Chard, 2000).

Students not only acquire new knowledge throughout the process but also apply skills. This authentic application of learned skills allows students to develop effective learning strategies that will serve them well throughout their lives. These strategies are most significant if a student's disposition to learn is enhanced. Katz and Chard (2000) are quick to point out that a disposition to learn cannot be taught directly but is strengthened through opportunities to engage in meaningful learning. Again, this is a tenet of progressive education. Life itself is considered development, and development is life; thus, the education process has no end (Dewey, 1916). For this process to continue throughout life, dispositions for learning must be cultivated at an early age and nurtured throughout school. While it is difficult to strengthen these dispositions to learn when children have never had opportunities to truly investigate and research matters of personal interest, that does not mean it is impossible for children to develop such dispositions after they have left their primary classrooms far behind.

Key to the project approach is another progressive idea—the idea that the purpose of education is to prepare students to participate in a democratic society. Dewey (1916) explained that democracy is a form of living that includes communicated experience. It is far more than just a governmental form. The project approach clearly reflects Dewey's thinking. The experiences within the project approach allow students to engage in the democratic process through collaborating, negotiating, contributing, and responding to each other's ideas. It involves working toward consensus to accomplish tasks and solve problems (Katz & Chard, 2000). By selecting topics that are worthy of deep thought and discussion, children can grow in their ability to accept other points of view (Helm & Chard, 2001). This is perhaps the most important, yet most difficult attribute to possess as a member of a democratic society.

Theme Immersion

While the project approach is associated with early childhood education (Helm & Katz, 2001), theme immersion is intended to be included in classrooms that contain students of all ages (Manning, Manning & Long, 1994). Also rooted primarily in the work of John Dewey, proponents of theme immersion seek to engage students in authentic investigations of real-life issues (Manning et al., & Long, 1994). While the project approach appears to favor specific topics for in-depth study, theme immersion, as its name implies, favors the use of overarching curricular themes. There are significant differences between traditional thematic units and theme immersion. Traditional units are teacher directed, with emphasis on products that are produced during the study. Assessment is summative and usually objective. Theme immersion, on the other hand, empowers students to generate their own curriculum, be it in part or in whole, with the emphasis on the processes in which students engage while they answer their own questions. The teacher's role is that of facilitator, with assessment being both formative and summative. In a theme immersion classroom, students play a vital role in the assessment process by reflecting on their own learning (Manning et al., 1994).

Structures, patterns, habitats, and transformations are examples of themes that have been explored in theme immersion classrooms. These broad, overarching themes are springboards for individual and group investigations. The topics explored are relatively narrow in scope, and reflect the natural curiosity of children. Topics continue to develop as children delve deeper and deeper into the guiding theme. Manning et al. (1994) believe that social issues lend themselves particularly well to thematic study. Sometimes these topics address social issues directly (i.e., homelessness, AIDS, human rights, or environmentalism) and sometimes they do not (bats, hurricanes, seeds, or butterflies). Social issues are inherently embedded in life, and consequently in the topics that children choose to explore. In other words, school is a social place and children are social beings. Social issues emerge naturally. There are those, however, (Hirsch, 1996) who do not feel that social issues are best explored as isolated topics or themes.

As a fifth-grade teacher, I decided that "journeys" would be an appropriate overarching theme to drive the curriculum in my classroom. This was decided after many months of thought and reflection. While I think that students are capable of determining their own theme as a learning community, I concluded that since my students have never been in classrooms in which they are allowed such voice in the curriculum, I needed to scaffold them into the experience. I believed that "journeys" was appropriate to the learning situation, because all my students had some prior knowledge and experience with trips and journeys. I could visualize countless topics that might find their way into our classroom via our theme. These included immigration, emigration, migration, circulation, digestion, the journey to independence, the journey aboard a slave ship, the water cycle, the process of recycling, the journey to the White House, the journey that all authors embark on when they hope to accurately express themselves through words. Rich social issues are a natural part of this theme. When exploring the journeys of Africans to this continent aboard slave ships, how can the issue of human rights not arise? When tracing the journey of a recycled can or bottle, how can environmentalism not be discussed? When investigating the political process and the electoral college system, how can the issue of fairness be ignored? Social issues are best addressed and understood within a larger curricular context, thus reflecting Dewey's goal of educating students for the role of citizen within a democratic society.

The Developmental-Interaction Approach

The developmental-interaction approach, also known as the Bank Street Approach, is another example of progressive education in action. Lucy Sprague Mitchell, founder of the Bureau of Educational Experiments, which later became Bank Street College, was profoundly influenced by family friend John Dewey (Wolfe, 2000). Like Dewey, Mitchell believed that schools should strive to know more about how children learn and what their inherent interests are. Today, the developmental-interaction approach also emphasizes the progressive idea that education is a vehicle for social change and social justice (Nager & Shapiro, 2000).

There is a strong relationship between theory and practice in the developmental-interaction approach. The influence of Erikson, Piaget, Freud, Lewin, and Vygotsky are noticeable (Nager & Shapiro, 2000). This is obvious in the Bank Street School's Curriculum Guide (2000), which explains the six principles that guide the developmental-interaction approach. First, development occurs when people change the way they cope with the environment, moving from simple to more complex ways of responding. Second, development is not viewed as a linear process in which older, more immature ways of thinking are left behind. Instead, the less mature ways of thinking are used more effectively in increasingly complex ways. Third, disequilibrium is a necessary ingredient for development. The role of the practitioner is to help the child in finding a sense of intellectual balance. Fourth, humans by nature are interactive explorers of the environment. These interactions tend to move from physical interactions to more symbolic interactions as students get older. Fifth, a child's sense of confidence, self-worth, and well-being are built upon interactions with other people. Finally, conflict, both external and internal, is a necessary part of growth and development.

The curriculum is thus organized to reflect these principles. For example, teachers decide on overarching concepts (themes) and thus "design activities that will lead children to make discoveries about those ideas" (Bank Street School Curriculum Guide, 2000, p. 2). Very similar to both the project approach and theme immersion, individual students and small groups build on prior knowledge to inquire about the world. Following the thinking of Lucy Sprague Mitchell, the concepts that guide learning are related to the social sciences. Work in social studies is believed to help children with problem solving, posing and answering questions, integrating skills, developing relationship thinking, and helping children develop a sense of social responsibility and caring (Bank Street School Curriculum Guide, 2000). Relationships among subject areas are considered a natural result of in-depth study and are never forced.

Unfortunately, like so many other curriculum models and approaches that address the needs of young children, the implications of the developmental-interaction approach for older learners is unclear. Even at the Bank Street School, older learners are treated somewhat differently than their younger counterparts. According to the curriculum guide, each grouping of students, which is usually a very small multiage community, follows a course of study that is somewhat prescribed. As children grow, the curriculum becomes more and more narrow and for all intents and purposes, departmentalized. For example, students in the 10/11-year class study the medieval societies of Africa, Southwest Asia, and Western Europe and or Pre- and Post-Columbian Latin America. As argued earlier, these topics of study do not represent a single overarching theme that drives learning. Engaging in predetermined topics is no better than investigating teacher-directed topics.

The curriculum guide goes on to describe for parents what they can expect their older children to learn and how they will learn it, as well as how they will feel before, during, and after learning. While the curriculum guide goes on to state that the curricula addressed will be determined based on the needs and interests of the group, the school states that ideally both medieval societies and Pre and Post-Columbian Latin America should be explored. So much for a generative curriculum for older students! What would happen if the interests of the group were not in synchrony with the stated curriculum guide?

Current Criticisms of Progressive Education

Perhaps the strongest critic of progressive education today is E. D. Hirsch Jr. (1996). According to Hirsch, "from kindergarten through high school, our public educational system is among the worst in the developed world. For over fifty years, American schools have operated on the assumption that challenging children academically is unnatural for them, that teachers do not need to know the subjects they teach, that the learning 'process' should be emphasized over the facts taught. All this is tragically wrong" (book cover). Hirsch's words are in many ways the antithesis of a progressive pedagogy. He believes that the way to build enthusiasm for learning is to emphasize the learning of facts, to work hard, and to take rigorous tests.

Encouraging the knowledge of specific facts, Hirsch is the editor of the *Core Knowledge Series (1991–96)* in which a collection of books titled *What Your Kindergartner Needs to Know; What Your First Grader Needs to Know*; all the way through sixth grade has been published. Hirsch and his collaborators have arbitrarily decided what a child at each grade level needs to know. This is especially interesting since Hirsch has spent little if any, time as an elementary school teacher.

Hirsch attributes much of the undoing of American education to the progressive education movement. Ironically, he believes that progressive education is currently rampant in the schools and that a return to the basics and a core curriculum is what is needed. Apparently he has not visited many schools in the 21st century where few, if any, progressive ideas are in practice due to the heavy emphasis on standardized testing, the teaching of basic facts out of context, and rote learning.

Conclusions

State courses of study that read like Trivial Pursuit questions and countless standards established by a plethora of professional organizations have so dissected the curriculum, especially in grades 3–12, that many public school teachers, including myself, feel pressure to cover the curriculum, not uncover it. I have never participated in staff development that was aimed at hashing out the differences between overarching themes and narrow topics. I have, however, spent many hours correlating newly adopted textbooks to State Course of Study objectives and the SAT-IX Test for Student Achievement objectives. In many cases, elementary school teachers are required to note in their lesson plan books each and every time a state or SAT-IX objective has been addressed. In some extreme cases, those are the *only* objectives that are noted in lesson plan books. No one seems to be very interested in the prior knowledge that students bring into the classroom, the questions they ask, the questions they answer, the conflicts they resolve, or the community they build. After June, my students are a set of numbers to be published in a local newspaper. To outsiders, nothing else that took place in our classroom will matter. For us, however, what happened in our classroom has changed us forever.

Progressive educators across the country share in my frustration. Alfie Kohn, author of *The Case Against Standardized Testing* (2000) argues that the very idea of standardizing student achievement is contrary to democratic ideals. Kohn (2000) notes that the control of education has been taken away from teachers and placed in the hands of business leaders and know-nothing politicians with standardized tests fueling the engine of learning.

Recently, a young preservice teacher who had just completed her practicum asked to observe my students and me for a few hours. Remembering my own fear and trepidation just eight short years ago, I welcomed her to learn with us. I could tell by the initial expression on her face that I would be answering many questions about the kinds of learning that were taking place in the room. One small group of students was engaged in deep conversation about the novel they were reading together. Another group was researching the setting of the novel they were reading. A third group was writing, and yet another group was reading picture books to help them better understand the plot of the Arthurian legend they were tackling together. I moved from group to group to monitor and assess. When the students left their literature discussion groups and moved into their research groups, she asked me to explain what the students were studying. I explained my beliefs about how children learn as best I could in a few minutes, and showed her that each group was investigating different, self-selected aspects of America's journey from the New World to an independent nation. I saw her meander over to the large chart on the wall that showed our theme at the center of a large web, with the many topics that have emerged from them connected by an array of colored lines. She then saw our agenda, the designated place in our classroom where students pose issues and concerns that need to be discussed in a class meeting, and rather skeptically asked if I really expected my students to resolve their own conflicts and problems. Of her many questions, her last was most puzzling. "Where did you learn so much about these new ways of teaching?" she wondered aloud. I did not know how to respond. My ways were anything but new. Progressive ideas have been at work in classrooms for over 100 years.

At the end of the day, I saw a small purple envelope peeking out of my mailbox. In it was a lengthy note from that student teacher. I was happy to read that she realized that like me, she had much to learn. She bemoaned the fact that now, at the end of her undergraduate degree, she had found something in an intermediate classroom that she had previously seen only in the primary grades. While the standard curriculum is continually being pushed downward, requiring younger children to compete in an academic curriculum, progressive education starts in early childhood and fizzles out somewhere along the way.

I feel the pressure of high-stakes testing, and I am sometimes envious of my colleagues who teach in primary grades. I watch as their students spend month after month engaged in rich thematic explorations that afford everyone in the room the opportunity to truly grow and learn. Children, not content, is the focus. No one asks them if they are certain that their students are "learning what they need to know." I also hear primary grade teachers mention a thing called recess. Unfortunately, recess is often not allowed in "testing" grades. Most of my colleagues who teach in primary classrooms realize, however, that their days, too, are numbered. It is only a matter of time before standardized testing comes to a classroom near them. The tension and contrast between traditional education and progressive pedagogy is ever present in the real world of my fifth-grade classroom.

REFERENCES

Bank Street School Curriculum Guide (2000). New York: Bank Street Publications.

Chard, S. C. (1998). Drawing in the context of a project. In J. H. Helm (Ed.), *The project approach catalog 2* (pp. 1:11–1:12). Champaign, IL: ERIC Clearinghouse on Elementary and Early Childhood Education.

Cuffaro, H., Nager, N., & Shapiro, E. (2000). The developmental-interaction approach at Bank Street College of Education. In J. L. Roopnarine and J. E. Johnson (Eds.), *Approaches to early childhood education*, (pp. 263–275). Upper Saddle River, NJ: Prentice-Hall.

Dewey, J. (1916). *Democracy and Education: An introduction to the philosophy of education.* New York: The Free Press/Macmillan.

DuCharme, C. (1993, November). *Historical roots of the project approach in the United States: 1850–1930.* Paper presented at the annual meeting of the National Association for the Education of Young Children. Anaheim, CA.

Edwards, V., Lindsay, D., Stainburn, S., & Rodman, B. (2000). Is progressive education dead? *Teacher Magazine, 7*, 23.

Helm, J. H., & Katz, L. G. (2001). *Young investigators: The project approach in the early years.* New York: Teachers College Press.

Hirsch, E. D. (1996). *The schools we need: Why we don't have them.* New York: Doubleday.

Katz, L. G., & Chard, S. C. (1989). *Engaging children's minds: The project approach.* Norwood, NJ: Ablex.

Katz, L. G., & Chard, S. C. (2000). *Engaging children's minds: The project approach.* Stamford, CT: Ablex.

Kilpatrick, W. H. (1918). The project method. *Teachers College Record, 19*(4), 1–18.

Kohn, A. (2000). *The case against standardized testing.* Portsmouth, NH: Heinemann.

Manning, G., Manning, M., & Long, R. (1994). *Theme immersion: Inquiry based curriculum in elementary and middle schools.* Portsmouth, NH: Heinemann.

Nager, N., & Shapiro, E. (2000). *Revisiting a progressive pedagogy.* Albany, NY: SUNY Press.

Peterson, F. H. (1986). *John Dewey's reconstruction in philosophy.* New York: Philosophical Library.

Wolfe, J. (2000). *Learning from the past: Historical voices in early childhood education.* Mayerthorpe, Alberta, Canada: Piney Branch Press.

Social Promotion, Retention, and Alternative Possibilities

8

JANICE N. COTTON

Thousands of children each year fail to acquire the skills necessary to experience success in the next grade. Some are retained with the intent of providing more time and opportunities to master needed concepts. Others are *socially* promoted in the belief that retention may possibly do more harm than help. Which is more effective in promoting immediate and long-term academic success—grade retention or social promotion? A review of the research indicates that neither is an appropriate course of action for students that are failing academically (Alexander, Entwisle & Dauber, 1994; Shepard & Smith, 1989; Thompson, 1999). Ironically, the evidence against the effectiveness of retention and social promotion continues to mount as more states develop rigorous promotion and graduation standards. If neither is effective, what course of action should schools take with struggling students? The purpose of this chapter is to present the research on retention and social promotion and then detail proven alternatives to these practices.

Social Promotion

Prevalence of Social Promotion

Social promotion is the practice of promoting students to the next grade even though they have not acquired minimum competencies expected of that grade. The number of students socially promoted each year is unknown since few school districts report these data and other districts have only limited data (United States Department of Education [USDOE], 1999). This practice appears to be fairly widespread, however, according to a 1997 survey conducted by the American Federation of Teachers (AFT). Results from the AFT (1997) survey showed that 85 large urban school districts do not have a policy endorsing social promotion. Even though social promotion is not officially endorsed in these districts, more than half of the teachers surveyed indicated that they had promoted unprepared students in the previous year. Reasons given for these social promotions were fear that high failure rates would reflect poorly on the school and school personnel, pressure exerted by principals and parents to promote unready students, knowledge that retention is ineffective, and the absence or insufficiency of effective educational alternatives to social promotion.

Negative Effects of Social Promotion

Educational leaders, governmental officials, and policy makers are clearly concerned about the prevalence of social promotion. In February 1998, President Clinton recommended that the United States Department of Education put an end to social promotion (USDOE, 1999). In the past 15 years, 15 states have established specific standards for grade promotion and others are planning such policies (Northwest Regional Educational Laboratory [NWREL], 1999).

Social promotion is problematic for students, teachers, and parents. Social promotion gives some students the false sense that they have mastered skills necessary for later success. It sends a message to other students that their effort and achievement do not count. Having socially promoted students in the classroom is challenging, since teachers must plan for and teach to a group of children with widely divergent skills and knowledge. Furthermore, it creates frustration among teachers who feel powerless to expect hard work from all students. Social promotion sends parents the false message that their children are adequately prepared to be successful in school and in the labor force (AFT, 1997; National Association of State Boards of Education [NASBE], 1999).

Colleges, universities, and businesses also encounter negative side effects from the practice of social promotion. Data from the National Center for Education Statistics (NCES) showed in 1995 that about one in three freshmen had to take a remedial class in math, science, or writing (NCES, 1996). In addition, college professors are finding that they must lower their standards to assist students who are not prepared for college work. The business community is now investing substantial funds to reeducate students who lack skills needed to be successful in the labor force (AFT, 1997; NASBE, 1999; Thompson, 1999).

Implications and Findings from Local Social Promotion Policies

An increasing number of state and local school districts have created promotion policies that guide decisions regarding students' advancement to the next grade level. The long-term results of these promotion policies are unknown. Recent events with the Los Angeles Unified School District provide an interesting case study of the possible fallout from implementing such standards.

The Los Angeles Unified School District reported on January 31, 2000, that if they retained all the students that had not met grade-level standards, two-thirds of all eighth graders and 40–60 percent of second through eighth graders would flunk. Therefore, the district redefined or loosened their standards and it now appears that 6,000 second graders and 4,000 eighth graders will not be promoted. Even though the number is substantially reduced, Los Angeles still faces several significant problems. School officials plan to tailor a curriculum for these students rather than have them repeat the same material. However, they have no place to house the retainees, so they are investigating leasing space from hospitals and setting up bungalows in school parking lots. In addition, they have not identified teachers to work with these students nor provided training to give them the skills they need to be successful. Teachers, administrators, and parents are all questioning why the district did not adequately prepare for the possible consequences of the tougher promotion standards (Sahagun & Sauerwein, 2000).

A research study examining Chicago's promotion standards also provides information on the effect of promotion standards on student academic achievement. In 1997, Chicago established promotion standards for Grades 3, 6, and 8. Students who do not meet the standards are required to attend a summer program and retake the promotion test. Those who fail in the summer are retained, promoted, or sent to an alternative school. The Consortium on Chicago Research completed a study examining the efficacy of the 1997–1998 promotion standards on student achievement (Roderick, Byrk, Jacob, Easton & Allensworth, 1999). Results from this study showed that the summer program was successful in raising students' performance, but these students remained at-risk because the gains were not sustained in the following academic year. The students who were retained fared poorly. Only about one in three retained students were able to meet the test cutoff score after two years in the same grade. Furthermore, the retained students did no better than comparable children who had been socially promoted.

Conclusions about Social Promotion

Social promotion is a widespread practice that is being questioned by school personnel and the community at large. Districts are implementing policies to eliminate or severely curtail the practice because of the negative short- and long-term effects. Even though this practice is not in the best interest of students, schools, businesses, colleges, or the community, school officials are struggling with how to best eliminate social promotion and at the same time provide manageable, cost-effective programs that promote positive student achievement.

Grade Retention

Educators and researchers have examined the effectiveness of grade retention for decades. From the early 1980s to the present time, opinions regarding the merit of grade retention have varied from being positive for some students and in some circumstances, to being overwhelmingly negative and of little value in promoting academic achievement. Several conclusions regarding the helpfulness and harmfulness of retention can be drawn from the wealth of research that has been conducted. Overall, one point is clear—retention is not effective in producing significant gains in student achievement or in having lasting benefits for struggling students (Alexander et al., 1994; Shepard & Smith, 1989; Thompson, 1999).

Prevalence and Cost of Grade Retention

The prevalence of grade retention, much like social promotion, is unknown, since school districts rarely keep records of how many children are retained each year. Estimates can be derived, however, from census data. These estimates show that the number of grade retained children ranges from 6–9 percent annually (Association of California School Administrators [ACSA], 1999); Center for Policy and Research in Education [CPRE], 1990). For students in urban school districts, the retention rate has been estimated to be approximately 50 percent (AFT, 1997). The cost of retaining or reeducating U.S. students for at least one year, is staggering. For example, in 1996–1997 there were about 46 million children enrolled in public schools in the United States with an average cost per pupil expenditure of $5,923 (NCES, 1999). Using these figures, this means that at least 3.2 million children (7 percent) were retained in grade at a cost of almost $19 billion.

Retention and Academic Achievement

Retention can help some students and in certain circumstances, but there are serious risks associated with it (Thompson, 1999). The majority of studies show that retention is not effective in promoting positive academic achievement, especially in the long run. Holmes (1989) conducted a meta-analysis of 63 empirical studies that examined the effectiveness of retention. Fifty-four of the 63 studies showed that at-risk children who were promoted achieved at the same or higher levels than comparable peers who were retained and spent two years rather than one in a grade. Other studies have also confirmed these findings and found that when retained and promoted students of like ability were compared, the promoted students outperformed the retained students the next year (Norton, 1990; Walters & Borgers, 1995).

Children are often retained in kindergarten or first grade in the belief that if a student must be retained, it is best to do so very early in a child's school career. Several well-designed studies show, however, that retaining children in kindergarten and first grade ultimately can be ineffective and harmful. A large study in the Chicago Public Schools showed that retained children, especially in first grade, did not improve over time (Reynolds, Temple & McCoy, 1997). Alexander et al. (1994) followed 775 students in the Baltimore City Schools for eight years. They found that children retained in first grade improved their achievement test scores the year they were retained. However, these same retainees achieved in second grade and every grade thereafter at the same relative level as their first year in first grade. Researchers speculate first-grade retention may be especially difficult for young children because of the difficulty they experience transitioning into a formal school environment. Being removed from peers with whom they have formed a relationship appears to hinder their development rather than foster positive growth (Entwisle & Alexander, 1993).

There is a considerable amount of research that also shows that kindergarten retention and use of transition grades (i.e., 2-year kindergarten programs) have no lasting academic advantage over other children that were never retained but were also equally unready because of immaturity or low achievement. Children who spent the extra year in kindergarten were just as likely as their promoted counterparts to be at the bottom of the third-grade class (Gredler, 1984; Holmes, 1989; Meisels, 1992; Nason, 1991; Rose, Medway, Cantrell & Marus, 1983; Shepard & Smith, 1986, 1989).

Retention and Social and Health Implications

Children who are retained tend to feel more poorly about their capabilities, score lower on measures of personal and psychological adjustment, and display more discipline problems. Clinical interviews with students showed that they felt angry or sad about the retention and feared the reaction of family and friends. Some were teased by neighbors and reported having a difficult time adjusting to school (Byrnes, 1989; Holmes, 1989; Norton, 1990; Shepard & Smith, 1989).

Being retained in a grade has also been strongly correlated with dropping out of school. Children who are retained one year are five times more likely to drop out of school than those who have never been retained. Children who are retained two or more years have almost a 100 percent probability of becoming dropouts as compared to similar low performers who are promoted (CPRE, 1990).

School failure has also been linked to participation in health-risk behaviors (cigarette use, alcohol use, and weapon-related violence) for adolescents, according to data from the National Longitudinal Study of Adolescent Health. In-home interviews with a nationally representative sample of about 10,000 students ages 12–17 and their families showed that school failure is more likely to predict participation in violent activities, use of alcohol, and involvement in sexual activity than is poverty, race, or family structure. The researchers concluded that school failure should be viewed as a public health problem (Blum et al., 2000).

Conclusions about Retention

Even though a few studies have found that retention can have a positive short-term benefit (Alexander et al., 1994; Holmes, 1989), the vast majority have shown either no long term advantage, harm, or a consistent "wash-out" effect (Gredler, 1984; Holmes, 1989; Mantzicopoulos & Morrison, 1992; Meisels,

1992; Nason, 1991; Reynolds et al., 1997; Rose et al., 1983; Shepard & Smith, 1986, 1989). This indicates that the potential benefit does not warrant the risk. Even researchers who otherwise support retention do not view it as a tool for helping children *succeed* in school (Alexander et al., 1994).

Alternatives to Social Promotion and Grade Retention

In 1998, the Secretary of Education urged school districts to find alternatives to social promotion and retention. The White House Press Office stated that promoting unprepared students and retaining students in the same grade are not appropriate responses to low student achievement because these practices presume that academic failure is unavoidable and acceptable. Instead, they recommended, schools should implement research-based practices that help students meet standards the first time they are exposed to them (NWREL, 1999).

As schools create plans to prevent school failure, two key points should be emphasized. Schools must

1. be proactive and attempt to prevent failure, and
2. identify at-risk children as soon as possible and immediately take action to implement best practices.

One of the best means to ensure student success is to provide a program that strives to prevent school failure, and provides intervention at the first indication of a problem (USDOE, 1999). Yet all too often, intervention is provided too late to truly be effective. Often schools step in to help children after an academic problem has escalated out of control, rather than identifying and providing assistance in preschool, kindergarten, or first grade. Many children who enter school with insufficient skills, especially those two or more years behind their peers, are never able to meet grade-level standards and fall further and further behind their peers. A longitudinal study with about 800 students found that children retained in elementary or middle school were those who were having significant problems in first grade or had insufficient skills upon entering school (Alexander et al., 1994). It is incumbent on schools to identify and provide remediation with proven practices early in a child's school career.

The following research-based strategies have proven to be effective in preventing school failure and in curtailing potential academic failure. Each should be considered in a total plan to reduce or eliminate grade retention and social promotion.

1. *Provide high-quality preschool programs, especially for children at greatest risk for academic failure due largely to starting "way behind" in kindergarten.*

A number of longitudinal research studies have demonstrated that early intervention programs can provide immediate and long-term benefits for children at-risk for failure and special education placement. Programs that are intensive and individualized are more likely to improve the developmental outcomes for children (Ramey & Ramey, 1999).

Two long-term research studies demonstrate the efficacy of early intervention programs for children at greatest risk. The Abecedarian Project studied the potential benefits of early childhood education for economically disadvantaged children. It provided intensive, individualized full-day preschool education five days a week for children from 6 weeks to 5 years of age. Long-term findings from this study revealed participating children scored higher on reading and math tests through age 15 and had lower rates of special education placement and grade retention (Campbell & Ramey, 1995). At age 21, these children continued to have higher cognitive test scores and higher academic achievement in both reading and math. These individuals were more likely to postpone parenthood until their young adult years. In addition, they were more likely to attend a 4-year college (Frank Porter Graham Child Development Center, 1999).

The Perry Preschool Project focused on 3- and 4-year-old children with low IQ scores and tracked these children to age 27. It was found they were less likely to be placed in special education, had fewer grade retentions, attained greater academic achievement, had lower teen pregnancy rates, and lower juvenile crime rates (Schweinhart, Barnes, Weikart, Barnett & Epstein, 1993). A cost-benefit analysis completed in 1985 showed that for every dollar invested in this early intervention program, $7 were saved in the costs associated with additional or special schooling, juvenile crime, and welfare (Barnett, 1985).

2. *Provide teachers with intensive, quality professional development opportunities focused on: (a) raising student achievement and (b) meeting the diverse needs of struggling students.*

One of the most effective remedies for school failure is skillful teaching. Skillful teachers are those who know their students' strengths and needs, are familiar with and utilize a wide range of successful teaching strategies, and continuously adapt strategies to meet their students' needs. Not surprisingly, studies conducted in several states showed that good teaching makes a positive difference in academic performance that is sustained over time (Education Trust, 1998). Specifically, a Tennessee study showed that students who have highly effective teachers for 3 straight years score about 50 percentile points higher than those that had ineffective teachers for 3 years (Sanders & Rivers, 1996). A 1991 study involving over 900 Texas school districts shows, after controlling for socioeconomic status of students, that teacher qualifications and expertise accounted for over 40 percent of the difference in student academic achievement (Ferguson, 1991).

These studies provide convincing evidence that teacher expertise is a significant predictor of student academic success.

Such expertise and knowledge typically do not come naturally. "One-shot" workshops are the most frequently used format for professional development and have consistently been shown to be highly ineffective (Fullan & Stielgebauer, 1991). Professional development opportunities that are intensive and sustained over time are more likely to produce skillful teachers. Research findings and practices of exemplary schools show that effective professional development practices (1) reflect best research and practices in teaching, (2) engage teachers in continuous study, (3) create networks for them to plan collaboratively, (4) encourage professional inquiry and exchange, and (5) require substantial time and resources (Office of Educational Research and Improvement [OERI], 1997). Well-prepared teachers who are engaged in continuous, high-quality professional development opportunities can prevent student failure.

3. *Provide research-based intervention strategies that meet the individual needs of struggling students.*

   The U.S. Department of Education (1999) recommends that schools utilize different approaches if students are not responding to traditional methods. A number of intervention strategies have proven to be successful in remediating academic difficulties. These include:

   a. Looping—Looping is a practice where the teacher works with the same group of children for more than one year. Looping supports academic success because the teacher develops long-term relationships with students. Since teachers spend less instructional time becoming acquainted with students and their needs, they are able to focus more of their time on instruction (USDOE, 1999; Yang, 1997).

   b. Class Size Reduction—A large 4-year study conducted in Tennessee evaluated the effect of small class size on student performance in kindergarten through third grade. This study showed that classes with 13–17 students made significantly greater gains than classes with 21–25 students, with and without a classroom aide. The small-class-size advantage was evident in all four grades, but especially in kindergarten and first grades (Word et al., 1990).

   c. One-on-One Tutoring—One-on-one tutoring has consistently been highly effective in preventing early reading failure. A synthesis of research studies that meet stringent criteria found that one-on-one instruction by adults produced large educationally significant gains. In addition, the use of certified teachers, as compared to paraprofessionals, produced significantly larger educational gains. The studies that evaluated the lasting effects of one-on-one tutoring in the early grades found that the initial positive effects continued to grow on into second and third grades (Wasik & Slavin, 1994).

d. Extended Learning Time—Providing extra time after school or in the summer in and or of itself is not enough to make a difference in the lives of struggling students (Karweit, 1989). Programs that have the greatest likelihood of improving student achievement are after-school *and* summer programs that build on the regular curriculum and address students' specific needs. The use of appropriate techniques and the quality of teacher instruction are also critical elements in producing positive gains, especially for children at-risk (Leinhardt & Palley, 1989).

4. *Actively address the social needs and provide social support as well as academic assistance for struggling students.*

Young people who are struggling academically need not only effective intervention strategies focused on academic deficiencies, they also need the support that comes from teachers, peers, family, and other interested individuals. Personal relationships, or social support, motivates students to learn, builds confidence that academic success is possible, and instills a sense of trust and safety that allows them to be risk takers and "bounce back" when they experience failure (Lee, Smith, Perry & Smylie, 1999; Wehlage, Rutter, Smith, Lesko & Fernandez, 1989).

One study with over 28,000 sixth and eighth graders showed that students who experienced a strong emphasis on academic success *and* had high social support achieved significantly higher levels than students who experienced only a strong emphasis on academic standards (Lee et al., 1999). An in-depth study of 14 schools showed that the provision of social support is critical in preventing school failure and school dropout (Wehlage et al., 1989). This social support is found in schools where personnel actively create positive and respectful relationships with students and address students' personal problems through communication and direct support. It is likely that training on how to provide social support to students is needed.

5. *Develop rigorous, specific, grade by-grade standards that provide direction for curriculum development and help teachers assess individual learning needs.*

Grade standards provide multiple benefits. Overall, standards provide a means for teachers, parents, and the community at large to consistently judge adequate student performance. This consistency will help ensure that teachers from school to school are judging performance by the same criteria. Standards also serve as the foundation for curriculum development and student assessment, and can demonstrate the need for additional educational services. They give parents and students an overview of the academic focus and expectations (AFT, 1997; NASBE, 1999). A study with over 28,000 students showed that conformity to academic standards produces greater academic gains (Lee et al., 1999).

Grade standards should encompass more than simply designating a standardized test score as an indicator for student achievement. The American Federation of Teachers (1997) recommends a number of criteria when developing or critiquing existing standards. They believe standards should be based on the core disciplines, that they reflect the essential components of the academic curriculum, and that they be rigorous and comparable to standards of other high-achieving countries. In addition, they believe standards should delineate different levels of student performance and include content and performance standards.

6. *Involve parents as team members in improving student performance.*

Teachers should be prepared and willing to work jointly with parents on supporting students' educational progress. Studies have shown that regardless of parental income, level of education, or work status, it is the schools' efforts and the teachers' practices that determine the success of parent involvement programs (Epstein, 1988; USDOE, 1997). Parents need teachers to provide direction. In addition, excellent parent involvement programs include teacher training as an essential component to ensure that teachers are adequately prepared to support parent involvement activities (Decker, Gregg & Decker, 1996; Shartrand, Weiss, Kreider & Lopez, 1997). Parents are more likely to be involved when schools welcome parents, make it easy for them to be involved, and when parents and teachers respect each other (NCES, 1997).

7. *Continue to monitor and provide assistance on an "as-needed" basis to students who graduate from intervention programs.*

Unfortunately, numerous studies have shown that the academic gains made in most intervention programs for at-risk students fade or "wash out" over time (Alexander et al., 1994; Gredler, 1984; Holmes, 1989; Mantzicopoulos & Morrison, 1992; Meisels, 1992; Nason, 1991; Reynolds et al., 1997; Shepard & Smith, 1986, 1989). Continuing intervention is needed to address new and different challenges that children face at various points in their school career (Karweit, 1994). Therefore, it is essential that schools continue to monitor children who have participated in intervention programs and provide assistance if problems reoccur. This assistance should come as soon as possible to prevent accelerated deterioration of academic performance.

The Bottom Line

Current systems for preventing school failure and social promotion in most schools do not work and will require comprehensive reform to provide equity and excellence in education. Implementing proven practices will require in some situations a total restructuring of schools and reeducation of school personnel. School systems must be informed of current research and provided opportunities to explore and adopt strategies that have the greatest potential of enhancing student development and achievement. Adopted strategies should be consistently evaluated to determine their effectiveness in enhancing student achievement. A total commitment on the part of teachers, administrators, parents, and school board members is needed to identify and implement effective strategies that will dramatically reduce the incidence of social promotion and retention and at the same time help students attain their academic potential.

REFERENCES

Alexander, K. L., Entwisle, D. R., & Dauber, S. L. (1994). *On success or failure: A reassessment of the effects of retention in the primary grades.* Cambridge: Cambridge University Press.

American Federation of Teachers. (1997, September). *Passing on failure: District promotion policies and practices.* Washington, DC: Author.

Association of California School Administrators. (1999). *Student success in a standards based system: Moving beyond social promotion and retention* [On-line]. Available: http://www.222.acsa.org/publications/EDCAL/EDCAL_05_24 1999/master_plan.html

Barnett, W. S. (1985). Benefit-cost analysis of the Perry Preschool Program and its long-term effects. *Education Evaluation and Policy Analysis, 7,* 387–414.

Blum, R. W., Beuhring, T., Shew, M. L., Bearing, L. H., Sieving, R. E., & Resnick, M. D. (2000). The effects of race/ethnicity, income and family structure on adolescent risk behaviors. *American Journal of Public Health, 90*(12).

Byrnes, D. A. (1989). Attitudes of students, parents, and educators toward repeating a grade. In L. A. Shepard & M. L. Smith (Eds.), *Flunking grades. Research and policies on retention* (pp. 108–131). London: The Falmer Press.

Campbell, F. A., & Ramey, C. T. (1995). Cognitive and school outcomes for high risk students at middle adolescence: Positive effects of early intervention. *American Educational Research Journal, 32,* 743–772.

Center for Policy Research in Education. (1990). *Repeating grades in school: Current practices and research evidence* (CPRE Publication No. RB-04-1/90). Brunswick, NJ: Author.

Decker, L., Gregg, G., & Decker, V. (1996). *Teacher's manual for parent and community involvement.* Alexandria, VA: National Community Education Association.

Education Trust. (1998). *Thinking K–16 report: Good teaching matters. How well qualified teachers close the gap, 3*(2)[On-line]. Available: http://www.edtrust.org/pubs-online.html

Entwisle, D. R., & Alexander, K. L. (1993). Entry into schools: The beginning school transition and educational stratification in the United States. *Annual Review of Sociology (19),* 58–59.

Epstein, J. (1988). How do we improve programs for parent involvement? *Educational Horizons, 66*(2), 58–59.

Ferguson, R. F. (1991). Paying for public education: New evidence of how and why money matters. *Harvard Journal on Legislation, 28,* 465–498.

Frank Porter Graham Child Development Center. (1999). *Early learning, later success. The abecedarian study* [On-Line]. Available: http://www.fpg.unc.edu/~abc

Fullan, M. G., & Stiegelbauer, S. (1991). *The new meaning of educational change.* New York: Teachers College Press.

Funkhouser, J. E., & Gonzales, M. R. (1997). *Family involvement in children's education: Successful local approaches* [On-Line]. Available: http://www.cd.gov/pubs/FamInvolve/title.html

Gredler, G. R. (1984). Transition classes: A viable alternative for the at-risk child? *Psychology in the Schools, 21,* 463–470.

Holmes, C. T. (1989). Grade level retention effects: A meta-analysis of research studies. In L. A. Shepard & M. L. Smith (Eds.), *Flunking grades: Research and policies on retention* (pp. 16–33). London: The Falmer Press.

Karweit, N. L. (1989). Time and learning: A review. In Slavin, R. (Ed.), *School and classroom organization* (pp. 69–95). Hillsdale, NJ: Erlbaum.

Karweit, N. L. (1994). Can preschool alone prevent early learning failure? In Slavin, R. E., Karweit, N. L., & Wasik, B. A. (Eds.), *Preventing early school failure: Research, policy, and practice* (pp. 58–77). Boston: Allyn and Bacon.

Lee, V. E., Smith, J. B., Perry, T. E., & Smylie, M. A. (1999, October). *Social support, academic press, and student achievement: A view from the middle grades in Chicago* [On-Line]. Available: http://www.consortium-chicago.org/acrobat/social%20support.pdf

Leinhardt, B., & Pallay, A. (1989). Instruction's the thing wherein to catch the mind that falls behind. In Slavin, R. E. (Ed.), *School and classroom organization* (pp. 197–226). Hillsdale, NJ: Erlbaum.

Mantizicopoulos, P., & Morrison, D. C. (1992). Kindergarten retention: Academic and behavioral outcomes through the end of second grade. *American Educational Research Journal, 29*(1), 182–198.

Meisels, S. J. (1992). Doing harm by doing good: Iatrogenic effects of early childhood enrollment and promotion policies. *Early Childhood Research Quarterly, 7,* 155–174.

Nason, R. B. (1991). Retaining children: Is it the right decision? *Childhood Education, 67*(5), 300–304.

National Association of State Boards of Education. (1999, March). *Policy update: Social promotion and retention of students, 7*(3). Alexandria, VA: Policy Information Clearinghouse.

National Center for Education Statistics. (1996, October). *Statistical analysis report: Remedial education at higher education institutions in fall 1995* [On-Line]. NCES Publication No 97-584. Available: http://www.nces.ed.gov/pubs/97584.html

National Center for Education Statistics. (1999, April). *Statistics in brief: Public school student, staff, and graduate counts by state, school year 1997–1998* [On-Line]. NCES Publication No. 1999327. Available: http://www.nces.ed.gov/pubs99/1999326.pdf

National Center for Education Statistics. (1999, June). *Statistics in brief: Revenues and expenditures for public elementary and secondary education: School year 1996–1997* [On-Line]. Available: http://www.nces.ed.gov/pubs99/1999301

Northwest Regional Educational Laboratory (1999, July). *When students don't succeed: Shedding light on grade retention* [On-Line]. Available: http://www.nwrel.org/request/july99/index.html

Norton, M. S. (1990). Practical alternatives to student retention. *Contemporary Education 61*(4), 204–208.

Office of Educational Research and Improvement [OERI]. (1997). *National awards program for model professional development 1998 application.* Washington, DC: Author.

Ramey, S. L., & Ramey, C. T. (1999). Early experience and early intervention for children "at risk" for developmental delay and mental retardation. *Mental Retardation and Developmental Disabilities Research Reviews, 5*(1), 1–10.

Reynolds, A., Temple, J., & McCoy, A. (1997, September 17). Grade retention doesn't work: Three reasons why and what should be tried instead. *Education Week, 17*(3), 37.

Roderick, M., Byrk, A. S., Jacob, B., Easton, J. Q., & Allensworth, E. (1999, December). *Finding social promotion: Results from the first two years* [On-Line]. Available: http://www.consortium-chicago.org/Html_web_store_3.0/Html/end_social_promo.html

Rose, J. S., Medway, F. J., Cantrell, V. L., & Marus, S. H. (1983). A fresh look at the retention-promotion controversy. *Journal of School Psychology, 21*(3), 201–211.

Sahagun, L., & Sauerwein, K. (2000, January 31). L.A. schools brace for task of holding back thousands. Education get tough policy on promotions could bring campus crowding, confrontations with parents. *The Los Angeles Times,* p. A1.

Sanders, W. L., & Rivers, J. C. (1996). *Cumulative and residual effects of teachers on future student academic achievement.* Knoxville, TN: University of Tennessee.

Schweinhart, L. J., Barnes, H. V., Weikart, D. P., Barnett, W. S., & Epstein, A. S. (1993). *Significant benefits: The High-Scope Perry Preschool study through age 27.* Ypsilanti, MI: High Scope Press.

Shartrand, A., Weiss, H., Kreider, H., & Lopez, M. (1997). *New skills for new schools: Preparing teachers in family involvement*. Cambridge, MA: Harvard Family Research Project.

Shepard, L. A., & Smith, M. L. (1986). Synthesis of research on school readiness and kindergarten retention. *Educational Leadership, 44*(3), 786–788.

Shepard, L. A., & Smith, M. L. (Eds.). (1989). *Flunking grades: Research and policies on retention*. London: The Falmer Press.

Thompson, C. L. (1999). *Research on retention and social promotion: Synthesis and implications for policy*. Chapel Hill: The North Carolina Education Research Council.

U.S. Department of Education. (1997). *Parent involvement and participation*. Washington, DC: Author.

U.S. Department of Education. (1999). *Taking responsibility for ending social promotion*. Washington, DC: Author.

Walters, D. M., & Borgers, S. B. (1995). Student retention: Is it effective? *School Counselor 42*(4), 300–310.

Wasik, B. A., & Slavin, R. E. (1994). Preventing early reading failure with one-to-one tutoring: A review of five programs. In Slavin, R. E., Karweit, N. L., & Wasik, B. A. (Eds.), *Preventing early school failure: Research, policy, and practice* (pp. 143–174). Boston: Allyn and Bacon.

Wehlage, G., Rutter, R., Smith, G., Lesko, N., & Fernandez, R. (1989). *Reducing the risk: Schools as communities of support*. Philadelphia: Falmer Press.

Word, E., Johnston, J., Bain, H., Fulton, B., Zaharias, J., Lintz, N., Achilles, C. M., Folger, J., & Breda, C. (1990). *Student/teacher achievement ratio (star): Tennessee's K–3 class size study. Final report and final report summary*. Nashville, TN: Tennessee State Department of Education.

Yang, X. (1997, February). *Educational benefits in elementary school through looping and Friday in-services, part 2: Benefits of looping*. Paper presented at the Annual Seminar of the National Association for Year-Round Education, San Diego, CA.

CHAPTER

9   Teaching in
Inclusive Settings

Consider the following perspectives:

1. "Why should students with disabilities be excluded? Why not exclude children with red hair, children with dimples, or kids who play basketball?"
2. "Don't talk to me about inclusion if you are just considering children with disabilities. There are a lot of children who are excluded within regular classrooms for a variety of reasons such as gender, race, ethnicity, weight, height, looks, and who knows what else."
3. "I'm against inclusion, especially full inclusion, because neither regular education or special education teachers are prepared for it. It won't work."
4. "Theoretically I'm for full inclusion, but it doesn't work for two reasons—money and time. For full inclusion to work, more personnel are needed to support regular education teachers who teach students with special needs. No one is going to pay for that. So, it takes too much extra time for a regular teacher to modify instruction and help those children who would have been in special education. Regular education students should have rights. With full inclusion too much time is spent with special kids."
5. "Special education has been just another way to marginalize those who do not fit the traditional mold. This has been true for many years. More minority students and more males have been labeled as mentally retarded. This is not true for giftedness. Categories such as mental retardation are not characteristics of specific individuals. These labels are social constructions used to discriminate against those who are different. It's time all people were included in regular education and the labels reconsidered and probably thrown out."

Need we say more about inclusion being a hot topic in the 21st century? This chapter poses several questions about inclusion. First, we will consider what inclusion is. Then we will address how we got to inclusion. The following difficult questions will also be addressed: Is inclusion better than full inclusion? What are the advantages of inclusive schools? What are the barriers? What would make full inclusion work? Finally, are there any results that support or refute inclusion?

What Is Inclusion?

As with most educational trends and issues, the debate over inclusion often begins, "What are we talking about?" What is inclusion? To begin with, inclusion is not the same thing as mainstreaming. Mainstreaming is defined as integrating children with special needs into the regular classroom with the understanding that there is a resource room or special education class to which they can go to receive assistance. Mainstreaming is still part of a pullout model in which students can go to another class for the help they need. Inclusion, on the other hand, is a movement that was designed to bring special education services into the general classroom. In such settings children with disabilities are "considered as full members of the classroom learning community, with their special needs met there" (Friend & Bursuck, 1996, p. 4). This movement is a significant change from the traditional practice of having students "pulled out" of regular education to receive special services in a resource room or self-contained special education classroom (Henley, Ramsey & Algozzine, 1999).

An inclusive program has a "zero reject philosophy"; no one is turned away because of the presence of a disability (Thousand & Villa, 1989). Unlike mainstreaming, inclusion maintains an open door to all students regardless of abilities. Inclusive schools reflect the heterogeneous makeup of society. Instruction is designed around individual strengths and concerns rather than placement of students in programs where instruction is based on the type or severity of the students' disabilities. Inclusion assumes a positive attitude in which all students are accepted as members of the school and classroom environment (Bradley, King-Sears & Tessier-Switlick, 1997).

Support for inclusion has been based on the ethical, legal, and educational benefits to members. Educators, parents, and legislators continue to question existing separateness between regular and special education (Sailor, 1991; Stainback & Stainback, 1992; Willis, 1994).

How Did We Get Here?

The purpose of this section is not to provide a full review of the history of special education but to describe the general events that led up to inclusive practices. (For a historical review of special education see Winzer, 1986 or 1993.)

At the beginning of the 21st century, special education has quite a colorful history. The historical route of students with disabilities started with neglect. It progressed to institutionalization, residential schooling, and other isolated schools and classes. This can be described as full segregation. Students who were different were placed in institutions or entirely separate schools. Later, pullout programs and eventually mainstreaming became the fashion. Today inclusion is the trend. However, *how much* inclusion is quite an issue.

Should We Have Inclusion or Full Inclusion?

In the early 1800s, pioneers such as Thomas H. Gallaudet and Louis Braille established special schools and communication that assisted children who were hearing impaired or blind to learn. The first organized arrangements in the United States for the education of students with disabilities were copied from European asylums that had been established for the purpose of providing custodial care and "protecting persons with disabilities from the outside world" (Halvorsen & Sailor, 1990, p. 114). After it was proved that students with various disabilities were educable, residential schools were established.

Many states by the late 19th century were demonstrating public acceptance for the education of people with disabiltiies. Even some residential institutions began to train specialized teachers for special programs in some local schools. It was not, however, until the middle of the 20th century that parents of children with disabilities organized for political action. State and federal governments began to show support for special education in the form of research, training, and legislation (Turnbull, 1990).

The past three decades have witnessed dramatic changes in legal, social, and economic forces that have affected both regular and special education. Educational practices have been continually refined to reflect changes that should benefit a wide variety of learners.

In 1975 Congress passed Public Law 94-142, the Education of All Handicapped Children Act. Among the requirements of this law were the guarantee of a free appropriate public education for children and youth with disabilities. The law also stipulated that these students be educated in the "least restrictive environment." This meant that these students be educated to the maximum extent possible along with their peers without disabilities in the school that they would have attended if they did not have a disability. However, the law did not specify how this was to occur. To meet the intent of this law, many school systems responded by creating segregated programs rather than by providing services to students *within* general education classrooms. Today, many of these programs continue to provide service in segregated programs (Bradley et al., 1997).

The results of the continued segregation of students with disabilities are fragmentation promoted by separate training, administration, labels, and buildings that increasingly isolate special education from general education. Many separate categories of students with special needs have been created to form the creation of many categorical programs (i.e., Title I programs, bilingual programs, programs for students with mental retardation, programs for students with emotional disturbance, etc.). This fragmentation encourages competition between special needs groups for resources such as money, materials, and personnel.

Mainstreaming.   The 1980s saw progressive moves toward inclusion in the general education of students with challenging learning and behavioral needs. Additional federal legislation passed such as Public Law 99-457 in 1986, which extended services toward a younger population with special needs. Public Law 101-476, passed in 1990, required students with disabilities to be educated in general education to the maximum extent possible. The response of the educational community to these laws was to mainstream students whenever possible.

The Regular Education Initiative. The regular education initiative (REI) is founded on the premise that students with mild disabilities should be viewed as the shared responsibility of all educators rather than the sole responsibility of special educators (Will, 1986). General education classes are adapted to meet the needs of a variety of individual learners (Semmel, Abernathy, Butera & Lesar, 1991).

Inclusion completely changes the way all students are educated. Rather than having pull out special education services, special education teachers work collaboratively alongside regular educators in the same setting. This significantly restructures service delivery. All teachers and support personnel have a new and different role than previously conceived. A fourth-grade teacher is no longer a person with her own classroom, separate from the rest of the school. She must share her room and students with a collaborative special educator, a Title I teacher, and other professionals and paraprofessionals, which might include speech therapists, physical therapists, and occupational therapists. However, neither special educators nor regular educators have been prepared for this (Fuchs & Fuchs, 1998).

Is Inclusion Better than Full Inclusion?

Regular classrooms typically have a large number of children, ranging from 25 to 45. Although it has been shown that students' academic performance improved when their class size ranged from 13 to 17 (Viadero, 1998), inclusionists wonder whether such small classes are possible in the foreseeable future (Fuchs & Fuchs, 1998). In addition, the 25 to 45 students are not all performing on grade level. For example, a typical fifth-grade class includes a few students reading below second-grade level, a handful of students reading above the sixth-grade level, and the majority of students reading somewhere in between. Even in traditional, noninclusive classrooms, few teachers differentiate their instruction to address this broad variety of academic achievements (Baker & Zigmond, 1990; McIntosh, Vaughan, Schumm, Haager & Lee, 1993). Many teachers present the same lesson and instructional materials to all students. A reason for this is that not all teachers use best practices such as cooperative learning and classwide peer tutoring. About 30 percent of children with disabilities typically fail to respond to these best practices, suggesting that even very knowledgeable and devoted teachers using effective practices are not responsive to *all* children (Fuchs & Fuchs, 1998).

Willis Walter (2000), principal of an urban elementary school serving children from kindergarten through fifth grade, describes his views on inclusion versus full inclusion.

> I am against full inclusion because I believe some students can benefit from smaller class settings and more one-on-one interaction with a special education teacher. I am for inclusion and mainstreaming for the majority of our students because children learn as much from one another as they do from the teacher. This is especially true for social habits in dealing with differences. This learning would not usually occur in a sterilized classroom.
>
> The teachers in my school are uncomfortable with full inclusion for several reasons. One of their biggest complaints is that professional development has lagged behind a lot of the issues they face—particularly [for] inclusion.
>
> Many of the teachers in my school believe [inclusion for] some special education students hinder[s] the learning community of the other students more than it helps their disability. This is particularly true of emotionally disturbed students—those who act out on a regular basis. These students do not have an aide or one-on-one support.

Kathy Blackwell (2000), a veteran fourth grade teacher who also teaches in an urban setting, echoes Mr. Walter's remarks.

> I don't have a problem with full inclusion if you get true support. I don't think that will ever happen. I believe the regular child in the classroom has rights also. There is so much emphasis placed on students with special needs we forget about the others—the average, normal child. Special education students take a lot of time. If we had full support, that would be different. But what is full support? If I had an aide in every classroom and 17 children, I don't think I would have a problem. This will never happen. It's purely a money issue.
>
> I would love for the resource teacher to come to my room. I would have no problem with that. The three students with special needs I teacher this year are wonderful children. I personally don't have enough time to devote to them. It's a matter of time. So, time, money, and help are the big issues for me with regard to full inclusion.

When we consider the large numbers of students per class, the wide variability of academic accomplishment among students without disabilities, and the significant number of students with disabilities who are not helped by best practices, we must conclude that full placement in regular classes will not service the academic needs of some children with disabilities. Instead, they need to be placed in special education settings where they are more likely to benefit (Fuchs & Fuchs, 1998).

The differences between inclusionists' and full inclusionists' positions are threefold. First, inclusionists stress that the primary objective of schooling is to help children master skills and knowledge necessary for future successes in and out of school. Full inclusionists believe schools are most important to provide opportunities for friendship making, changing stereotypic thinking about disabilities, and strengthening socialization skills. Second, inclusionists maintain that the continuum of special education placement is vital. Full inclusionists insist that the proper place for all children is in the regular classroom. Third, inclusionists believe that whereas regular classrooms can and should be made more accommodating of special needs, there is a limit to what one realistically can expect of such settings. In contrast, full inclusionists believe all things are possible (Fuchs & Fuchs, 1998).

How can these fundamental differences between inclusionists and full inclusionists exist? The answer is fairly simple if one considers that inclusionists and full inclusionists advocate for different children with different needs. Most inclusionists speak for children with high-incidence disabilities such as children with behavior disorders, learning disabilities, and mild mental retardation. Many full inclusionists represent children with severe mental retardation. Their major concern is more with socialization opportunities than academic or vocational development (Fuchs & Fuchs, 1998).

What about Full Inclusion and the Law?

Special education services and the rights of children with disabilities are topics that constitute the fastest-growing areas of school law. Most of the controversies center around the interpretations of the Individuals with Disabilities Education Act (IDEA). Although the term *inclusion* is not mentioned in the federal law, the 1990s courts have interpreted IDEA as entailing a strong preference for inclusion (McCarthy, 1998). They have, accordingly, placed the burden on school personnel to establish that a regular education placement is not appropriate for a given child with disabilities. Courts consider some of the following criteria in making this determination: the educational benefits of the inclusive versus segregated settings; the noneducational (e.g., social) benefits of both placements; the costs of the respective placements; and the impact of the inclusive placement on other children in the class (McCarthy, 1998).

School authorities do not necessarily support the more restrictive environment. In several court cases, it was the parents who contested the school district's proposed inclusive placement. Parents have requested instead residential or other segregated settings for their children.

Courts are not requiring inclusive placements under all circumstances although they are interpreting IDEA as entailing a presumption that children with disabilities should be placed in regular education. The court will review the specific circumstances for each case. Certainly, it is not impossible for school authorities to substantiate that the welfare of the child or classmates would be jeopardized in the regular classroom.

In several cases involving students with hearing impairments, courts have upheld centralized programs, some of which are in segregated settings. The courts believed that the language needs of these children would be served most appropriately in these more restrictive placements where the services are superior to what could be provided in a regular classroom (McCarthy, 1998).

Should We Prepare for Full Inclusion or Just Inclusion?

The underlying philosophy that embraces inclusion of students into regular education is based on welcoming all neighborhood students into the community school. It also is based on meeting these students' needs in that educational system. Several critical goals need to be considered when making the transition from a "segregated" to an inclusive school:

1. to promote a school philosophy and create an atmosphere based on egalitarianism and democracy
2. to win the support and value the ideas of all who will be involved
3. to integrate students, personnel, and resources so that regular and special educators can work together
4. to incorporate Best Practices of education throughout the school

In order for inclusion to operate at its best, several best practices of education have been identified (Bradley, 1993; Fox, 1987). Students with or without special needs benefit from the following:

1. Students with special needs are to be included for at least part of the day in the regular program with peers who do not have disabilities.
2. Whenever possible, heterogeneous grouping should take place.
3. Technical expertise and equipment should be utilized.
4. Adaptations in the curriculum should be made when necessary.
5. Assessments should be curriculum based and focus on how students learn instead of what is wrong with them.
6. Techniques for behavioral management may need to be employed.
7. A curriculum based on social skills may be used.
8. Students should feel empowerment through the use of such techniques as peer teaching, cooperative learning, and self-developed rules.
9. The staff should engage in ongoing development. (Bradley & Switlick, 1997)

Preparing the System

The current directions of school reform for the 21st century emphasize not only improvement in general education but also improved performance for more challenging populations. We should use the opportunities that now exist in educational reorganization to merge the goals of regular and special education to work toward a "shared educational agenda" (Sailor, 1991, p. 8).

Preparing Teachers

Stainback & Stainback (1990) pointed out that although regular educators cannot educate students with disabilities alone, neither can special educators. Teachers in the past saw students who were not successful in the mainstream as needing special education programs. The problems were attributed to the student. A new paradigm is emerging that says that all students can learn if instruction and materials meet their needs (Bradley & Fisher, 1995). This shift in thinking requires both special and regular educators to work together for each student.

General and special educators must work collaboratively to gain understanding about how the best teaching and learning takes place. Materials and teacher expertise need to be shared. To help both teachers and students who require specialized instruction, Miller (1990) recommends a merger of (1) material, (2) knowledge, (3) skills, (4) personnel, (5) resources, and (6) categorical programs such as Title I or bilingual (Bradley et al., 1997).

Preparing Families

Families play a critical role in creating an inclusive school philosophy. They need to be included in all decisions that affect the instructional program of their children. Families are being asked to think differently about what is best for their children. Previously they were told that a self-contained classroom was the best setting for quality instruction. Now they are being told that the general education classroom with modifications and services will be best for their child's education. Offering families information about inclusion can help make a smoother transition to inclusive practices.

Preparing Students

The inclusion process needs to be explained to students *before* it is put into practice. Students should be asked to make suggestions. When students believe that their input is valued, they are more likely to feel vested and support the program (Bradley & Fisher, 1995). All students should have the opportunity to discuss their questions, fears, and concerns. They need to know how, when, and why to aid students with disabilities.

Students with disabilities need to be notified about what changes to expect and what new responsibilities come with inclusion. Students who receive special education services may need extra time to adjust to the changes. They may need more help to prepare them for the physical move to the regular education setting such as learning how to follow schedules, finding locations in the school, and using lockers. Establishing networks of peer support can address many of these changes and help in making a smooth transition from a special education setting to a general education setting (Bradley et al., 1997).

What Are the Advantages of Full Inclusion?

Academic Advantages

A major purpose of academics is to prepare students for the world of work. Unfortunately, follow-up studies of special education students show that graduates of self-contained programs are employed less and often have lower self-esteem than those who received their education in the mainstream (Lipsky & Gartner, 1996).

When students are in inclusive programs, the number of IEP objectives that are accomplished increase, according to Halvorsen and Sailor (1990). In other studies (Peterson, 1989), results indicated that students who have been placed in heterogeneously grouped programs showed significantly more improvement than those who were grouped by ability levels. In addition, students with special needs who were placed in mixed ability groups participated more in class activities and presented fewer discipline problems.

When special education moves away from labeling and toward instruction, more of the special education teacher's time can be spent in direct service to students rather than in attending meetings or administering tests. Also, continuity with grade-level academic programs more likely will take place. Students' time for instruction is better spent because they are not moving from class to class in order to receive special services (Bradley & Switlick, 1997).

Gains in Socialization

When special needs students are placed in inclusive settings, they have greater opportunity for normalization, i.e., the exposure to the norms and cultural patterns of the society in general (Halvorsen & Sailor, 1990). Special needs students also should be provided with opportunities for participation in programs to facilitate the acquisition of skills that will enhance their functioning in the general environment (Brown et al., 1987; Halvorsen & Sailor, 1990). When planned programs of interaction are made possible, both students with and without special needs can learn to interact, communicate, develop friendships, work together, and help one another. This interaction assists both groups to develop understanding, respect, sensitivity, and comfort with individual similarities and differences.

Inclusive settings allow students with special needs to have access to a range of learning opportunities and social models. With these opportunities, more appropriate social development can take place. The stigma and isolation that come with segregated programs decrease.

Benefits to Regular Education Students

Regular education teachers express concern that having students with disabilities, particularly severe disabilities, will adversely affect students without disabilities (Bradley & Switlik, 1997). Results of studies (Hollowood, Salisbury, Rainforth & Palombaro, 1995) showed that the regular education students did not suffer detrimental effects. It was shown that no losses of instructional time were incurred when students with severe disabilities were included in classrooms. In addition, in inclusive settings no significant differences existed for the two groups, students with or without disabilities, in either academic or behavioral performance.

Students without disabilities gain skills and insights that are beneficial to them, such as developing increased tolerance and appreciating human differences (Willis, 1994). "The greatest gain for students without disabilities who are educated with peers who have disabilities is that they develop values that enable them to support the inclusion of all citizens in the various aspects of community life" (Bradley & Switlik, 1997, p. 15).

What Are Barriers to Inclusion?

Changing Roles for Educators

Currently we do not have good data on the attitudes of regular education teachers toward inclusive schools (Bradley & West, 1994). For more than 20 years, regular education teachers were told that they do not know how to teach students with disabilities. Now they are told that since good teaching is good teaching, you will be able to do a good job. Regular teachers, therefore, are "skeptical and scared" (Miller, 1990, p. 32). They also feel caught between inclusion and test score accountability. Changes in instructional preparation, delivery, and assessment will be required of them to meet the needs of such a diverse group—from students who are gifted to those with severe physical, academic, and emotional challenges. Regular educators are concerned with the more comprehensive record-keeping systems that special education requires. They sometimes anticipate that inclusion will require them to do more with less. They fear a lack of support from special educators and have expressed fear that these supports may likely be eliminated altogether (Bradley & Switlik, 1997).

Special educators may also experience some disadvantages as a result of the inclusion model. Confusion may occur as to who is responsible for what—the implementation of IEP goals, for example, as well as the behavior and general achievement of students with disabilities (Bradley & Fisher, 1995). Special educators often run highly structured classrooms with a strong behavior management system in place. When classrooms are open to students without disabilities, this system may not be easy for them to follow.

Funding formulas encourage separateness between special and general education. These formulas encourage restrictive placements and reward systems for labeling and placing students in special education (Bergan, 1995; Katsiyannis, Conderman & Franks, 1995). Schools housing students with disabilities for the first time face space and accessibility limitations. In sparsely populated areas, service delivery can be very difficult and require cooperative agreements between school systems.

Adverse Effects on Students

Some parents who in the past have had their children served in special settings within small groups and with considerable individual attention wonder if programming in regular education settings is adequate to meet the needs of their children with disabilities. Sailor (1991) expresses concern that social discrimination can occur if students with disabilities enter an inclusive setting.

What Would Make Full Inclusion Work?

A review of the research and a National Center survey identified seven factors that are necessary if inclusion is to succeed (Lipsky & Gartner, 1996).

1. *Visionary leadership.* The comments of a Vermont special education director, who stated that several years ago his district came to view inclusion as a subset of the restructuring of the entire educational system, are illustrative of the kind of leadership necessary. They no longer viewed special education as a means to help students meet the demands of the classroom. Rather, they view special education as a part of the classroom services that must be available to accommodate the learning needs of *all* children in a restructured school.

2. *Collaboration.* No one teacher can or should be expected to have all the expertise required to meet the educational needs of all the students in the classroom. Support systems that provide collaborative assistance and enable teachers to engage in cooperative problem solving must be in place and available to teachers. Tools necessary for collaboration must be accessible and must include planning teams and scheduled time for teachers to work together.

3. *A redirected use of assessment.* In the past, students' assessments have been used as screening devices to determine where students "fit." In special education many studies have addressed the inadequacy of this screening. The inclusive movement has called for more authentic assessments including the use of portfolios of students' work and performances.

4. *Staff and student support.* Systematic staff development and flexible planning time for regular and special education teachers to meet and work together

are critical for inclusion to work successfully. Students need supplementary aides and support services available to them. School aides, needed therapy services that are integrated into the regular school program, peer support, buddy systems, effective use of computer-aided technology, and other assistive devices prove helpful to students.

5. *Funding.* Changes in funding are necessary because current special education funding formulas tend to encourage separation placements. Funds should follow the students. When this happens, inclusive education programs are no more costly overall than segregated models (McLaughlin & Warren, 1994).

6. *Parental involvement.* Effective inclusive programs encourage and welcome parental participation through family support services and the development of educational programs that engage parents as co-learners with their children.

7. *Adaptation of curricula and adoption of effective instructional practices.* Inclusive programs should consider multilevel instruction, cooperative learning, activity-based learning, mastery learning, use of instructional technology, peer support, and tutoring programs.

Students with special needs have numerous legitimate needs that may go beyond the seven factors provided here. A simplistic, generalized agenda for success would make a mockery of the complexities concerning special education and inclusive practices. However, some delivery models have produced promising results so far.

Delivery Models that Work

Teachers, both regular and special educators, need to ask two questions: (1) How do kids learn best? (2) Does specialized instruction work to the extent we had hoped it would? The goal of setting up a program is to serve students most effectively. Teachers should ask which model is best for students' long-term needs, not what is most accommodating to teachers. For example, a pullout program is easier for all teachers involved to schedule and implement but not necessarily in the best interest of students (Elliot & McKenney, 1998).

Before choosing approaches to inclusion, teachers need to determine what attitudes staff members have about students with special needs. The school's approach to inclusion will depend heavily on staff beliefs. Because negative attitudes will impede inclusion, it is important to address these attitudes in the form of different delivery models. Ideally, we would like to adhere to one belief and therefore one model of inclusion. However, teachers, like students, work in an environment that accommodates their particular needs.

According to Elliot and McKenney (1998) as well as Rogers (1993), several approaches appear effective in including students with special needs in general classroom settings. These approaches include consultation, team teaching, aide services, and a limited pullout service. Elliot and McKenney (1998) describe four approaches that have been used successfully within their program to provide inclusive services for children with special needs and meet the belief systems of the teachers.

Consultation. Consultation in general involves *no* direct services to students in the classroom setting. The exceptions, however, include assessment, observation, and planning meetings. Special time allotments are granted to general and special educators to meet and discuss student needs and services. Adaptations and modifications are made as needed. The special educators may provide additional instructional materials based on individual need.

With this model the student's environment is modified to meet attention, visual, hearing, and behavioral needs. Academic adjustments are also modified. For example, teachers should alter classroom assignments. Teachers may provide materials to aide students with organizational difficulties. They may supply different writing tools, assignment formats, or a word processor.

To be successful, consultation requires a strong trust and communication between two teachers, the regular and special education teachers, as well as parents. Some regular education teachers may find inclusion very difficult to accept. They may have concerns that other students in the classroom may be neglected because of the considerable needs of students with special needs. They may feel ineffective working with students with disabilities. Other, less inclusive models, such as team teaching, may work for some teachers more effectively (Elliot & McKenney, 1998).

Team Teaching. Team teaching involves the general and special education teachers working together in the classroom and instructing the entire class. It can be done in a variety of ways. Co-teaching is the least restrictive approach. Teachers teach together at the same time or switch subjects or days teaching. Other approaches involve small-group work as well as individual tutorial assistance. The team-teaching approach lends itself to flexibility in delivery. The advantage of team teaching over consultation is the ability to change, as needed, on the spot.

The problem with team teaching is the comfort level of the teachers involved. Co-teachers may not hold the same belief systems and therefore are not working in a comfortable environment. In contrast, compatible teams have found team teaching to be successful and positive (Elliot & McKenney, 1998).

Aides' Services. The use of instructional aides in the classroom is one way to avoid tracking students by ability. Realistically, it is not possible for special education teachers to meet the needs of students placed in several different classrooms at different grade levels without the use of instructional assistance. It is important that the general education teacher also assume ownership. The success of this approach is dependent on the competency of the aides and the willingness of the school system to budget sufficiently. Further, it is recommended that the special education teacher have direct contact at least monthly with the students in the classroom to observe and evaluate progress.

Aides typically work in the classroom where one to four students with disabilities are placed. Their responsibility is to check the students' progress, provide assistance on an individual or small-group basis, assist the classroom teacher, and report back to the special education teacher. Occasionally, the aide may take a small group of students out of the classroom to work on a test or project in order to avoid distractions.

Most teachers value aide services as long as the aides are well trained and helpful to them. The problem with this service model is the inconsistency of personnel and funding from year to year (Elliot & McKenney, 1998).

Limited Pullout Service.   The pullout service is the more traditional approach that special educators have used for years. It has relieved the regular educator from considerable responsibility involving students with disabilities. The special education teacher does not need to collaborate as frequently with the regular education teacher. Both teachers can independently direct their classroom and curriculum.

Although a pullout program often allows for more individualized instruction, it breaks apart the student's day and the student's learning. Students must leave the general classroom at certain times and travel to and from the resource room. Time is wasted gathering supplies and traveling the halls. Much of the material learned in the resource room is not transferred to the general classroom because the material is sometimes out of context. It is almost impossible to coordinate curriculum between regular and special education on a daily basis. Stigmas are associated with pullout programs and students are often uncomfortable and do not feel part of the general class because they are not "smart enough" to remain the whole day.

Students with severe disabilities may need pullout services. For example, students may need to be pulled out to work on skills that are extremely low for their grade placement and cannot realistically be taught within the regular classroom. If the disability creates a distraction that prevents other students from learning or the teacher from teaching, the pullout program could be used.

Elliot and McKenney (1998) propose that a pullout program should be used only on a limited basis within an inclusion model. Their goal is to use the pullout program only when there is no way for students with disabilities to succeed in the classroom without the more individualized instruction and tutoring. They consider the pullout approach the most restrictive model within their program.

Peer Tutoring.   Fischer, Schumaker, and Deshler (1996) reviewed the literature in search of validated inclusive practices. Peer tutoring is one of these. During peer tutoring, one student (the tutor) acts as a teacher, providing instruction to a peer (the tutee). The tutor helps the tutee master needed skills, providing instruction, opportunities for practice, clarification, and feedback by following a structured, teacher-developed lesson. Proponents of peer tutoring stress the importance of training tutors how to tutor. It is also essential that teachers interact with each group to keep students focused. The tutee's progress must be assessed continually and the sessions must be scheduled regularly (Jenkins & Jenkins, 1985).

Teaching Devices.   In reviewing the literature on inclusive practices, researchers (Fischer et al., 1998) identified instructional tools teachers use that can be considered a part of inclusive practices. Many types of teaching devices (e.g., mnemonic devices, role-play activities, and manipulatives) have been developed and described in both regular and special education literature. However, only two types of teaching devices met the criteria established for review by the researchers (Fischer et al., 1998). These were graphic organizers and study guides. Teachers use graphic organizers as visual displays to organize information in a manner that makes information easier to comprehend and learn. Synonyms for graphic organizers include *tree diagrams*, *semantic maps*, *flow charts*, and *webs*. Theoretically, graphic organizers allow students to consolidate information into a meaningful whole rather than a set of unrelated terms and concepts. Horton, Lovitt, and Bergerud (1990) reported a series of studies undertaken to determine the effectiveness of graphic organizers as an inclusive practice.

Are There Any Results that Support or Refute Inclusion?

Given that inclusive education programs have been implemented relatively recently, few full-scale evaluations of outcomes are available. Several studies are under way. We will consider some of the initial findings from studies of inclusion here.

1. Students with learning disabilities who were included in the regular classroom made academic gains as reflected in their scores on criterion-referenced tests and report cards (Chase & Pope, 1993).
2. Students with significant disabilities experienced greater success in achieving Individual Education Plan (IEP) goals than did matched students in traditional programs (Ferguson, Meyer, Jeanchild, Juniper & Zingo, 1992).
3. Benefits to students with disabilities happened without limiting the educational program available to students without disabilities (Co-teaching, 1991).
4. Gains were evidenced in student self-esteem, classmate acceptance, and social skills (Burrelo & Wright, 1993).

Where Do We Go from Here?

As with any issue, where we go from here is debatable. Here are some questions to consider as we contemplate whether we can move into full inclusion or not.

1. Will the money be made available to support inclusive services? If so, where will it originate? Ideally, special education and regular education funding should merge.
2. How will educators be prepared for inclusion? (Remember, teachers who have been teaching for some time were trained in a different model.)
3. How can we assist children, teachers, and parents in becoming more tolerant of diversity?
4. Can class size in an inclusive setting be reduced to match the nature and needs of diverse children?
5. Will adequate support personnel be provided to assist in inclusive settings?

REFERENCES

Ayres, C. B. (1988). Integration: A parent's perspective. *Exceptional Parent, 18*, 22–25.

Baker, J., & Zigmond, N. (1990). Are regular education classes equipped to accommodate students with learning disabilities? *Exceptional Children, 56*, 515–526.

Bennett, T., Deluca, D., & Burns, D. (1997). Putting inclusion into practice: Perspectives of teachers and parents. *Exceptional Children, 64*, 115–131.

Bergan, J. R. (1995). Evolution of problem-solving model of consultation. *Journal of Educational and Psychological Consultation, 6*, 125–144.

Blackwell, K. (2000). Personal communication, April 25.

Bradley, D. F. (1993). Staff training for the inclusion of students with disabilities: Visions for educators. Unpublished doctoral dissertation. Walden University, Minneapolis, MN.

Bradley, D. F., & Fisher, J. F. (1995). The inclusion process: Role changes at the middle level. *The Middle School Journal, 26*, 13–19.

Bradley, D. F., King-Sears, M. E., & Tessier-Switlick, D. M. (Eds.). (1997). *Teaching students in inclusive settings.* Boston: Allyn and Bacon.

Bradley, D. F. & Switlick, D. M. (1997). The past and the future of special education. In D. F. Bradley, M. E. King-Sears & D. M. Tessier-Switlick (Eds.), *Teaching students in inclusive settings.* Boston: Allyn and Bacon.

Bradley, D. F., & West, J. F. (1994). Staff training for the inclusion of students with disabilities: Visions from school-based educators. *Teacher Education and Special Education, 17*, 112–128.

Burrello, L. C., & Wright, P. T. (Eds.). (1993, Winter). Strategies for inclusion of behaviorally challenged students. *The Principal Letters, 10*.

Chase, V., & Pope, E. (1993, February 24). Model for mainstreaming: The synergistic approach. Paper presented at the Learning Disabilities of America Conference, San Francisco, CA.

Co-teaching: Regular education/special education and co-teaching reference guide. (1991). Lansing, MI: Michigan State Department of Education.

Elliot, D., & McKenney, L. (1998). Four inclusion models that work. *Teaching Exceptional Children* V, 54–57.

Ferguson, D., Meyer, G., Jeanchild, L., Juniper, L., & Zingo, J. (1992). Figuring out what to do with the grownups: How teachers make inclusion "work" for students with disabilities. *Journal of the Association for Persons with Severe Handicaps, 17*, 218–226.

Fischer, J. B., Schumaker, J. B. & Deshler, D. D. (1996). Searching for validated inclusive practices: A review of the literature. In E. Meyen, G. A. Vergason & R. J. Whelan (Eds.), *Strategies for teaching exceptional children in inclusive settings* (pp. 123–154). Denver, CO: Love

Fox, T. (1987). *Best practices guidelines.* Burlington, VT: Center for Developmental Disabilities.

Friend, M., & Bursuck, W. (1996). Including students with special needs: A practical guide for classroom teachers. Boston: Allyn & Bacon.

Fuchs, D., & Fuchs, L. S. (1998). Inclusion versus full inclusion. Annual Theme Issue, *Childhood Education*, 309–316.

Halvorsen, A. T., & Sailor, W. (1990). Integration of students with severe and profound disabilities: A review of research. In R. Gaylor-Ross (Ed.), *Issues and research in special education* (pp. 110–172). New York: Teachers College Press.

Henley, M., Ramsey, R. S., & Algozzine, R. F. (1999). *Characteristics of and strategies for teaching students with mild disabilities* (3rd ed.). Boston: Allyn & Bacon.

Hilton A., & Henderson, C. J. (1993). Parent involvement: A best practice or forgotten practice? *Education and Training in Mental Retardation, 28,* 199–211.

Hollowood, T. M., Salisbury, C. O., Rainforth, B., & Palombaro, M. M. (1995). Use of instructional time in classrooms serving students with and without severe disabilities. *Exceptional Children,* 61, 242–253.

Horton, S. V., Lovitt, T. C., & Bergerud, D. (1990). The effectiveness of graphic organizers for three classifications of secondary students in content area classes. *Journal of Learning Disabilities, 23,* 12–22.

Hunt, P., Goetz, L., & Anderson, J. (1986). The quality of IEP objectives associated with placement on integrated versus segregated school sites. *The Journal of the Association for Persons with Severe Handicaps, 11,* 125–130.

Jenkins, J. R., & Jenkins, L. M. (1985). Peer tutoring in elementary and secondary programs. *Focus on Exceptional Children, 17,* 1–12.

Jenkins, J. R., Odom, S., & Speltz, M. L. (1989). Effects of social integration of preschool children with handicaps. *Exceptional Children, 55,* 420–428.

Katsiyannis, A., Conderman, G., Franks, D. J. (1995). State practices on inclusion: A national review. *Remedial and Special Education, 16,* 279–287.

Lipsky, D. K., & Gartner, A. (1996). Inclusive education and school restructuring. In W. Stainback & S. Stainback (Eds.), *Controversial Issues Confronting Special Education* (2nd ed.) (pp. 3–15). Boston: Allyn & Bacon.

Lord, C., & Hopkins, J. M. (1986). The social behavior of autistic children with younger and same-age non-handicapped peers. *Journal of Autism and Developmental Disorders, 16,* 249–262.

McCarthy, M. M. (1998). Inclusion of children with disabilities: Seeking the appropriate balance. *Educational Horizons,* 116–118.

McIntosh, R., Vaughn, S., Schumm, J. S., Haager, D., & Lee, O. (1993). Observations of students with learning disabilities in general education classrooms. *Exceptional Children,* 60, 249–261.

McLaughlin, M. J., & Warren, S. H. (1994). *Resource implications of inclusion: Impressions of special education administrators at selected sites.* Palo, Alto, CA: Center for Special Education Finance.

Miller, L. (1990). The regular education initiative and school reform: Lessons from the mainstream. *Remedial and Special Education, 11,* 17–22.

Peterson, J. M. (1989). Remediation is no remedy. *Educational Leadership, 6,* 24–25.

Piuma, F. (1989). *A benefit-cost analysis: The economic impact of integrated and segregated education service delivery models on the employment of individual with severe disabilities.* San Francisco: San Francisco State University, National Institute on Disability and Rehabilitation Research.

Rogers, J. (1993). The inclusion revolution. *Research Bulletin, 1,* 1–6.

Ryndak, D. L., Downing, J. E., Jacqueline, L. R., & Morrison, A. P. (1995). Parents' perceptions after inclusion of their children with moderate or severe disabilities. *Journal of the Association for Persons with Severe Handicaps, 20*, 147–157.

Sailor, W. (1991). Special education in the restructured school. *Remedial and Special Education, 12*, 8–22.

Sasso, G., & Rude, H. A. (1988). The social effects of integration on nonhandicapped children. *Mental Retardation, 23*, 18–23.

Semmel, M. I., Abernathy, T. V., Butera, G., & Lesar, S. (1991). Teacher perceptions of the regular education initiative. *Exceptional Children, 58*, 9–24.

Slavin, R. E. (1990). General education under the regular education initiative: How must it change? *Remedial and Special Education, 11*, 40–50.

Stainback, S., & Stainback, W. (1990). *Support networks for inclusive schooling: Interdependent integrated education.* Baltimore: Paul H. Brookes.

Stainback, S., & Stainback. W. (1992). Introduction. In J. Pearpoint, M. Forest & J. Snow (Eds.), *The inclusion papers: Strategies to make inclusion work.* Toronto: Inclusion Press.

Thousand, J. S., & Villa, R. A. (1989). Enhancing success in heterogeneous schools. In S. Stainback, W. Stainback & M. Forest (Eds.), *Educating all students in the mainstream of regular education* (pp. 89–103). Baltimore: Paul H. Brookes.

Turnbull, H. R. (1990). *Free appropriate public education: The law and children with disabilities.* Denver, CO: Love.

Viadero, D. (1998, February 18). Small classes: Popular, but still unproven, *Education Week, 17*, 1, 16.

Voeltz, L. M. (1982). Effects of structured interactions with severely handicapped peers on children's attitudes. *American Journal of Mental Deficiency, 86*, 380–390.

Walter, W. (2000). Personal communication, March 13.

Will, M. (1986). *Educating children with learning problems: A shared responsibility.* Washington, DC: Office of Special Education and Rehabilitative Services, U. S. Department of Education.

Willis, S. (1994, October). Making schools more inclusive. *Curriculum Update*, Association for Supervision and Curriculum Development (ASCD), 1–8.

Winzer, M. A. (1986). Early developments in special education. Some aspects of enlightenment thought. *Remedial and Special Education, 7*, 42–49.

Winzer, M. A. (1993). *The history of special education: From isolation to integration.* Washington, DC: Gallaudet University Press.

Yell, M. S. (1995). Least restrictive environment, inclusion, and students with disabilities. *Journal of Special Education, 28*, 389–404.

CHAPTER

10

Multicultural Education and the Cultural Curriculum

Charlotte is a teacher of eighth-grade social studies in a small Midwestern community. She uses the project approach because she believes that students should be able to relate what they study to their own personal lives. She is quite proud of the fact that her students are investigating the impact of the town's only traffic light on downtown congestion. Many of her students are actively engaged in this endeavor and take a personal interest because most have lived in this community all of their lives and remember when there was not even a stop sign at the town's only major intersection. However, this is not true of all Charlotte's students. She has several in her classroom who moved to the area from a large urban area in Mexico only a few months ago. Their background knowledge and primary language are quite different from the mainstream students'. They are puzzled as to what the issue at hand really is because, for most of their lives, they have dealt with congested traffic in one of the world's largest cities. Charlotte is doing the best she can, but how can she teach both process and content in such a way as to reach all her students?

Teachers must be prepared to meet the needs of all children in their classrooms and this includes students from diverse backgrounds (Kirmani & Laster, 1999). According to Ronald Takaki, multiculturalism challenges the traditional narratives of American history. Multicultural education "is not only more inclusive, but also more *accurate* to recognize this diversity. The intellectual purpose of multiculturalism is a more accurate understanding of who we are as Americans" (Halford, 1999, p. 9).

This chapter will pose many questions related to cultural diversity and the curriculum. We will consider misconceptions about multicultural education, dilemmas teachers face in the 21st century, issues related to students who are limited English proficient (LEP), and finally consider what and how we should teach. The issues are extremely complex. The goal of this chapter is to present numerous ideas for debate and discussion rather than provide simplistic, and thus unrealistic solutions.

Misconceptions about Cultural Diversity

As we begin to look at culture and what is taught in schools, let's consider some current misconceptions about multicultural education. According to Aldridge, Calhoun, and Aman (2000) there are at least 15 common misconceptions about cultural diversity in schools today. These include:

1. *People from the same nation or geographic region, or those who speak the same language, share a common culture.* There are numerous examples across the planet which indicate this misconception is false. The people of Nicaragua, the Dominican Republic, and Chile may all have Spanish-speaking citizens but their dialects and cultures are vastly different.

2. *Families from the same culture share the same values.* People from nondominant cultures live out their cultural pluralism in numerous ways. According to Lynch and Hanson (1998), there are at least four ways individuals from minorities express their cultural identities in the United States. These include: "(a) mainstreamers, (b) bicultural individuals, (c) culturally different individuals, and (d) culturally marginal individuals" (p. 19). Grandparents might be culturally marginalized because they maintain their original culture and have limited participation in the dominant culture while their grandchildren may be either mainstreamers or bicultural (Aldridge et al., 2000).

3. *Children's books about another culture are usually authentic.* Texts and periodicals written about specific cultures may be inaccurate. This is particularly true in the 21st century, when virtually anything can be published on the Internet. However, there are published guidelines that help in selecting culturally appropriate and bias-free sources. These include *Guidelines for Selecting Bias-Free Textbooks and Storybooks* (see Derman-Sparks & The A.B.C. Task Force, 1989) and *Teaching Multicultural Literature in Grades K–8* by Rudine Sims Bishop (1993).

4. *Multicultural education includes only ethnic and racial issues.* Gender and socioeconomic diversity are also important and should be included in multicultural explorations. Children come from many types of homes, including those headed by lesbian or gay parents. Further, children from lower socioeconomic environments often have more in common with one another than those of similar ethnic or racial heritage from higher income levels (Strevy & Aldridge, 1994).

   Gollnick and Chinn (1990) recommend considering other issues in multicultural education beyond ethnic and racial considerations. They advocate promotion of social justice and equity, the acceptance of alternative life choices for people, and an emphasis on equal distribution of power among marginalized groups.

5. *The tour and detour approach are appropriate for teaching multicultural education.* Merely visiting a culture would be considered tourist-multiculturalism

(Derman-Sparks, 1993). There is also the detour approach in which many elementary teachers incorporate the study of Native Americans during Thanksgiving or Martin Luther King during Black History Month without integrating these topics into the mainstream curriculum. According to Aldridge et al., (2000) "students come away from such teaching with even more biases" (p. 3).

6. *Multicultural education should be taught as a separate subject.* This would add something else to teachers' already full plates. James Banks (1994) recommends a transformative approach to teaching multicultural education. For example, in the past, history has been taught from one perspective. This is usually the perspective of the victor. Students who study the Alamo may only get the American perspective. What about the Mexican point of view? By presenting multiple viewpoints, teachers can infuse cultural issues into the mainstream curriculum.

7. *Multicultural education is already an accepted part of the curriculum.* This is simply not true. E. D. Hirsch (1996) and Rush Limbaugh (1994), among many others, are harsh critics of multicultural education. In fact, Limbaugh suggests multicultural education is really an excuse for people who have not made it in what he refers to as the American way.

8. *Multiculturalism is divisive.* Some people believe that when ethnicity is turned into a defining characteristic, it promotes divisiveness rather than unity. Multiple diversities have always existed in the United States. A counter suggestion to this myth is to consider the United States as a salad bowl rather than a melting pot. With a melting pot, all people are put into the system and come out alike. There is no distinction in this metaphor. However, a salad is rich with diversity. The onions, tomatoes, and celery play an important part in the unity of the salad (Aldridge, 1993).

9. *In predominantly monocultural or bicultural societies, there is no need to study other cultures.* Monocultural or bicultural societies are fading fast. Increasingly, all students need to learn about the cultures to which they will live in close proximity in the near or immediate future (Greenfield & Cocking, 1994). With a major influx of Hispanic and Asian immigrants, many if not most public schools represent a variety of cultures, languages, and religions.

10. *Multicultural education should be reserved for older students who are less egocentric or ethnocentric.* Young children establish cultural understanding by the age of five and more easily adapt to and learn from new cultural patterns than adults (Lynch & Hanson, 1998). Young children are capable of learning likenesses and differences when presented in developmentally appropriate ways. One way to begin might be to look at pictures of children's families and discuss their similarities and diversities.

11. *When multicultural education is implemented, the commonality is lost.* As more and more diverse cultures enter the schools, conflicts may arise as with the

civil rights movement. However, multicultural education can assist in helping students become more tolerant, equitable, and inclusive (Ravitch, 1991/1992).

12. *We do not need multicultural education because America already acknowledges its cultural diversity.* Critics are quick to point out that we have Martin Luther King's Birthday as a holiday in most states and celebrate Black History Month. As we have pointed out, this tour or detour approach can often be more divisive than transformative (Aldridge et al., 2000).

13. *Historical accuracy suffers in multicultural education.* Educators who subscribe to this viewpoint object to the notion that Cleopatra might have been Black or that Western Civilization may have started in Egypt (Africa) rather than Greece. However, if students are taught healthy skepticism, not cynicism, then they will seek out multiple sources to support and refute what they are learning in school.

14. *Most people identify with only one culture.* Increasingly, children and families are multiethnic. Take the following example. Alex is of Chinese heritage but was born and raised in Trinidad. He and his parents do not speak Chinese. Recently they moved to Buffalo where Alex is attending middle school. Alex has a multiethnic heritage that defies stereotyping.

15. *There are not enough resources about multicultural education.* While this may have been a real issue 20 years ago, it is not true in the 21st century. At the end of this chapter we have provided numerous references, including multicultural Websites.

While Aldridge et al., (2000) have identified these as misconceptions, several critics disagree. Strotsky (1999) believes, "today's version of multiculturalism has led to the suppression of the stories of most immigrant groups to this country" (p. 19). She suggests that historical accuracy suffers because few students today read about scientific and technological discoveries. They are too busy reading books in which they learn words in Spanish, Japanese, or Swahili, which will be of little use to them in the real world. Strotsky is even bold enough to assert, "the present version of multiculturalism may well be largely responsible, through its effect on classroom materials and instruction, for the growing gap between the scores of minority students and other students on the National Assessment of Educational Progress examinations in reading" (p. 21).

Criticisms also spill over into the issue of affirmative action in higher education. Clegg (2000) provides multiple arguments against affirmative action. He maintains, "skin color does not equal ideas, and ethnicity does not equal experiences. The position to the contrary used to be called stereotyping. Moreover, since the invention of the printing press, it has not been necessary to meet people in order to learn their perspectives" (p. 22). He goes on to say, "When we impose diversity upon an institution, we create resentment and stigmatization, break the law, compromise a college's mission, and tell some people that they aren't going to be admitted or hired or promoted, because they have the wrong melanin content or ancestry. Whatever the dubious benefits of diversity, is it worth all that?" (p. 23).

This might be a good time to examine your own personal beliefs about diversity and multicultural education. In doing so, it is important to note that everyone has prejudices whether they admit it or not (Aldridge et al., 2000). Recognizing and acknowledging your own prejudices can sometimes open up a dialogue and help make better communication among groups. For example, at a seminar in the early 1990s on diversity, Charles suggested that everyone has prejudices and that recognizing them is important. Jerry thought to himself, "Not me. Maybe other people do, but not me." However, one day while driving, Jerry began to notice that many people had what looked like a crown in the middle of their car dashboards. On closer examination Jerry realized that most of these drivers were African American. He commented to an African American colleague about this, but she didn't seem to know what they were. Jerry thought she was being evasive, that this must be some secret Black Power sign. Maybe, he thought, it had something to do with Martin Luther King, Jr., since it was a crown. Later he found out it was just air freshener.

Jerry called Charles, who is African American, and they had a good laugh about this. It didn't stop here, however. Charles told a relative, who also thought the story was most amusing. Without ever meeting Jerry, she went out and bought him an elaborate crown air freshener with blinking lights. Not all interactions turn out this positive. Still, a dialogue and camaraderie were established in this instance because Jerry acknowledged his own misconceptions.

Cultural Dilemmas Teachers Face in the Twenty-First Century

Teachers in the twenty-first century will be faced with numerous cultural dilemmas and opportunities to make decisions about how and what they teach about these episodes. The following are examples of dilemmas that have actually happened in the real world. The only changes we have made is in names and in some cases the ethnicity to protect the students and teachers who experienced them. As you read, determine what you might do in these situations. What information do you need to make an informed choice? What is the context and nature of the community in which this occurred? What are the shared values of the dominant culture in that community? We do not have simple answers to the experiences described. The question is, How can you find the information needed to make an informed decision when such instances arise in your classroom? A brief commentary follows each dilemma. These commentaries are meant to enhance further discussion of each of the scenarios presented here.

A director of a preschool program with a diverse population decides to have an Easter egg hunt. Children are to assist in painting and decorating eggs. Do you believe this is appropriate? Why or why not?

Kirmani and Laster (1999) provide more information related to this situation. They describe a child named Mukesh who is Hindu and faced with a similar situation. He says, "I am 9 years old and in the fourth grade. I am a Hindu, and I am a strict vegetarian. Strict vegetarians neither touch nor eat meat and eggs. We view them as life or as a source of life and believe they shouldn't be destroyed. I appreciate Easter celebrations, but in some ways they are difficult for me. I have a hard time handling eggs. Painting eggs and egg hunting can be fun, but I always feel I am doing something wrong" (p. 61).

What should a teacher do? Should students like Mukesh just not participate? Should the activity be adapted. For example, would it be appropriate for Mukesh to draw eggs on construction paper? Should he draw some other symbol of springtime? What about Mukesh's feelings related to socialization with the other children? Will he feel he's a part of the group if the activity is modified for him? Is there something Mukesh can share about his own background and religion with the class that will broaden their experiences? Should the teacher be having the Easter egg hunt in the first place? What do you believe and how would you handle this?

The PTA president has developed a parent education group and worked closely with them throughout the year. The president asks the parents to bring a present for exchange with another parent at the December PTA meeting. What are your thoughts about this? If you were a parent, how would you handle this if you disagreed or thought it was a bad idea? Also, what are some reasons a person might disagree with this practice?

Some parents may not have enough resources to provide their own children with presents. Further, certain cultures and religions do not focus on material things but still want to participate in the PTA and other school activities. What would you do?

You have a child whose parents are Christian Scientists. The parents do not believe in traditional medicine. The child falls and breaks a leg and the parents cannot be reached. The child is in your care. What would you do?

Many schools have policies related to this. Teachers need to discuss this with the parents *before* an incident like this occurs to discuss alternatives. Parents may be willing to provide a signed document as to what should occur. However, since teachers are not medical specialists, it is within their right and moral obligation to call the paramedics and let them decide the appropriate course of action. How would you handle this?

You notice Kham (a child of Hmong heritage) has red marks on his arms and back. What is happening here? How would you find out? What would you do?

According to Lynch and Hanson (1998) this may be a religious practice. The Hmong "practice animism as well as ancestor worship" (p. 284). They also use *coining*, rubbing the skin until it is red to get rid of evil spirits. If this is a religious practice, should you report it to social welfare agencies? If so, what about circumcision, which would certainly be more painful? Would you report this? What would you do?

A child in your class has parents who are Jehovah's Witnesses. The principal of your program has planned for the entire school to have a Valentine's Day Celebration. The child from the Jehovah's Witness background is not allowed to participate. What would you do?

A key issue in this vignette is the fact that the principal has planned for the entire school to participate. Derman-Sparks and the A.B.C. Task Force (1989) suggests that schools not use a seasonal curriculum in which Halloween, Thanksgiving, Christmas, and Valentine's Day are emphasized. This would alleviate some of the problem. However, in this situation, the celebration has already been "mandated." A child in kindergarten or first grade might not be able to comprehend the reasons for not participating. How would you deal with this dilemma?

A boy in your class is being raised by his uncle, who belongs to a group that worships satan. The boy has been told to poke his enemies in the eye with two fingers. The child has attempted this several times on the playground. What would you do?

In schools we generally have common rules. Three common rules include (1) you cannot hurt other people; (2) you cannot hurt yourself; and (3) you cannot destroy property. Would these be helpful in working with this child? How would you discuss or approach this with the uncle or guardian? What would you do?

You are a teacher in a middle school. You have a new student in your classroom. This child is originally from Nepal but has just moved to your community. You ask the person to tell something about herself to her new classmates. She describes herself and indicates she is a Buddhist. Another child responds, "Well, you're going to hell." How would you handle this?

The community in which this happened is Southern, rural, conservative, and predominantly Protestant. Most of the children in this student's class have never seen or interacted with anyone from Nepal. Many of the children come from Evangelical or fundamentalist backgrounds. They are probably echoing the beliefs of their parents and a large portion of the community at large. Considering this context, what actions would you take?

You are an elementary teacher and your volunteer room mother has been very helpful. You are Jewish but your spouse is Christian and you have chosen to incorporate both religious backgrounds into your home. In an interaction with your room mother, she states, "Wouldn't the world be better if everyone were white and Evangelical Christian?" How would you respond?

This might be an appropriate time to share your background with the parent. What would you tell this parent? What approach would you take to teaching diversity with the understanding that some of the students you teach may have parents who believe like this parent?

During a special education placement meeting with a parent of Native American heritage, the transdisciplinary team is asking the mother lots of questions but she does not appear to respond. She does *speak English. What is happening here? What would you do? (What information do you need to make an informed decision?)*

Different families within and among various cultures communicate in different ways. Without stereotyping the family, child or culture, it would have been helpful to find out as much as possible about them *before* the special education placement meeting. In this particular situation, the mother was providing the team with answers by looking up and down. When she looked up, she meant "yes," when she looked down, she meant "no."

Javier is a kindergarten student from Nicaragua. His teacher is constantly scolding him for not looking at her when she calls his name. Why does Javier look down? If you were his teacher what would you do?

Javier has been told in his family to look down when your name is called. If you have done something wrong it brings shame the family and to show your respect, you look downward. Javier's kindergarten teacher has two options. She can honor Javier's home culture and allow him to look down when she calls his name. *Or*, she could teach him how to *code switch*, meaning that she would explain to him, "At home you look down when your name is called. When I call your name, please look at me." The issue here is one of teaching the child to survive in the dominant culture while respecting his family and culture. Which do you believe is more appropriate—following the cues from home or teaching Javier to code switch?

How Can We Work with Students Who Are Limited English Proficient?

Every year more and more students who are limited English proficient (LEP) enter schools in the United States (Menken & Look, 2000). Who are limited English proficient students? Who teaches them? How do students with limited English proficiency learn best in an English-speaking classroom? The issue of how best to work with children whose primary language is other than English is a growing concern for many educators.

Who Are Limited English Proficient Students?

According to Peregoy and Boyle (1993), "students who speak English as a non-native language live in all areas of the United States" (p. 3). Non-English-speaking students come from all over the world. "Many recent immigrants have left countries brutally torn by war or political strife in regions such as Southeast Asia, Central America, and Eastern Europe; others have immigrated for economic reasons. Still others come to be reunited with families who are already here or because of educational opportunities they may find in the United States" (p. 3). Besides these, there are many limited English proficient children who were born in the United States. These include groups such as Native Americans and second- or third-generation immigrants (Peregoy & Boyle, 1993).

By 2003 there will be well over 4 million students who have English as a second language. Currently about 1 in 10 children in the United States is not fluent in English. Limited English proficient students are the fastest-growing group in our schools, with an increase of 104 percent during the past 10 years (Menken & Look, 2000).

Who Teaches Students with Limited English Proficiency?

In some schools, all of the teachers in the school teach some children with limited English proficiency. Nationally, it can be said that half of all teachers will experience LEP students during their teaching careers (Menken & Look, 2000). Peregoy and Boyle (1993) describe the first day of class for a first-grade teacher named Mr. Bertolucci. They report, "It may surprise you to learn that more than half of the children in Mr. Bertolucci's class are new to the English language, coming from homes in which languages such as Spanish, Cantonese, and Japanese are spoken. Such linguistic variety was not always the case, but changes in the neighborhood over the past ten years have been dramatic" (p. 2). Mr. Bertolucci's class is not unusual. First grades all over the United States have children from many cultural and linguistic backgrounds.

How Do Students with Limited English Proficiency Learn Best in an English-Speaking Classroom?

While all children have individual learning styles, most limited English proficient students learn best in classrooms that provide the following five things:

1. *Integrated instruction.* When students study topics around connected units or themes, they are better able to construct relationships among content areas. "By integrating language instruction and content instruction, language learners will not fall behind in developing grade-level content skills" (Menken & Look, 2000, p. 17).

2. *Meaningful communication.* When limited English proficient students have many opportunities to use language, they learn English faster. Cooperative and collaborative learning, peer tutoring, and pupil pairs encourage meaningful communication (California State Department of Education, 1994; Menken & Look, 2000).

3. *An interactive hands-on approach.* We have always known that students learn by doing. This is even more important for limited English proficient students. Experimenting with objects in science and exploring the environment in social studies is just good teaching. However, this is even more important for limited English proficient students. They are able to construct their own knowledge before being able to communicate it in English (Menken & Look, 2000, Peregoy & Boyle, 1993).

4. *Clear classroom procedures and guidelines.* A consistent and clear classroom structure can help students travel through the maze of classroom activities. While guidelines and procedures are crucial, making sure these are communicated to the limited English proficient students and that they understand them is just as important (California State Department of Education, 1994).

5. *Cultural connections.* Teachers need to familiarize themselves thoroughly with each child's culture so that connections between the child's culture and classroom learning can be encouraged (Aldridge et al., 2000; Menken & Look, 2000).

What Should We Teach with Regard to Culture?

There are basically two types of cultural literacy—mainstream and marginalized. Many of us were taught mainstream literacy in school. For example, Who discovered America? What we learned was Christopher Columbus in 1492. However, there were people who were already living here, and rumors that Leif Erikson came here before Columbus. If we consider that question from multiple viewpoints, we move into marginalized cultural literacy—different perspectives that are not addressed in mainstream literacy.

With regard to culture, both mainstream and marginalized literacy are not enough. Another option is *critical literacy*. If we teach students to consider multiple viewpoints from varying sources, then we also need to teach them how to evaluate these sources. Who said that? Who is served by this perspective? Who is marginalized? Who has been left out in telling their side of the story? All knowledge has political and cultural content. Absolutely no knowledge is value free. What we learn in school is highly political, social, and cultural in nature. This is a given. Isn't it our job to point this out to students and have them evaluate everything we ask them to read?

How Should We Teach with Regard to Culture?

To answer this question we have to consider how the dominant culture emphasizes certain values while minority groups often share different ones. A big issue is *collectivism* versus *individualism*. "Collectivism is a cluster of interrelated values that emphasize the interdependence of family members. Within this value system, children are taught to be helpful to others and to contribute to the success of any group they belong to—beginning with the family" (Rothstein-Fisch, Greenfield & Trumbull, 1999, p. 64). Individualism, on the other hand, is most often promoted in the dominant culture and in the schools and promotes individual achievement, independence, and competition (Rothstein-Fisch, 1998; Triandis, 1989).

Many of the more recent arrivals from Mexico, Central America, South America and Asia share more collectivist values (Lynch & Hanson, 1998). There are several ways teachers can incorporate teaching strategies that more effectively reach a wide variety of students from many different cultures. These include promoting collaborative learning and cooperation, encouraging helpfulness through such avenues as peer tutoring, and sharing group success as well as individual triumphs.

While teachers often feel the frustration of not knowing enough about each of their children's cultures and home backgrounds, they can incorporate collectivist practices to reach more children from a broad range of cultural histories. Collectivism can be used "to understand the underlying motivation behind specific cultural practices, including those of the school" (Rothstein-Fisch et al., 1999, p. 66).

REFERENCES

Aldridge, J. (1993). *Self-esteem: Loving yourself at every age*. Birmingham, AL: Doxa Books.

Aldridge, J., Calhoun, C., & Aman, R. (2000). 15 misconceptions about multicultural education. *ACEI Focus on Elementary, 12,* 1–6.

Banks, J. (1994). *An introduction to multicultural education*. Boston: Allyn and Bacon.

Bishop, R. S. (1993). Multicultural literature for children: Making informed choices. In V. J. Harris (Ed.), *Teaching multicultural literature in grades K–8*. Norwood, MA: Christopher-Gordon.

California State Department of Education. (1994). *Building bilingual instruction: Putting the pieces together*. Sacramento, CA: Bilingual Education Office.

Clegg, R. (2000). The perversity of "diversity." *Education Digest, 66*(1), 20–23.

Derman-Sparks, L., & The A.B.C. Task Force. (1989). *Anti-bias curriculum: Tools for empowering young children*. Washington, DC: National Association for the Education of Young Children.

Gollnick, D., & Chinn, P. (1990). *Multicultural education in a pluralistic society* (3rd ed.). New York: Macmillan.

Greenfield, P., & Cocking, R. (Eds.). (1994). *Cross cultural roots of minority child development*. Hillsdale, NJ: Lawrence Erlbaum.

Halford, J. M. (1999). A different mirror: A conversation with Ronald Takaki. *Educational Leadership, 56*(7), 8–13.

Hirsch, E. D. (1996). *The schools we need and why we don't have them*. New York: Doubleday.

Kirmani, M. H., & Laster, B. P. (1999). Responding to religious diversity in classrooms. *Educational Leadership, 56*(7), 61–63.

Limbaugh, R. (1994). *See, I told you so*. New York: Simon and Schuster.

Lynch, E., & Hanson, M. (Eds.). (1998). *Developing cross-cultural competence: A guide for working with children and their families* (2nd ed.). Baltimore: Paul H. Brookes.

Menken, K., & Look, K. (2000). Making chances for linguistically and culturally diverse students. *Education Digest, 65*(8), 14–19.

Peregoy, S. F., & Boyle, O. F. (1993). *Reading, writing, and learning in ESL: A resource book for K–12 teachers* (2nd ed.). New York: Longman.

Ravitch, D. (1991/1992). A culture in common. *Educational Leadership, 49*(4), 8–11.

Rothstein-Fisch, C. R. (1998). *Bridging cultures: A pre-service teacher training model*. San Francisco: WestEd.

Rothstein-Fisch, C. R., Greenfield, P. M., & Trumbull, E. (1999). Bridging cultures with classroom strategies. *Educational Leadership, 56*(7), 64–67.

Strevy, D., & Aldridge, J. (1994). Personal narrative themes of African American mothers. *Perceptual and Motor Skills, 78*, 1143–1146.

Strotsky, S. (1999). Is it really multicultural illiteracy? *Education Digest, 65*(4), 17–21.

Triandis, H. C. (1989). Cross-cultural studies of individualism and collectivism. *Nebraska Symposium on Motivation, 37*, 43–133.

11 Gender Equity and Education

L. KAY EMFINGER

Try this activity. Write down all the famous women that you can think of in three minutes. Do not use actresses or presidents' wives. Many people who attempt this activity end up with less than ten women after three minutes. What does this outcome tell us about gender and education?

Title IX

Although the 1972 enactment of Title IX prohibited sex discrimination in schools, significant gender differences in academic performance persist. Studies have indicated that subtle practices in schools are denying girls the opportunity to reach their full potential (American Association of University Women, 1992/1995; Streitmatter, 1994). The current status of gender issues and theories of innate and sociocultural causes for sex differences are examined here. This chapter will present a general overview of gender inequity in schools followed by a more detailed description of the areas deemed most crucial to some educators, namely math and science. Intervention strategies currently utilized in classrooms as well as new paradigms for bias-free education are outlined.

The issue of gender equity is complex. Even though educational equity programs have been in existence since Title IX, sex differences in educational performance persist. This situation has instigated a myriad of questions surrounding the issue. What is the current status of gender issues? What are the specific issues? Can the educational system impact gender differences? What intervention programs are in existence? How can these programs be applied in the primary school?

American Association of University Women

The American Association of University Women (AAUW) published a meta-analysis of gender-related research in 1992/1995. Sadker and Sadker (1994) cited this work as one of the most influential publications concerning gender issues. "The report made national headlines, salvaged gender equity from the backwaters of backlash, and put it squarely on the American agenda" (p. 279). The meta-analysis concluded that the most significant gender differences exist in the areas of science and mathematics. There are no gender differences in math performance at age 9, minimal differences at age 13, and significant differences favoring males at age 17. However, the AAUW report indicated that "gender differences favoring boys in mathematics are declining" (p. 24). The converse is true with regard to science. Gender differences in science achievement and performance increased between 1978 and 1986. Male achievement is higher in the areas of physics, chemistry, earth science, and space sciences. Females score lower on advanced placement examinations and are even less likely than males to take them (Bae, Choy, Geddes, Sable & Snyder, 2000). Currently, females outperform males in reading and writing (Bae et al., 2000).

Gender Differences and Genetics

Gender differences have been attributed to genetics (Benbow & Stanley, 1980; Gray, 1981) and to gender-role socialization (Fennema & Leder, 1990; Fox, 1980; Gilligan & Attanucci, 1988; Kelly, 1987; Sadker & Sadker, 1988, 1994). Hyde's (1981) study posited that "sex accounted for less than 5 percent of the differences [in academic performance] between boys and girls" (p. 21). Thus, gender-role socialization can account for most of the differences in academic performance. Caporrimo (1990) and Fox (1980) pointed out that even if it is proven that biological variables exist, they cannot currently be impacted by intervention strategies. Consequently, the educational community should focus on variables on which it can exert some influence.

Gender Differences and Intervention in Educational Settings

Worell (1982) more specifically addressed the issue of gender equity by defining interventions in educational settings. She assigned sex-role contributions as integral factors in understanding achievement behavior and defining group differences. She identified two major sources for change that influence children's sex-role development: natural and planned. "Natural change comes from contemporary political, social, and economic movements within the larger culture to modify their lifestyle activities and value systems" (p. 42). The women's movement and the civil rights movement are examples of natural change. "By the virtue of their position . . . schools will reflect and enact the contemporary themes that encourage gradual transition toward flexible and androgynous interpersonal roles" (p. 42). However, these "natural interventions" are not directly propagated by the teacher. Conversely, planned intervention, a proactive approach, does involve specific targets for change. Worell summarized the targeted goals of planned intervention programs.

1. Make sure students have equal access to school activities and educational resources.
2. Work toward flexible role definitions by revising textbooks, curriculum materials, testing, media, and counseling practices.
3. Develop new programs and curricular materials that encourage flexible roles and career development.
4. Work specifically on attitudes and values. This is particularly important, not only for students, but also for parents, teachers, and school counselors.
5. Teach both students and teachers new behaviors. Teach specifically toward gender equity and sex role flexibility.

Intervention Programs Related to Mathematics and Science

Intervention programs that specifically relate to gender differences in math and science tend to target the areas addressed by these five goals. Worell's model will be used to explore the specific variables that relate to gender differences in math and science and to identify proposed intervention strategies that are appropriate for use in classrooms.

Equal Access to Activities and Resources

The first goal of intervention is to make sure students have equal access to school activities and educational resources. Males and females have equitable access to preschool experiences (Bae et al., 2000). However, equal access does not ensure equitable opportunity for development (Sadker & Sadker, 1994). Although children learn through play, boys and girls play with different types of toys (Skolnick, Langbort & Day, 1982). Almost from birth, males and females are supplied by both teachers and parents with different kinds of toys, and they tend to play with those toys in different ways. A study conducted in Canada reported similar conclusions (Sadker & Sadker, 1994). When researchers visited the homes of children, they found "boys' rooms filled with sports equipment, toy vehicles, tools, and building kits. The girls' rooms contained children's furniture, kitchen utensils, and lots of dolls" (p. 255). "Girls tend to play with toys that favor verbal, interpersonal, and fine motor skills" (Skolnick et al., 1982, p. 27). Girls typically use objects to explore emotional relationships such as playing house, making up stories, and talking to dolls. Girls engage in fine motor activities like sewing and drawing, which tend to be solitary, sedentary, and structured. Boys tend to play with objects. Boys tend to be involved in taking things apart and putting them back together, grouping objects, and manipulating objects. The issue here is that boys develop a relationship with objects with a de-emphasis on play that promotes relationships with people (Skolnick et al., 1982). Boys typically participate in activities such as building with blocks, constructing model airplanes, fixing things, and experimenting with microscopes. Boys often participate in sports that involve science and math concepts (i.e., figuring batting averages, negotiating over game rules, and learning from which angle to hit the cue ball to propel it in the desired direction). In essence, the nature of the play experiences and toy choices of boys provides more opportunity for the development of spatial visualization and basic math and science skills than do the activities which girls typically engage in. Schwartz and Hanson (1992) reported what happens when girls first explore with notions of velocity and two- and three-dimensional geometry areas in the math classroom. Girls approach this as a new area of exploration while boys have experience with these core mathematical concepts through their play with action toys. However, toy selection is just the beginning.

Practical Ways for Teachers to Provide Equal Access to Materials

Vandell (1989) has described several examples of practical ways teachers can provide for equal access to materials in the primary classrooms. Primary teachers should note children's choice of toys and make sure that they have equal experiences. Teachers can encourage girls to freely build with blocks, construct models, and initiate science experiments. They can also provide guided play experiences with these materials to encourage equity of opportunity. Large-motor sports games should be a whole-class endeavor. Through parent workshops and letters, teachers can help parents become aware of the importance of providing a variety of toys and encouraging girls to participate in sports activities and other group games. Derman-Sparks and The A.B.C. Task Force (1989) suggested strategies for reorganization of play areas and the addition of new materials to play centers to encourage more cross-gender play.

Revision of Existing Programs

The second intervention goal involves the revision of existing curriculum programs. In reference to curricula revision, the AAUW report (1992/1995) suggested that restructuring in the areas of science and math should include programs that address awareness and identification of gender-role stereotypes and how they limit our lives and the broad range of career choices, in addition to content-area revision.

Several content-oriented models of curricular revision efforts in math and science were reviewed. These programs uniformly advocate the addition of problem solving, career awareness, and spatial visualization skills to the standard curriculum. Girls + math + science = choices (Arbanas & Lindquist, 1989) and EQUALS (Cobb & Conwell, 1988) are two such model programs that include activity handbooks for educators. Skolnick et al. (1982) and Spring (1985) propose similar activities.

The activities proposed are typical of what can be found in a well-built science and math curriculum. Based on these activities, Kelly (1987) posited that a good science program will not, solitarily or in combination with other factors, accomplish the mission of decreasing gender differences.

Revolutionary New Approaches

The third goal requires the development of revolutionary new approaches. In response to "failures" in curriculum revision, Kelly (1987) posed a radically different perspective in addressing gender issues and described why previous intervention programs have failed to successfully close the gender gap. She defined curriculum revision as a psychologistic approach. The traditional view is that if girls are not good at science, there must be something wrong with them or perhaps their perceptions of science. A better way to look at this, in terms of intervention, is to boost girls' confidence and to help correct any misconceptions they have about science.

For Kelly (1987), "science is not an immutable 'thing' but a socially constructed process" (p. 1). She called for a change in the nature of science, whereas other interventions involve a change in the child. In answer to this call, Bentley and Watts (1987) proposed the development of a new science—"feminist science" (p. 91). Characteristics of this theoretical new science are: (1) a holistic view of nature that involves a degree of subjectivity; (2) caring and cooperation as values, and (3) science viewed as an integral part of personal development. Kelly reviewed their approach as promising but in the developmental stages. Thus, the details of practical application are still in the process of being worked out.

Bentley and Watts (1992) used Carol Gilligan's (1982) groundbreaking research in the area of women's psychosocial development as a theoretical underpinning for their feminist science model. Gilligan (1982) questioned the notion of "sex differences as measured by standards derived by only one sex [males]" (p. 325). She noted the "dissonance between psychological theory and women's experience" (p. 325). According to Gilligan (1982), critical voices—women's voices—had been left out at the theory-building stages of developmental psychology. Brown & Gilligan (1992) defined their work as "revisioning . . . entering an old text from a new critical direction . . . by bringing women's voices into psychology and thus creating a new voice for psychology . . ." (p. 31). Additionally, educational applications inclusive of Gilligan's work have been proposed by Belenky, Clinchy, Goldberger & Tarule (1986); Leder and Fennema (1990), and Pappert (1987).

Attitudes and Values

The fourth and fifth intervention goals will be approached as one issue due to their interrelatedness. These goals, to work specifically on attitudes and values and to teach both students and teachers new behaviors, are the goals most frequently addressed by math and science education reform efforts. Leder & Fennema (1990) labeled two types of variables most directly related to gender differences in mathematics: the learner's beliefs, attitudes, and actions, and the attitudes and beliefs of the teacher. "Students face and interpret actions, events, and opinions around them . . . It has become apparent that students' perceptions of the experiences they have detract from potential equal educational treatment and opportunities to learn" (p. 198).

The Meyer and Kohler (1990) review of internal influences on gender differences in mathematics concluded that the beliefs or attitudes most consistently linked with gender differences in mathematics achievement are confidence, perception of the usefulness of mathematics, the sex-role congruency, and attributional style. Confidence influences task persistence and the degree of risk taking students exhibit when approaching new material. This confidence is reflected by continued participation in mathematics courses and student interest in quantitatively oriented career fields. Students' perceptions of the usefulness of mathematics affect their short-term and long-term participation and achievement. It is unlikely that students will continue to persist at a task or engage in additional mathematics courses if they do not see how it will benefit them. Tied to this view of usefulness is sex-role congruency. The value a female attaches to mathematics is affected by "whether or not she thinks studying mathematics is a sex-role appropriate activity" (p. 63).

Self-Concept of Ability

Attributional style is the way a student attributes the causes for success. Males tend to attribute success in mathematics to ability whereas females tend to attribute success in mathematics to luck. Attribution of success to ability is a predictor of student plans to take more mathematics. Meyer and Koehler (1990) point out that "the variable called self-concept of ability would encompass these [internal variables delineated above] and other components of the internal belief system" (p. 92).

How can this crucial internal variable, self-concept of ability, be addressed by educators? Fennema and Peterson (1985) proposed the Autonomous Learning Behavior Model as an intervention strategy to eliminate the internal variable influencing gender differences. "Autonomous learning behaviors require and develop one's ability to work independently in high-cognitive level activities" (p. 7). Vandell (1989) identified the teacher as the major impactor on learner beliefs and offered practical suggestions for "rewriting the script" to promote autonomy in the classroom. Teachers can foster girls' self-confidence and belief in themselves by encouraging them to explore and experiment, to find out answers for themselves, and to develop their own resources. Opportunities such as problem solving independently and cooperatively with boys will promote risk-taking in a secure environment and thwart sex segregation.

Examples of Subtle Sexism

However, Sadker and Sadker (1994) asserted that in order to provide truly anti-biased educational programs such as the ones outlined, teachers, parents, and society in general must become aware of the subtle sexist lessons that are perpetuated daily. "Today it [the school door] appears wide open for girls to pursue the curriculum of their choice . . . [However] school girls [suffer] . . . microinequities that appear seemingly insignificant when looked at individually but have a powerful cumulative effect" (p. ix).

Sadker and Sadker (1994) reported case after case of subtle sexism. The following are just a few examples of their findings.

1. Male students receive the most attention from teachers.
2. Learning problems in girls are not identified as often as in boys. When girls approach problem tasks, teachers complete it for them. Conversely, males are given directions and encouraged to do it for themselves.
3. Participants in a study perceiving an infant as male played with him and used a toy hammer to distract him when he became restless and cried. Infants perceived as female were held, cuddled, and given a doll when they cried.
4. Female representation in children's books is unequal to that of males.
5. Females in the media are often portrayed as passive, dependent, and submissive.

In order to combat sexism, it is imperative that we consciously evaluate the presence of gender differences in the classroom, reflect on student-teacher interactions, and continually make changes in response to these evaluations. Constant reflection, evaluation, and change can "transform our educational institutions into powerful levers for equity . . ." (Sadker & Sadker, 1994, p. 280) that will enable girls to develop their own voices.

REFERENCES

American Association of University Women. (1992/1995). *How schools shortchange girls*. Washington, DC: National Education Association.

Arbanas, R., & Lindquist, G. (1989). *Girls + math + science = choice* (Report No. SE-051-052). Lansing, MI: Michigan State University (ERIC Document Reproduction Service No. ED 313 242).

Bae, Y., Choy, S., Geddes, C., Sable, J., & Snyder, T. (2000). Trends in educational equity of girls and women. Washington, DC: National Center for Education Statistics [On-line]. Available: http://sces.ed.gov/pubs2000/quarterly/summer/6cross/q6-1.html

Belenky, M. F., Clinchy, B. M., Goldberger, N. R., & Tarule, J. M. (1986). *Women's ways of knowing: The development of self, voice, and mind*. New York: Basic Books.

Benbow, C. P., & Stanley, J. C. (1980). Sex differences in mathematical ability: fact or artifact? *Science, 210*, 1262–1264.

Bentley, D., & Watts, M. (1987). Courting the positive virtues: A case for feminist science. In A. Kelly (Ed.), *Science for girls?* (pp. 90–98). Philadelphia: Open University Press.

Brown, L. M., & Gilligan, C. (1992). *Meeting at the crossroads: Women's psychology and girls' development*. New York: Ballantine Books.

Caporrimo, R. (1990). *Gender, confidence, math: Why aren't the girls where the boys are?* (Report No. SE-052-161). Boston: American Psychological Association (ERIC Document Reproduction Service ED 334 074).

Cobb, K. B., & Conwell, C. R. (1988). *Science EQUALS success* (Report No. SE-051-542). Washington, DC: Office of Educational Research and Improvement (ERIC Document Reproduction Service No. Ed 324 199).

Derman-Sparks, L., & The A.B.C. Task Force. (1989). *Anti-bias curriculum: Tools for empowering young children*. Washington, DC: NAEYC.

Fennema, E., & Leder, G. C. (1990). Justice, equity, and mathematics education. In E. Fennema & G. C. Leder (Eds.), *Mathematics and gender* (pp. 1–9). New York: Teachers College Press.

Fennema, E., & Peterson, P. L. (1985). Autonomous learning behavior: A possible explanation of gender-related differences in mathematics. In L. C. Wilkinson & C. B. Marrett (Eds.), *Gender-related differences in classroom interactions* (pp. 17–35). New York: Academic Press.

Fox, L. H. (1980). Conclusions: What do we know and where should we go? In L. H. Fox, L. Broody & D. Tobin (Eds.), *Women and the mathematical mystique.* (pp. 195–209).

Gilligan, C. (1982). *In a different voice*. Cambridge, MA: Harvard University Press.

Gilligan, C., & Attanucci, J. (1988). Two moral orientations: Gender differences and similarities. *Merrill-Palmer Quarterly, 34*, 223–237.

Gray, J. A. (1981). A biological basis for the sex differences in achievement in science? In A. Kelly (Ed.), *The missing half: Girls and science education*. Manchester, UK: Manchester University Press.

Hyde, J. (1981). How large are cognitive gender differences? *American Psychologist, 36*, 894.

Kelly, A. (1987). Introduction. In A. Kelly (Ed.), *Science for girls?* (pp. 1–10). Philadelphia: Open University Press.

Leder, G. C., & Fennema, E. (1990). Gender differences in mathematics: a synthesis. In E. Fennema & G. C. Leder (Eds.), *Mathematics and gender* (pp. 188–201). New York: Teachers College Press.

Meyer, M. R., & Kohler, M. S. (1990). Internal influences on gender differences in mathematics. In E. Fennema & G. C. Leder (Eds.), *Mathematics and gender* (pp. 60–96). New York: Teachers College Press.

Pappert, S. (1987). The value of logic and the logic of values. In B. Inhelder, D. de Caprona & A. Cornu-Wells (Eds.), *Piaget today* (pp. 101–110).

Sadker, M. P., & Sadker, D. M. (1988). *Teachers, schools, and society*. New York: Random house.

Sadker, M. P., & Sadker, D. M. (1994). *Failing at fairness: how schools cheat girls*. New York: Touchstone.

Schwartz, W., & Hanson, K. (1992). *Equal mathematics education for female students*. New York: ERIC Clearinghouse on Urban Education, ED344 977.

Skolnick, J., Langbort, C., & Day, L. (1982). *How to encourage girls in math and science*. Englewood Cliffs, NJ: Prentice-Hall.

Spring, B. (1985). *What will happen if . . .* Washington, DC: Educational Equity Concepts.

Streitmatter, J. (1994). *Toward gender equity in the classroom: Everyday teachers' beliefs and practices*. Albany, NY: SUNY Press.

Watts, M., & Bentley, D. (1994). Humanizing and feminising school science: Reviving athropomorphic and animistic thinking in constructivist science education. *International Journal of Science Education, 16*(1): 83–97.

Worell, J. (1982). Psychological sex roles: Significance and change. In J. Worell (Ed.), *Psychological development in the early years* (pp. 1–52). New York: Academic press.

Vandell, K. (1989). *Equitable treatment of girls and boys in the classroom* (Report No. SO-030-446). Washington, DC: American Association of University Women (ERIC Document Reproduction Service No. ED 326 447).

CHAPTER

12 Private Schools

Gwendolyn is a third grader attending Catholic School in the Bronx. Tray is in high school attending a small private school in rural Alabama. Sara attended public school through the sixth grade. Now entering seventh grade, she attends a very expensive private school in Denver, Colorado. These students attend private schools, but for vastly different reasons. This chapter will discuss private school education by defining what constitutes a private school, describing the history of private schools, and explaining how private schools have influenced the American education system.

What Is a Private School?

The term *private school* entered the lexicon of American education at the end of the 19th century. Previously, few distinctions were made between institutions based on how they were financed and governed. When the "common school" arrived on the scene, any school that did not fit that mold was considered different (Archer, 1999).

In the United States, public and private education is generally distinguished by the distinct separation of both their governance and funding. Typically, *public* authorities govern and finance public schools while *private* authorities govern and finance private schools (Bertonneau, 1997). In this respect, the American system is atypical among developed countries. Many developed countries finance public, private, and religious schools with public funds. This funding process abroad does not raise the controversy that it does in the United States. In return for funding, the private sector honors government standards in matters such as curriculum and class size and their students must pass the same national examinations as their public school peers.

Public support of the private sector in the United States is meager. In a few states, parents receive tax credits equal to the amount of their tuition bills or students enjoy publicly provided transportation to private schools. Private schools also can receive federal assistance for poor children such as reduced-fee lunches or compensatory instruction. At the higher education level, private universities generally receive large amounts of public funds in the form of federal and state grants. All private schools receive property-tax relief (Dykgraaf & Lewis, 1998).

Public schools still educate almost 90 percent of the nation's school children. According to the *Newsletter* (1999) of the National Private Schools Association Group, there are approximately 130,000 individual private schools with 1,700,000 teachers and staff. The national demand for independent private schools, governed by a board of trustees separate from a church, has increased by 11 percent over the last decade (De Rouffignac, 1996).

What Is the History of Private Schooling?

The current arguments on school funding and governance are not new. Rather, they have been debated for thousands of years. Both public and private education existed among the ancient Greeks. Although the cities of Athens and Sparta were little more than 100 miles apart, philosophically and practically they were worlds apart. Athens was known for its thriving culture—poetry, philosophy, and literature. In sharp contrast, Sparta is remembered for its brutal, regimented control on many aspects of life.

In Sparta, the state, not the parents, was viewed as best equipped to make decisions. All young boys attended government-run schools and were fed a one-size-fits-all curriculum of physical activity. Little attention was paid to the arts or sciences.

Athens, on the other hand, put its faith in parental freedom. Anyone could open a school. All schools were run as private institutions. Through charity and competition, costs were kept low. Aristotle's Lyceum and Plato's Academy, among others, charged no tuition at all. Competition for students drove schools to offer an expanded curriculum. Parents demanded more education so secondary institutions emerged. Athenian children were exposed to mathematics, art, astronomy, philosophy, and a host of other disciplines. Spartan children were confined to the physical arts and warfare.

The results are recorded in numerous history books. Athens was the most literate society of the Western world and the birthplace of democracy, philosophy, and medicine. Sparta is remembered for its totalitarian ways and its ceaseless wars against Athens (Lynaugh, 1999).

The United States has a rich heritage of private schools. Many of the private schools originated years before the official founding of the nation. Americans have continued to be assertive about providing an education for their children. Over 100 years ago a band of settlers in Idaho cleared the land in the Boise Valley. The public school was too far away so they built a private school nearby. That school still prospers today (Smitherman, 1999). In the past century private schools have flourished for a variety of reasons. One of these reasons is the perception by many parents that public schools are failing.

Have Public Schools Failed?

Eberstadt (1997) notes that during these postmodern times, certain established secular creeds are being put to the test. Educational progressivism, both in theory and practice, "is fast losing ground." For almost twenty years, progressive education, grounded in Rousseau's philosophy and transplanted to the United States by John Dewey and his followers, has suffered numerous setbacks (Hirsch, 1996).

In 1983, the National Commission on Excellence in Education published *A Nation at Risk*. This report documented the distinct mediocrity of the nation's students and the failing of its schools. Certain observers drew to our attention the parallel ascendancy of progressive ideas in the public schools. E. D. Hirsch (1987), for example, attacked progressivism. He argued that progressive ideas in the schools are depriving all students, particularly those least advantaged, of the knowledge required for citizenship. He further argued that "the mistaken ideas" of progressivism have led to "disastrous consequences," and that since mistaken ideas have been the root cause of America's educational problems, the ideas must be changed before the problems can be solved (Eberstadt, 1999). The ideas in his books, along with his Core Knowledge Foundation and its grade-by-grade, content-laden K–6 curriculum, laid the groundwork for what is an antiprogressive educational counterculture.

Parents and school boards who were also alarmed by *A Nation at Risk* have seized on one educational experiment after another in hopes of improving their schools. For example, many school districts have opted for mandatory standardized testing. Some districts are experimenting with financial incentives such as merit pay for teachers or school vouchers for disadvantaged families. Some parents have voted with their feet, fleeing public schools toward private schools as well as into the home school movement, now numbering some one and a half million students (Eberstadt, 1999).

What Are the Benefits of Private Education?

The U.S. Department of Education conducted the National Educational Longitudinal Study (NELS). Results indicated that a larger percentage of students in private schools are enrolled in advanced courses than are students in public schools. Schools operating under the guidelines of the National Association of Independent Schools report that their students do twice as much homework as their counterparts, watch only two-thirds as much television, are significantly more likely to participate in sports, and are more likely to agree that students and teachers get along well, discipline is fair, and teaching is good (Archer, 1999).

Why do parents choose to send their children to private schools? There are many reasons, but the main reason is *quality* (Archer, 1999). These parents perceive that their children will benefit from a host of advantages such as smaller classes, more individual attention, teacher excellence, and higher academic standards.

Even though states guarantee a free education to all, some parents also believe that private education promises something that public education does not—the preservation of their religious and cultural identities. Because the United States is perpetually caught between the ideals of pluralism and the melting pot, the history of private education is an often tumultuous one (Archer, 1999).

Swilley (1999) believes the single most important differences that private schools have over public schools is that each private school is free to prescribe the conditions for admission, hire teachers for their competence rather than their certification, form its own curriculum, choose its own texts, set its own standards, and, in most cases, be in the charge of one person. He views the private school as self-contained, human in its proportions, and eminently manageable.

Private education also reduces the financial burden of government for the education of its citizens (Smitherman, 1999). Private schools generate their income through fees or tuition charged to the families participating, contributions by those interested in the programs being offered, and, at times, earnings generated by ancillary enterprises.

How Much Do Private Schools Cost?

When one thinks of private education, one thinks "expensive." Certainly costly schools such as Andover and Exeter cost in excess of $10,000 yearly. However, Education Department figures show that the average private elementary school tuition in America is less than $2,500. The average tuition for all elementary and secondary private schools is $3,110 or less than half the cost per pupil in the average public school, $6,785 (Boaz & Barrett, 1996).

Ken Smitherman (1999), a long-term administrator of private schools, makes several observations regarding the benefits of private schooling. These include:

1. Private school families develop strong bonds and social networks among other families whose children attend these schools.
2. Private school families provide strong support for one another's children. This support is reflected in student activities such as transportation pooling and assisting in times of stress, tragedy, or financial need. They show a sense of accountability for what happens to the children of other school families. They value that culturally, socially, and morally unacceptable conduct will be closely scrutinized by other school families.
3. High expectations for individual student achievement are a paramount issue among private school families. They have made large financial investments in their children's education and, therefore, are deeply involved in it.

4. Most families see the relationship with private schools as a *partnership* in the education of their children. The positive outcomes of this relationship are reflected in significant ways, from parental volunteerism to strong financial support above and beyond the regular tuition fees. Through this strong linkage, students have a more positive perception of authority and the importance of education. (Smitherman, 1999)

How Does Private Schooling Affect Students' Social and Civic Participation?

Although considerable research has been conducted on the positive relationship between the amount of education that people receive and their political partici-pation, little empirical research exists on whether different types of education such as private or public schooling have significantly different effects on these political outcomes. Greene, Giammo, and Mellow (1998) examined the effect of private education on political participation, social capital, and tolerance among Latinos. To determine social capital, subjects were asked whether they were members of voluntary organizations: charitable groups, social groups, and/or sports groups. The findings from this study were that private education con-tributes to higher levels of political participation, social capital, and tolerance than does public education.

Smith and Sikkink (1999) conducted a national survey including a repre-sentative sample of over 9,000 parents of school-age children. The survey exam-ined whether families with children in private schools were more socially isolated and withdrawn from participation in civic life than children in public schools. The content of the survey looked at participation in an ongoing community ser-vice activity, visits to the library for books, tapes, lectures, story hours, or library equipment, and participation in public meetings within the preceding year. The results showed that families choosing private and home schooling were consis-tently more fully involved in a wide spectrum of civic activities than were fami-lies of public school students. Private school families, by an average margin of 9 percent, were more likely than public school families to engage in all forms of civic participation. Twenty-six percent more private school families were mem-bers of community groups and were volunteering at local organizations than were public school families.

Do Private Schools Serve the Difficult to Educate?

Bertonneau (1997) comments that youth with special needs, whether troubled emotionally and/or learning disabled, are not often well served in the conven-tional public setting. Many people erroneously believe these youth at risk are not well served by the private sector. He points out that it is a misnomer to think that private schools "skim the cream" and leave the toughest kids to the public schools.

When the public schools cannot serve a particular student, they sometimes contract with the private sector to do the job. Approximately 3,000 special education schools and facilities are in the private sector, according to the Director for Exceptional Children. Costs vary widely, depending on the nature of the disability and may include medical care and transportation (Bertonneau, 1997).

Tom Bushness, president and director of the National Challenged Homeschoolers Associated Network, reports that some 30,000 American children with special needs are homeschooled. Bushness homeschools his own daughter, who is blind, a child with Down syndrome, and a child with cerebral palsy. He says that parents are greatly stressed when they have to face an Individualized Education Plan (IEP) meeting composed of a multidisciplinary team of six to eight professionals (Bertonneau, 1997).

Are There Differences among Teachers in Private and Public Schools?

Studies by the National Center of Education Statistics (Smitherman, 1999) reflect that full-time teachers in American public schools earn on average 55 percent more than teachers in private schools. On the positive side, however, the same studies reveal that private school teachers have significantly greater influence than public school teachers over issues of school discipline, school curriculum, textbooks, class content, and class size. Private school teachers also report less difficulty than public school teachers with attendance, robbery/vandalism, alcohol/drugs, physical conflict/weapons, apathy, poverty/racial tension, and dropouts.

What Is the Business Side of Private Schools?

Like most entrepreneurial ventures, the private school industry has experienced mixed results (De Rouffignac, 1996). Some local facilities have a healthy bottom line with long waiting lists. Others are "scratching" for students while barely making ends meet. In order to compete with the public sector, successful private schools usually have fewer administration costs. They must follow sound financial practices and have the flexibility to respond to market demands. The parents, who pay double in the form of private tuitions and public taxes, can be very demanding.

Private schools are no different than any other commercial enterprise, notes Ned Becker, headmaster of Episcopal High School in Houston, Texas. Private schools are little minibusinesses. They have to make money or break even. Otherwise, they go out of business (De Rouffignac, 1996).

Are Public Schools Really that Bad?

A report on case studies of eight public and eight private elementary schools in California examined whether there were any identifiable and transferable private school practices that public schools could adopt to improve student outcomes (Rothstein, Carnoy & Benveniste, 1999). The practices examined in the report included accountability to parents, outcome expectations, clarity of emphasis on both academic and moral objectives, and teacher selection and retention policies. It should be remembered that this report is based on a small sample. However, some results may be telling.

The report found the economic makeup of the community to be the key to differences between private and public elementary schools. Private schools in inner-city settings had more in common with public schools in low-income communities than with affluent suburban private schools. Suburban public schools shared more characteristics in common with suburban private schools than with urban public schools. The study further questioned the generalizations about the superiority of nonprofit private school practices. The authors of the study found the following:

1. Personnel in private elementary schools are not necessarily more accountable to parents than personnel in public elementary schools.
2. Outcome expectations for students in private schools are not more clearly defined than outcome expectations for students in public schools.
3. Private schools do not necessarily aim to produce higher nonachievement outcomes—behavior and values, for example—than do public elementary schools. In addition, private schools do not necessarily allocate more funds to these nonachievement outcomes than do public schools.
4. Neither private nor public schools surveyed indicated that formal evaluation, supervision, or mentoring of teachers was a meaningful indicator of variation (Rothstein et al., 1999).

Are School Vouchers Worthwhile?

Some people argue that school vouchers are a great idea since the State has to pay for public education. Since we pay for education through taxes, why shouldn't the taxpayers get the money directly in the form of school vouchers to pay for the schools their children actually attend? Others argue that the government doesn't give anyone money without strings attached as to how that money is spent. Once private schools accept government funds, the government will tell them how to spend those funds. All kinds of conditions and standards of private schools will be set in order to keep getting those funds. Some are concerned that a school voucher system would lead to the elimination of private and religious education (Perkel, 1999).

Currently, private schools can select their students whereas public schools are required to accept everyone. Once private schools start taking government money, they have to accept any child who wants to attend that school.

Critics of the voucher system further argue that if the government has to pay for school vouchers, then it will come out of money for public schools. When public schools become underfunded, taxes rise (Perkel, 1999).

In 1963, Alabama Governor George Wallace stood in a schoolhouse door in an attempt to keep blacks from entering. Through force, Federal marshals kept the doors open. Thirty-seven years later, a similar scenario is being played out in which a Florida judge has effectively barred minority and poor children from getting out of their failed schools and into private schools where they will get a better education (Thomas, 2000). The case involved 53 poor children in Pensacola, who were given state money to pay private-school tuition in Florida's groundbreaking voucher program. In their private schools they were learning to read and write, an accomplishment exceeding their previous attempts in their government-run school. Governor Jeb Bush has said the ruling will be appealed.

According to Thomas (2000), teachers' unions want to keep kids trapped in failed schools. These unions would prefer to keep their own power and perks rather than to give children and their parents real educational opportunities. Ted Forstmann, a Wall Street financier who heads the Children's Scholarship Fund, reports he will pay for the 53 Pensacola children to remain in their private schools (Thomas, 2000).

At the same time, the unions claim they are not to blame for failed schools. The late American Federation of Teachers president, Albert Shanker, concluded, "It is time to admit that public education operates like a planned economy. It's a bureaucratic system where everybody's role is spelled out in advance, and there are few incentives for innovation and productivity. It's not a surprise when a school system doesn't improve. It more resembles a Communist economy than our own market economy" (Thomas, 2000, p. 15a).

William Rasberry (2000) recognizes that too many public schools, including Florida's, are in poor health. He raises concerns that one can get lost in the battle between those who don't like public schools and those who are more concerned with defending public schools than improving them. He believes that the solutions to improving education are many, some replicable anywhere "true believers come together to implement them, some dependent on particular charismatic individuals and some whose success depends on local circumstances" (p. 15a).

Is There a Place for Charter Schools?

Charter schools are public schools that have autonomy from selected state and local rules in exchange for accepting more responsibility for student performance. As of July 1999, almost 1,100 charter schools operated in 36 states across the nation (ED-Sponsored, 1999).

Intense interest in charter schools has arisen. People want to know where they are located, who they serve, what programs they offer, and how well they serve students. To help meet the need for information, the U.S. Department of Education began a program of national studies in 1995 designed to answer these and other questions. The National Study of Charter Schools is a comprehensive, 4-year study of charter schools designed to examine what types of students attend charter schools, how charter laws and policies affect charter schools in each state, the conditions under which charter schools improve student achievement and other aspects of student learning, and how charter schools affect local and state systems of public education. The study included an annual telephone survey of all charter schools, intensive case studies of 90 charter schools and a smaller number of comparison schools, and interviews with staff at charter-granting agencies, state educational agencies, and school districts.

What about Public Attitudes Concerning Private Higher Education?

A study of attitudes of the American public toward higher education indicated that the public showed considerable support for the goals of higher education. However, there was overwhelming dissatisfaction with higher education and its faculty, according to Miller (1997). This issue is complex because public and private universities are very different institutions. The private school is generally a liberal arts college whereas the public setting is often a large university. The first is better for some students whereas the second is more to the liking of others. The two have basically different goals and missions. The public university is sometimes described as a general-purpose institution wherein the course offerings are abundant. Students who are enrolled can choose from a grand array of courses. The private school often has a more limited menu of choices. The public universities stress preprofessional studies and tend to minimize the general education requirements. In contrast, the private liberal arts college sees as its fundamental mission the preparation of its graduates for lives as productive citizens.

With regard to the faculty, Miller points out that most faculty members are dedicated, hard-working professionals. The primary mission of the liberal arts college is teaching. Research is secondary. At a large university, the primary mission has long been research. Teaching, particularly at the undergraduate level, is considered secondary. These distinctions, in Miller's opinion, are unfortunate.

The public further suspects that higher education, whether public or private, artificially inflates their costs. The price of college has risen dramatically over the last decade resulting in a 38 percent increase for private 4-year colleges and a 41 percent increase for public universities. Meanwhile, disposable personal income per capita has increased about 12 percent in constant dollars. College tuition and fees are currently rising at about twice the rate of inflation. Why? In this country students or their parents pay for college through a combination of ways. These include personal funds, government loans, state grants, and institutional grants. Half of all students in college nationwide receive financial aid (Miller, 1997).

Tuition pays for only half of the cost of attending college. The rest is subsidized by endowment earnings, gifts or, for public institutions, state taxes. Over the past ten years, the share of the cost covered by federal grants has been declining so that federal aid has been reduced to about half. This reduction in federal aid for students has produced the single largest push on college costs. Other rising expenses include the ballooning investments required in computers and telecommunications technology, the imperative of addressing facility maintenance needs that were deferred and backlogged in the 1970s and 1980s, the zooming prices of library periodicals, and the labor-intensive nature of teaching (Miller, 1997).

Conclusions

This chapter raises many issues related to private schools. As a student or teacher, you might want to ask the following questions related to private schools in your own community. As you respond to each, think about what your own views of public and private education are and the personal, political, economic, and social reasons for your attitudes.

1. Why do people attend private schools? What are the real reasons?
2. Why do some teachers teach at private schools instead of public schools?
3. What do you believe are the benefits of a private education over a public one?
4. How are private schools financed in your community?
5. What do you believe about vouchers?
6. Are charter schools a viable alternative to regular public education?
7. Who benefits most from a private education? A public education?

REFERENCES

Archer, J. (1999). A private choice, *Education Week*, *19*(8), 1 [On-line]. Available: http://www.edweek.org/ew/ewstory/cfm?slug=08intro.h19

Bertonneau, T. (1997). Private sector schools serve the difficult to educate [On-line]. Available: Wysiwgy://61http://edreform.com/forum/100697tb.htm

Boaz D., & Barrett, M. R. (1996, March 26). What would a school voucher buy? The real cost of private schools [On-line]. Available: http://www.cato.org/pubs/briefs/bp-025es.html

De Rouffignac, A. (1996). Private schools = big business. *Houston Business Journal* [On-line]. Available: http://www.amcity.com/houston/stories/1996/11/11/story2html

Dykgraaf, C., & Lewis, S. (1998). For profit charter schools: What the public needs to know. *Educational Leadership*, *56*, 51–54.

Eberstadt, M. (1999, October & November). The schools they deserve: Howard Gardner and the remaking of elite education. *Policy Review*, No. 97 [On-line]. Available: http://www.policyreview.com/oct99/eberstadt.html

ED-Sponsored charter school research and demonstration programs [On-line]. Available: http://www.uscharterschools.org/tech_assisted/edinitiatives.htm

Greene, J., Giammo, J., & Mellow, N. (1998). The effect of private education on political participation, social capital, and tolerance: An examination of the Latino National Political Survey [On-line]. Available: http://www.la.utexas.edu/research/ppc/lmps11_4.html

Hirsch, E. D. (1987). *Cultural literacy: What every American needs to know.* Boston: Houghton Mifflin.

Hirsch, E. D. (1996). *The schools we need and why we don't have them.* New York: Doubleday.

Hoerle, H. (1994). Choose the right school [On-line]. Available: http://www.schools.com/nais/pub/cjhoosing/choose01.html

Johns, D. (1996). Parents . . . what do they look for in a private school? [On-line]. Available: http://www.npsag.com

Lynaugh, B. S. (1999, April 14). History shows the value of a private education marketplace [On-line]. Available: http://www.conservativenews.org/Education/archive/EDU19990414a.html

Miller, S. (1997, September). Public attitudes about private higher education [On-line]. Available: http://www.wesley.edu/president/speeches/phlcatt.htm

Newsletter. (1999). Of the National Private Schools Association Group. [On-line]. Available: http://www.npsag.com/newsletter.html

Perkel, M. (1999). School vouchers: Government control of private schools [On-line]. Available: http://www.perkel.com/politics/issues/voucher.htm

Rasberry, W. (2000, March 17). Program's defeat no cause to celebrate. *The Birmingham News*, p. 15a.

Rothstein, R., Carnoy, M., & Benveniste, L. (1999). *Can public schools learn from private schools?* Aspen: Aspen Institute's nonprofit sector Research Fund.

Smith, C., & Sikkink, D. (1999). Is private schooling privatizing? [On-line]. Available: http://www.catholiceducation.org/education/ed0031.htm

Smitherman, K. (1999). The benefits of private education to society [On-line]. Available: http://www.acsi.org/conferences/China/

Swilley, L. (1999). The advantage of private schools [On line]. Available: http://administrators.net/chatboard/topic805/11.02.99.18.18.55.html

Thomas, C. (2000, March 17). Vouchers in trouble. *The Birmingham News*, p. 15a.

Wirt, J., Snyder, T., Sable, J., Choy, S., Yupin, B., Stennett, J., Gruner, A., & Perie, M. U.S. Department of Education: National Center for Education Statistics. The condition of education 1998, NCES 98-013.

INDEX